Dreamweaver 4

A Quick Reference of More Than 300 Dreamweaver Tasks, Terms and Tricks

From A to Z

Heather A. Williamson

FIREWALL MEDIA
(An Imprint of Laxmi Publications Pvt. Ltd.)
An ISO 9001:2015 Company
BENGALURU • CHENNAI • GUWAHATI • HYDERABAD
KOCHI • KOLKATA • LUCKNOW • RANCHI
NEW DELHI

Printed and bound in India

First Edition : 2004, Edition: 2026

ISBN *:*978-81-7008-330-6

Published in India by

FIREWALL MEDIA
(An Imprint of Laxmi Publications Pvt. Ltd.)

An ISO 9001:2015 Company
113, GOLDEN HOUSE, GURUDWARA ROAD, DARYAGANJ,
NEW DELHI - 110002, INDIA

Corporate Office : B-33, Sector-5, Noida,
Gautambuddha Nagar (U.P.) - 201 301, INDIA
Telephone : +91-120-44 46 900
www.laxmipublications.com
info@laxmipublications.com

Branches

✆	Bengaluru	080-26 75 69 30
✆	Chennai	044-24 34 47 26
✆	Guwahati	0361-254 36 69
✆	Hyderabad	040-27 55 53 83
✆	Kochi	0484-405 13 03
✆	Kolkata	033-40 04 77 79
✆	Lucknow	0522-430 36 13
✆	Ranchi	0651-224 24 64

INTRODUCTION

You should find *Dreamweaver 4 From A to Z* easy to use. You only need to know that the book organizes its information—key tasks and important terms—alphabetically in order to use the book. You'll find it helpful, however, if you understand what this book assumes about your computer skills, what you should know about the Dreamweaver program from the very start, and what editorial conventions this book uses. This short Introduction provides this information.

What You Should Know About Windows/ Macintosh

You don't need to be a computer expert to use either this book or Macromedia Dreamweaver. Definitely not. But you want to be comfortable working with your computer and Microsoft Windows or your Macintosh.

For example, you should know how to turn your computer on and off, how to start and stop programs, how to choose menu commands, and how to work with dialog boxes. This book, for the most part, doesn't provide this type of basic operating information.

If you need this operation's focused information, take the online tutorial, get a friend to give you a quick tutorial, or acquire another book on Windows or the Macintosh.

TIP *Any short book on Windows will tell you what you need to know, but if you find you like this book, you may want to acquire* Windows XP from A to Z.

What You Should Know About Dreamweaver

You don't need to know anything about Dreamweaver to use this book. But because understanding the Dreamweaver program window will make using Dreamweaver and this book easier, let me identify some of the more important parts of the window, as shown in Figure 1.

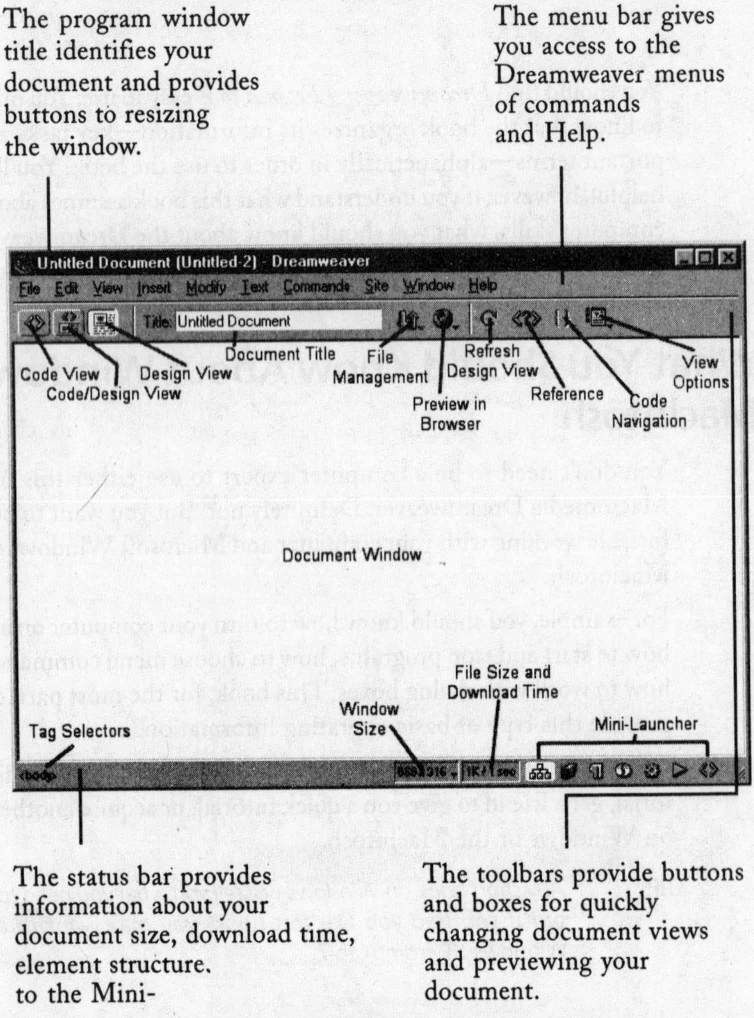

Figure 1 The Dreamweaver program window.

Let me also point out two important items about the Dreamweaver panels:

- Dreamweaver panels allow access to a variety of features that assist you in developing an HTML document using the Dreamweaver interface. These panels provide direct control over your Frames configurations, Layers configurations, JavaScript-based behaviors, and both Cascading Style Sheets and HTML styles. In addition to these panes, you can access a History (Shift+F10) of your past steps, view a Timeline (Shift+F9) of actions that will be taken, or just see a list of your site Assets (F11).
- You can merge Dreamweaver panels together by dragging the tab (showing the name of the panel) to another pane. For instance, dragging the History tab to the CSS Styles pane will merge these two individual windows. By merging, also called docking, panels together, you can have a single window that gives you access to multiple pieces of information about your document, without moving panes around your screen.

One other piece of information usually helps people just starting to use Dreamweaver. And here it is: The Undo Change option is your best friend. Unlike other programs, Dreamweaver doesn't include a preview pane to show you what effect your change will have on your document, so you don't have any idea of what your document will look like until you have completed your change. To undo an option, select Edit→Undo or press Ctrl+Z. You can also access the History panel (Shift+F10), shown in Figure 2, and undo multiple steps at once.

Figure 2 The History panel.

What You Should Know About This Book

You already know the most important feature of this book—that it organizes its task descriptions and term definitions alphabetically. But let me comment quickly on the book's other conventions.

- When this book refers to some box or button label, the label description appears in all initial capital letters. So, while the Type category of the CSS Styles dialog box includes a check box labeled "Decoration: underline," this book refers to the Decoration Underline check box. The initial capital letters signal you that the book refers to an onscreen label.
- This book's pictures of windows and dialog boxes may look a bit funny to you because they use a low display resolution to make the buttons, boxes, and text look larger. Less information fits on the screen when the resolution is low, unfortunately, but what you see you can read. If the book's screen pictures had used a higher resolution, images would be very difficult to see clearly.

And that's everything you should know to get started. Good luck. Be patient in your learning. Have fun with Macromedia Dreamweaver. It's an amazing program. And be sure to read the Troubleshooting entry if you encounter problems.

Heather A. Williamson

heather@catsback.com

Enterprise, Oregon, October 2001

DREAMWEAVER 4 FROM A TO Z

Absolute Links

An absolute link contains all of the information a computer requires to traverse from the current Web page to another Web page located on the local computer, a network, or the Internet. Absolute links specify the protocol (http, ftp, mailto) to be used, as well as the exact name and location of the document, as shown in the following examples:

```
http://www.wallowavalley.com/index.html

ftp://ftp.wallowavalley.com/pages/myprogram.zip

mailto:webmaster@wallowavalley.com
```

Absolute links, like relative links that reference a document based upon the location of the current document, are entered into the Dreamweaver Properties inspector's Link field, as shown in Figure A-1.

Figure A-1 The Link field of the Properties inspector.

SEE ALSO *Hyperlink, Link, Relative Links*

ActiveX

Microsoft's ActiveX technology provides the mechanism by which interactive content can be added to your Web page. ActiveX controls typically work only on Microsoft Web servers, although there are many other third-party programs that are providing support for these controls.

You can insert ActiveX controls into your Dreamweaver documents by selecting Insert→Media→PActiveX, clicking on the ActiveX icon in the Object panel's Special category, or by dragging an ActiveX control from the Assets Panel into your document. The following code is added to your document until you provide the rest of the ActiveX control information in the Properties inspector, as shown in Figure A-2.

```
<object width="32" height="32">

</object>
```

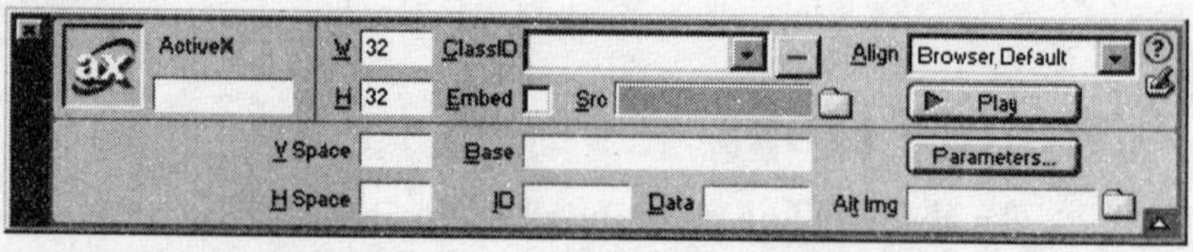

Figure A-2 ActiveX control Properties inspector.

Complete the following fields on your Properties inspector for your ActiveX control to function:

- Align - Controls the alignment of the control on your document.
- Alt Img - The name of the image to be displayed in the event that a Web browser doesn't support the <object> tag.
- Base - The address of the ActiveX control to be used.
- Borders - The width of the border around the ActiveX control.
- Class ID - Creates and identify for the control for the Web browser. You can either enter an ID, or select one from the pop-up list.
- Data - The address of the data file loaded by the ActiveX control.
- Embed - Forces Dreamweaver to use the <embed> tag as well as the <object> tag when using the control. The <embed> tag starts the control for Netscape browser users.
- H (Height) - Specifies the height of the ActiveX effect.
- Hspace - The amount of reserved white space to the left and right of the object.
- ID - The name of the object to be used by other scripting languages.

- Name - Specifies the name used for the control by scripting applications.
- Parameters - Provides a list of parameters (or instruction) that are passed to the control in order to configure it to run the way you intended.
- Src - The address of the text file used to provide information to the Navigator plug-in if the <embed> tag is used.
- Vspace - The amount of reserved white space above and below the object.
- W (Width) - Specifies the width of the ActiveX effect.

SEE ALSO *Embed, Media Objects, Object*

Apple Macintosh

Dreamweaver is available for the Apple Macintosh operating system. You can move Dreamweaver documents from Windows computers to Apple Macintosh computers and vice versa. Dreamweaver on either system will open HTML documents created on either system.

Application Window

The window that a program like Dreamweaver displays is called an application window, or program window. Document windows appear inside application windows.

Assets Panel

The Dreamweaver Assets panel, shown in Figure A-3, provides a list of all of the assets, or items, used to create the current Web site, not only the current document. It contains a series of tabs that provide lists of the Images, Colors, URLs, Flash movies (including Flash Buttons and Flash Text), Shockwave movies, MPEG and QuickTime movies, Scripts, Templates, and Library items, used on the Web site. You can open the Assets panel by selecting Window→Assets or by pressing F11.

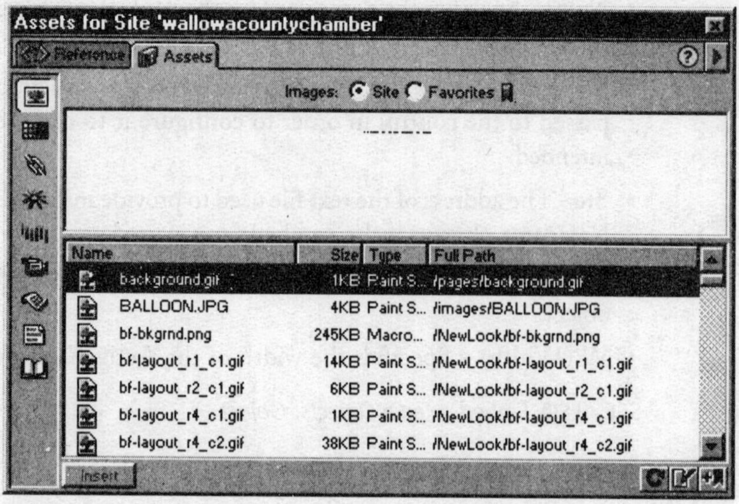

Figure A-3 The Assets panel Image tab.

To use the Asset's panel, select the asset, whether color, image, or movie on the panel, and drag it into your Web document. The Asset's panel has the following effects:

- Dropping an image inserts the image into the document at the point it was dropped.
- Dropping a color over preselected text changes that text to that color.
- Dropping an URL over a selection of text turns that text into a link to that URL.
- Dropping a Flash, Shockwave, MPEG, or QuickTime movie into the document inserts that movie into the document at that point.
- Dropping a Template onto your document applies that template to the document.
- Dropping a Library item into your document places that item in the location it was dropped.

Assets are automatically added to your Assets panel if you have created a cache of your Web site as discussed in the Defining Sites entry.

SEE ALSO *Defining Sites, Flash, Library Items, Scripting, Shockwave/Director, Templates*

AutoFormat HTML

Dreamweaver provides you with the ability to automatically format your HTML code to make it more legible to people, without affecting its usability by Web browsers. Imagine that you have code that looks like the following on your Web site:

```
<body bgcolor="#FFFFFF" background="wbbkg.jpg"
text="#000000" link="#663333" vlink="#330066"
alink="#FF0000"> <table border="0" width="600"
height="400" cellpadding="0" cellspacing="0">
<tr>   <td width="100%" colspan="4">
<img src="titlebar.gif" width="600" height="80"></td>
</tr> <tr>  <td width="170" rowspan="3">
<img src="leftbar.gif" width="170" height="319"
border="0" href="contact.htm"><td>
<td width="30" rowspan="3"><img src="leftofbox.gif"
width="30" height="320"></td>
<td width="350" height="30"><img src="topofbox.gif"
width="350" height="30"></td>  <td width="50"
rowspan="3"><img src="rightofbox.gif" width="50"
height="320"></td>  </tr> <tr>  <td width="350"
height="250" bgcolor="#FFFFFF"></td> </tr> <tr>
<td width="350"><img src="bottomofbox.gif"width="350"
height="40"></td> </tr></table></body> </html>
```

Reading this information, you don't know at first look, if there is a table in the Web page, or whether there are any images. To make this code much easier to read, select Command→Apply Sort Formatting. This will make your code much more readable, as shown in the following example:

```
<body bgcolor="#FFFFFF" background="wbbkg.jpg"

text="#000000" link="#663333" vlink="#330066"

alink="#FF0000">

<table border="0" width="600" height="400"

cellpadding="0" cellspacing="0">

  <tr>

    <td width="100%" colspan="4">
      <img src="titlebar.gif" width="600"
       height="80"></td>
```

```
    </tr>

    <tr>

      <td width="170" rowspan="3">

      <img src="leftbar.gif" width="170" height="319

           border="0" href="contact.htm">

      </td>

      <td width="30" rowspan="3">

      <img src="leftofbox.gif" width="30"
       height="320"></td>

      <td width="350" height="30">

      <img src="topofbox.gif" width="350"
       height="30"></td>

      <td width="50" rowspan="3">

      <img src="rightofbox.gif" width="50"
       height="320"></td>

    </tr>

    <tr>

      <td width="350" height="250" bgcolor="#FFFFFF"></
  td>

    </tr>

    <tr>

      <td width="350">

      <img src="bottomofbox.gif" width="350"
       height="40">

      </td>

    </tr>

  </table>

  </body>
```

SEE ALSO *Clean Up FrontPage HTML, Clean Up HTML, Clean Up Word HTML*

Base Element

The <base> tag provided a reference point for the processing of all relative links. These links use the absolute address provided in the href attribute of the base element to provide a starting location from which all relative links are evaluated. The base element has the following structure:

```
<base href="http://www.wallowavalley.com"
target="_self">
```

To use the base element with Dreamweaver, select Insert→Head Tags→ Base. In the Insert Base dialog box, shown in Figure B-1, type the address of the computer or select the name of a file, using the Browse button, from which you wish all relative addresses to be considered against into the Href field. Provide the name of the target from or document window in the Target field.

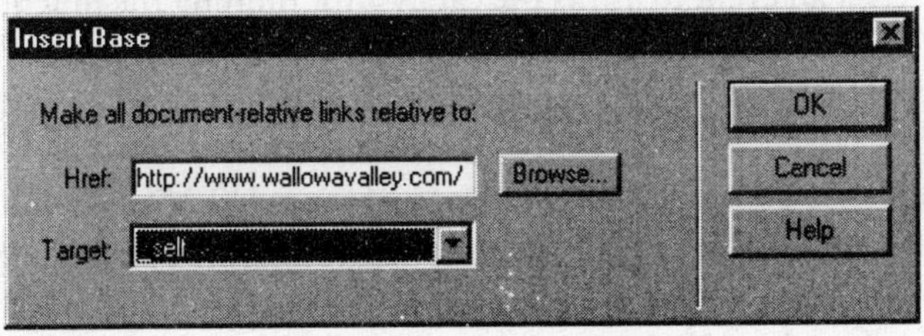

Figure B-1 The Insert Base dialog box.

Behaviors

A wide variety of behaviors are available with Dreamweaver. The following sections describe each behavior.

NOTE *If these behaviors don't meet your development needs, visit Dreamweaver Exchange and explore the over 475 behaviors available there.*

Call JavaScript

JavaScript is one of the scripting languages that provides for the automation of Web pages. The Call JavaScript behavior loads a prewritten JavaScript function whenever a specific event occurs.

To start the Call JavaScript behavior, follow these steps:

1. Select an object and select the plus (+)→Call JavaScript command on the Behaviors panel. This opens the dialog box shown in Figure B-2.

Figure B-2 The Call JavaScript dialog box.

2. Type the name of the function you wish to call in the JavaScript field.
3. Click OK.
4. Select an event to use as the catalyst for running the function from the Events list in the Behaviors panel.

Change Property

Properties control the appearance of your HTML elements. The Dreamweaver Change Property behavior allows you to modify those properties on the fly so you can create the appearance of a dynamically changing Web page.

To use the Change Property behavior, follow these steps:

1. Select an object and select the plus (+)→Change Property command on the Behaviors panel. This opens the dialog box shown in Figure B-3.

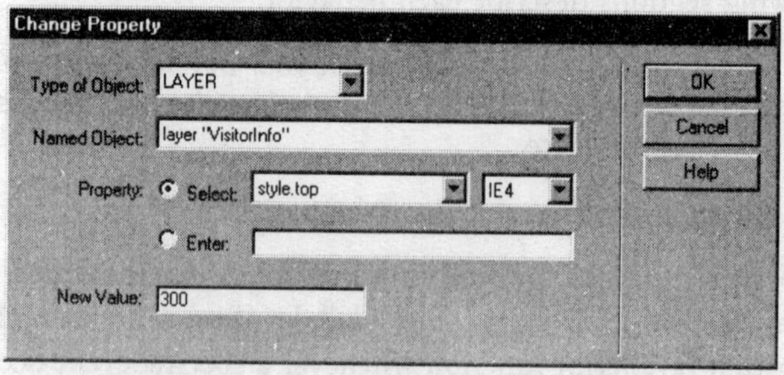

Figure B-3 The Change Property dialog box.

2. Select the type of object that you wish to modify from the drop-down list provided.
3. Select one of the named objects on your document from the Named Object drop-down list.
4. Select the property you wish to modify from the Property Select drop-down list. There are different properties available for Internet Explorer (IE4) and Netscape (NS4) browsers. Alternatively, you can type in your own property by selecting the Property Enter radio button.
5. Provide the new value for the property, the one it is being changed to, in the New Value text field.
6. Click OK.
7. Select an event to use as the catalyst for running the function from the Events list in the Behaviors panel.

Check Browser

The Check Browser property identifies the type of browser that is viewing the Web page. This can be used to load an alternative document for older browsers, if your page has a lot of automation on it.

To use the Check Browser behavior, follow these steps:

1. Select an object and select the plus (+)→Check Browser command on the Behaviors panel. This opens the dialog box shown in Figure B-4.

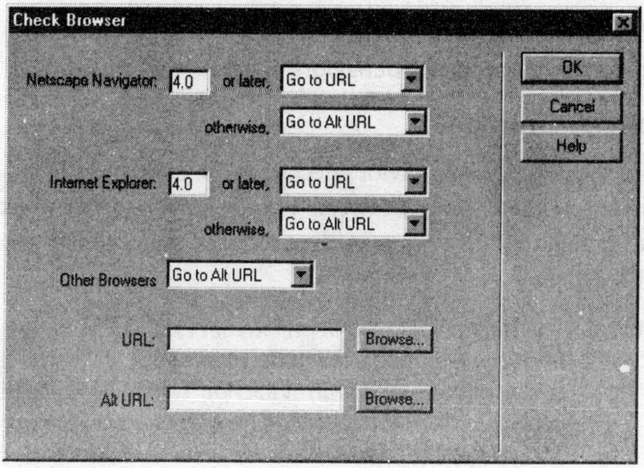

Figure B-4 The Check Browser dialog box.

2. In the Netscape Navigator field, provide the version number that you wish to check for, then select the action that needs to be taken if the version is found to be correct. Your options are Go To URL (visit the page specified in the URL field), Go To Alt URL (visit the page specified in the Alt URL field), or Stay On This Page. If the browser is Netscape Navigator, but not the version that you tested for, then the values specified in the Otherwise field will be used.
3. In the Internet Explorer field, provide the version number that you wish to check for, then select the action that needs to be taken if the version is found to be correct. Your options are Go To URL, Go To Alt URL, or Stay On This Page. If the browser is Internet Explorer, but not the version that you tested for, then the values specified in the Otherwise field will be used.
4. Select the action to be taken if neither of the browsers being tested for is found. Your options are the same as for either the Netscape Navigator or the Internet Explorer selections.
5. In the URL field, type (or select using the Browse button) the name of the file that you wish to be loaded for all options that the Go To URL selection has made.
6. In the Alt URL field, type (or select using the Browse button) the name of the file that you wish to be loaded for all options that the Go To Alt URL selection has made.
7. Click OK.
8. Select an event to use as the catalyst for running the function from the Events list in the Behaviors panel.

Check Plugins

The Check Plugins behavior checks for the existence of the selected plug-in on the visitor's browser. This behavior allows you to send visitors to alternative pages in the event the plug-in is not found, or if it is located.

NOTE *You can't detect plug-ins in Internet Explorer on the Macintosh. JavaScript can't be used to detect plug-ins on Internet Explorer on Windows, although VBScript can. This behavior adds JavaScript to do the detection on Netscape Navigator browsers, and VBScript to provide detection services for Internet Explorer.*

To use the Check Plugins behavior, follow these steps:

1. Select an object and select the plus (+) →Check Plugins command on the Behaviors panel. This opens the dialog box shown in Figure B-5.

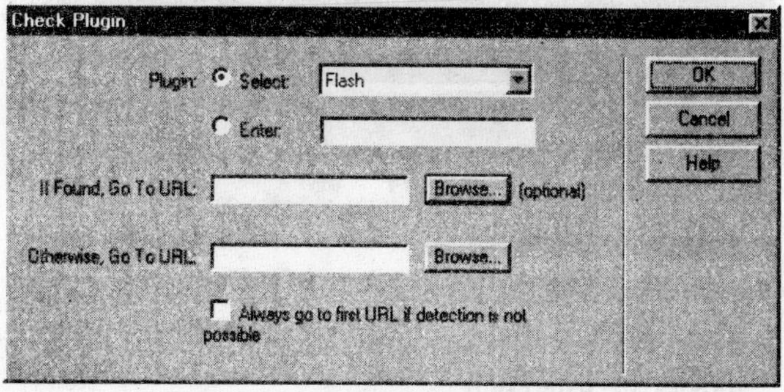

Figure B-5 The Check Plugins dialog box.

2. Select the plug-in from the Plugin Select list or type its name into the Plugin Enter text field. Dreamweaver provides automatic detection scripts for Flash, Shockwave, LiveAudio, Netscape Media Player, and QuickTime movies.
3. In the If Found Go To URL field, type (or select using the Browse button) the URL of the documents to be opened when the plug-in's presence is found on a site visitor's computer.
4. In the Otherwise Go To URL field, type (or select using the Browse button) the URL of the documents to be opened when the plug-in's presence is not found on a site visitor's computer.
5. Check the Always Go To First URL If Detection Is Not Possible check box if you wish to assume the presence of the plug-in even if it can't be determined by the script.
6. Click OK.
7. Select an event to use as the catalyst for running the function from the Events list in the Behaviors panel.

Control Shockwave or Flash

The Control Shockwave or Flash behavior is only available if you have a Flash or Shockwave movie embedded in your page. This behavior allows you to Play, Stop, Rewind, or go to a specific destination frame in that movie.

To use the Control Shockwave or Flash behavior, follow these steps:

1. Select a link on your document, and then select the plus (+)→Control Shockwave Or Flash command on the Behaviors panel. This opens the dialog box shown in Figure B-6.

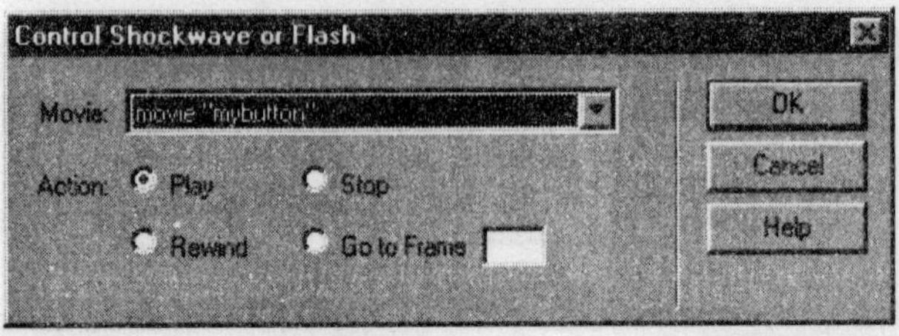

Figure B-6 The Control Shockwave Or Flash dialog box.

2. Select the name of the movie from the Movie field. Only named movies are listed here.

NOTE *If you have unnamed Flash behaviors on your document, they will be listed as pairs of objects and embedded items. Make sure you have named all of your Flash or Shockwave movies before applying this behavior.*

3. Select the Action radio button you wish to enact Play (starts the movie from its current frame), Stop (stops the movie at its current frame), Rewind (rewinds the movie to the first frame), or Go To Frame (takes you to the specified frame of the movie).
4. Click OK.
5. Select an event to use as the catalyst for running the function from the Events list in the Behaviors panel.

Drag Layer

The Drag Layer behavior is only available if you have a layer on your document. This behavior allows you to drag a layer on your screen and control how that layer's position is manipulated. This technique is often used to create online jigsaw puzzles.

To use the Drag Layer behavior, follow these steps:

1. Select a link on your document, then select the plus (+)→Drag Layer command on the Behaviors panel. This opens the Drag Layer dialog box at the Basic tab, as shown in Figure B-7.

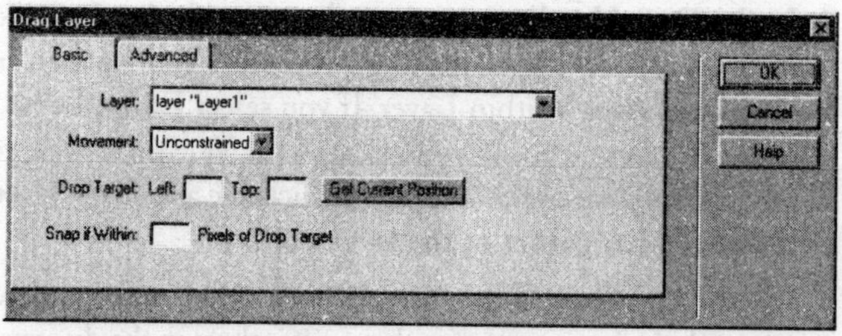

Figure B-7 The Basic tab of the Drag Layer dialog box.

2. Select the name of the layer from the Layer drop-down list.
3. Select the style of movement from the Movement drop-down list. Your options include Unconstrained (free moving) or Constrained (must move within a specific horizontal or vertical space). If you select Unconstrained, go on to the next step. If you select Constrained, then you need to provide the number of pixels the layer can be moved Up, Down, Left, and Right from its current location.
4. Provide the Drop Target Left and Top coordinates for the location of the top left corner of the layer for when it is released. Use the Get Current Position button to get the current position of the layer on your document. It is often easier to place the layer in its end position before creating this behavior. You can then move the layer to its intended start position before saving the document.
5. Use the Snap If Within _ Pixels Of Drop Target to identify how close to the target you must have the layer positioned. If you create a jigsaw puzzle, this option allows people to be within a few pixels of correct positioning and the script adjusts the piece to the puzzle.
6. Click the Advanced tab. This opens the dialog box shown in Figure B-8.

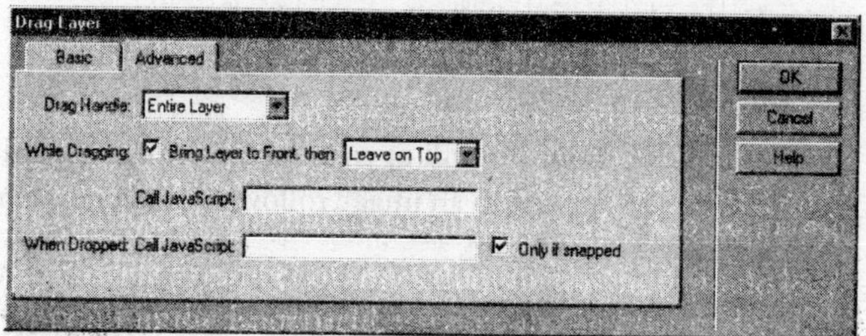

Figure B-8 The Advanced tab of the Drag Layer dialog box.

7. In the Drag Handle drop-down list, specify the clickable area of the layer used to initiate the drag procedure. Your options are Entire Layer and Area Within Layer. If you select Entire Layer, then go on to the next step. If you select Area Within Layer, you must provide the pixel coordinates of the clickable area in the layer, relative to the top left corner of the layer itself.
8. Check the While Dragging _ Bring Layer To Front check box if you wish the layer to appear above any others in the document while you are dragging the layer. This prevents the layer you are moving from becoming hidden behind other layers in the document.
9. Make your selection from the Bring Layer To Front Then drop-down list to control how the layer is treated once it is dropped. Your options include Leave On Top and Restore To Z-Index (place back at its current level in the document).
10. Provide the name of the JavaScript function to run in the Call JavaScript field. This field runs the JavaScript function when the layer is being dragged. You can leave this blank if there is no script that needs to be run and you are only using the drag-and-drop function.
11. Provide the name of the JavaScript function to run when the layer is dropped in the When Dropped Call JavaScript field. You can leave this blank if there is no script that needs to be run and you are only using the drag-and-drop function. Use the Only If Snapped check box to run the JavaScript only if the Drag Layer behavior snapped the layer into place. This JavaScript function could be something as simple as an alert box stating There I helped you out a bit.
12. Click OK.
13. Select an event to use as the catalyst for running the function from the Events list in the Behaviors panel.

Go to URL

The Go to URL behavior will open a document in a specified location. This can be applied to an image rollover to load new banner ads as people traverse your site.

To use the Go to URL behavior, follow these steps:

1. Select a link on your document, then select the plus (+)→Go To URL command on the Behaviors panel. This opens the dialog box shown in Figure B-9.

Figure B-9 The Go To URL dialog box.

2. Select the name of the window to load the document into from the Open In field. Only named windows opened by other scripts and behaviors are listed here.
3. In the URL field, type (or select using the Browse button) the file that will be loaded into the specified window.
4. Click OK.
5. Select an event to use as the catalyst for running the function from the Events list in the Behaviors panel.

Jump Menu

The Jump Menu behavior allows you to turn a standard Form List Menu into a hyperlinked site navigation tool. This behavior can only be added to your document if a List Menu has already been created.

To use the Jump Menu behavior, follow these steps:

1. Select the List Menu on your document, then select the plus (+)→Jump Menu command on the Behaviors panel. This opens the dialog box shown in Figure B-10.

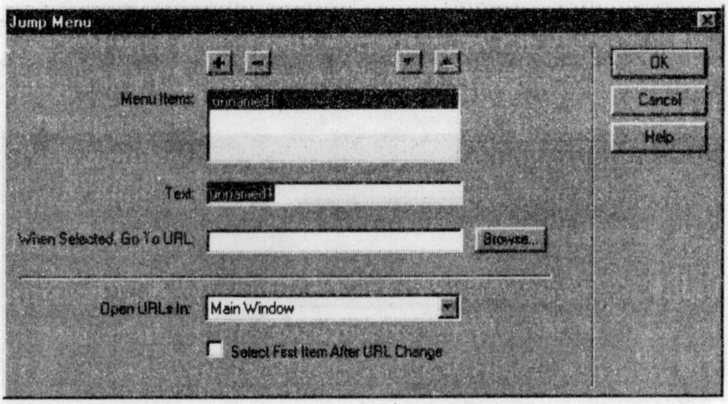

Figure B-10 The Jump Menu dialog box.

2. In the Text field, type the name of the menu entry to create. This is the name that will appear within the Jump Menu for site visitors.
3. In the When Selected Go To URL field, type (or select using the Browse button) the name of the file that will be loaded when this option is selected.
4. Click the plus (+) button to add a new menu item. Repeat steps 2 through 4 until all of your menu items have been created.
5. Use the minus (-) button to remove any entries that you wish to no longer use. Select the entry to be removed before clicking minus (-).
6. Use the up and down arrows to adjust the order of your menu entries.
7. In the Open URLs In field, select the name of the window that serves as the destination for the documents loaded by the Jump Menu.
8. Check the Select First Item After URL Change check box to make the first link, or form field, active whenever the new document is completely loaded.
9. Click OK.
10. Select an event to use as the catalyst for running the function from the Events list in the Behaviors panel.

Jump Menu Go

The Jump Menu Go behavior adds a Go (or Submit) button to your Jump Menus. This allows people to make multiple selections in the menus without automatically being taken to every page they select.

To use the Jump Menu Go behavior, follow these steps:

1. Select a link on your document, then select the plus (+)→Jump Menu Go command on the Behaviors panel. This opens the dialog box shown in Figure B-11.

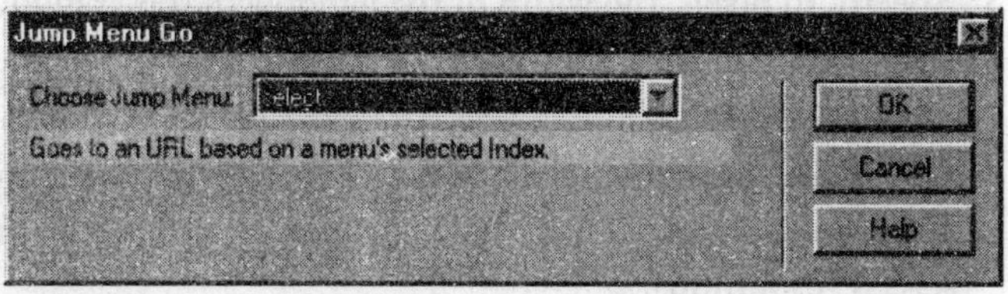

Figure B-11 The Jump Menu Go dialog box.

2. Select the name of the Jump Menu that will be used by the Go button.
3. Click OK.
4. Select an event to use as the catalyst for running the function from the Events list in the Behaviors panel.

Open Browser Window

The Open Browser Window behavior allows you to open a new browser window. You can control the size, name, loaded document, and screen attributes of the window when it loads. This is how all of those annoying popup ads are created, but they can be used for many items that are more informative.

To use the Open Browser Window behavior, follow these steps:

1. Select a link on your document, then select the plus (+)→Open Browser Window command on the Behaviors panel. This opens the dialog box shown in Figure B-12.

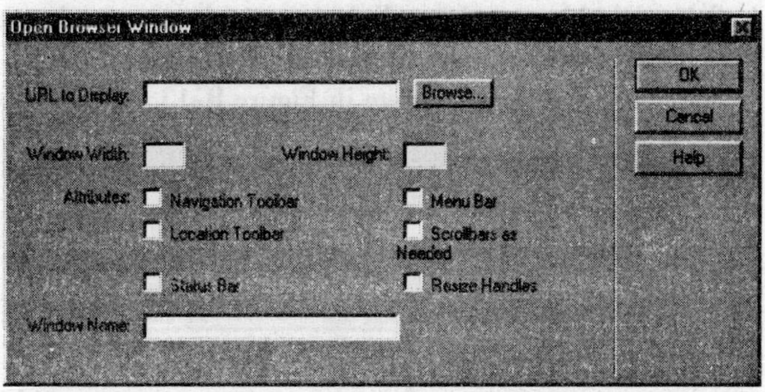

Figure B-12 The Open Browser Window dialog box.

2. Type in the URL of the document to be loaded in the URL To Display field. Alternatively, you can select the document using the Browse button.
3. Specify, in pixels, the width of the window in the Window Width field. Keep in mind that most users have under 800-pixels-wide screen resolutions.
4. Specify, in pixels, the height of the window in the Window Height field. Keep in mind that most users have under 600-pixels-tall screen resolutions.
5. Select the screen attributes to load from the following list: Navigation Toolbar, Location Toolbar, Status Bar, Menu Bar, Scrollbars As Needed, Resize Handles. If you select none of these, the window being created will only have a border and the document contents. Generally, you will need to check Scrollbars As Needed to ensure that people will be able to scroll through the information you have provided them if it doesn't all appear on their screen.
6. Type a name for the window in the Window Name field.
7. Click OK.
8. Select an event to use as the catalyst for running the function from the Events list in the Behaviors panel.

Play Sound

To play a background sound, or even one that is started whenever you move your mouse over a button, you need to install the Play Sound behavior. This behavior embeds a sound file into your document.

To use the Play Sound behavior, follow these steps:

1. Select an object, such as a link, on your document, then select the plus (+) →Play Sound command on the Behaviors panel. This opens the dialog box shown in Figure B-13.

Figure B-13 The Play Sound dialog box.

2. In the Play Sound field, type the address of the sound file you wish to play. Alternatively, use the Browse button to select it from your hard drive.
3. Click OK.
4. Select an event to use as the catalyst for running the function from the Event's list in the Behaviors panel.

Popup Message

The Popup Message behavior allows you to create a popup alert box on your Web page. This can be used to provide a note to the site visitor, or even remind them about information that may affect them.

To use the Popup Message behavior, follow these steps:

1. Select an object, such as a link or image, on your document, then select the plus (+)→Popup Message command on the Behaviors panel. This opens the dialog box shown in Figure B-14.

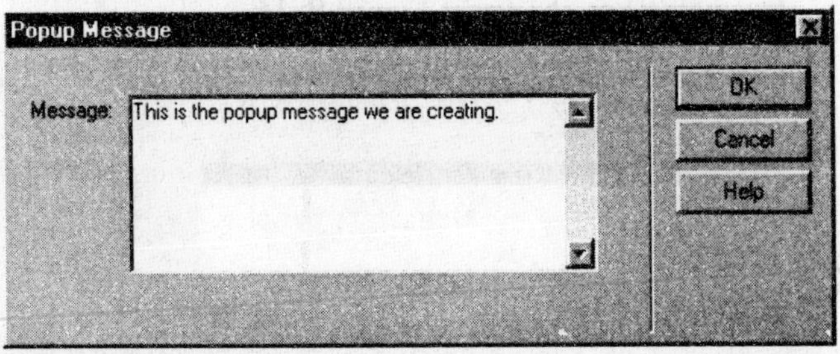

Figure B-14 The Popup Message dialog box.

2. In the Message field, type the message that you want to appear in the alert box.
3. Click OK.
4. Select an event to use as the catalyst for running the function from the Events list in the Behaviors panel.

When this behavior is used, it will appear in the same fashion as the dialog box shown in Figure B-15.

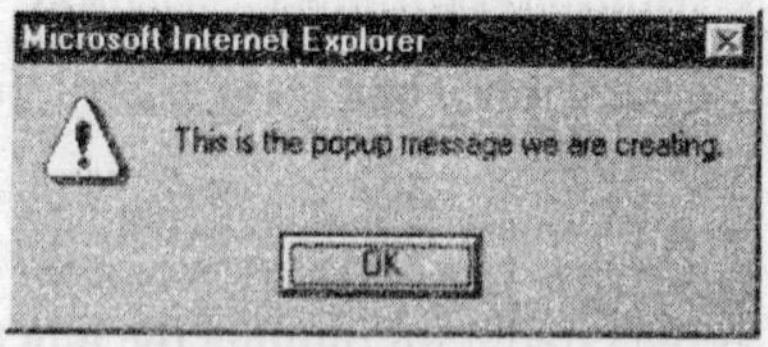

Figure B-15 An alert box created with the Popup Message behavior.

Preload Images

When you use a series of images in your document that are part of image rollovers, or navigation bars, you want to preload those images so that they are already loaded before they are needed by the image effect.

To use the Preload Images behavior, follow these steps:

1. With your cursor anywhere in your document, select the plus (+)→Preload Images command on the Behaviors panel. This opens the dialog box shown in Figure B-16.

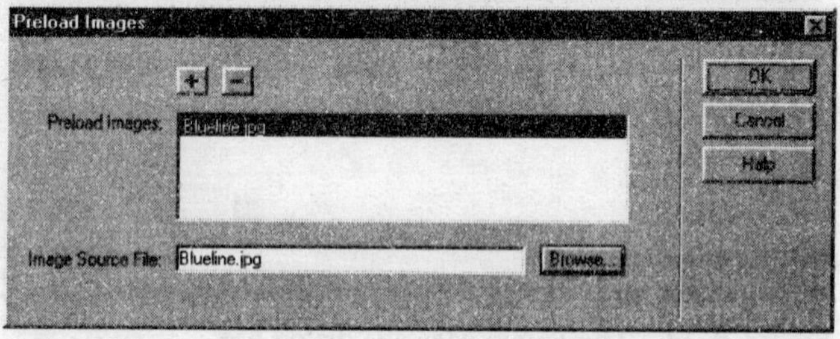

Figure B-16 The Preload Images dialog box.

2. In the Image Source File field, type the address of the image file you wish to preload. Alternatively, use the Browse button to select it from your hard drive.
3. Click the plus (+) button and repeat step 2 to add another image. Repeat these two steps until you have listed every image you wish to preload.
4. Click OK.
5. Select an event to use as the catalyst for running the function from the Events list in the Behaviors panel.

Set Nav Bar Image

The Set Nav Bar Image behavior allows you to create a navigation bar out of a series of images on your document. A navigation bar is a series of images that provide the menu, or navigational structure, for maneuvering through a Web site. There are four possible states of each image used in a navigation bar. You should have those images created before you apply the Set Nav Bar Image behavior. It is also easier to use the Insert→Interactive Images→Navigation Bar command if you are creating a page from scratch. Navigation bars are designed to be used on Frames-enabled sites.

To use the Set Nav Bar Image behavior, follow these steps:

1. Select an image in your document, then select the plus (+)→Set Nav Bar Image command on the Behaviors panel. This opens the Set Nav Bar Image dialog box at the Basic tab, as shown in Figure B-17.

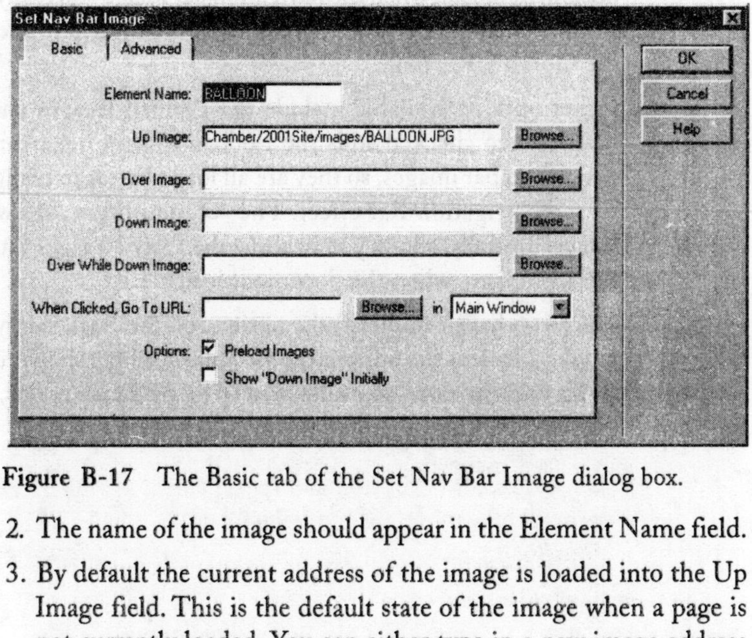

Figure B-17 The Basic tab of the Set Nav Bar Image dialog box.

2. The name of the image should appear in the Element Name field.
3. By default the current address of the image is loaded into the Up Image field. This is the default state of the image when a page is not currently loaded. You can either type in a new image address or use the Browse button to replace this image if it is not the default image you wish to use.

4. In the Over Image field, type in (or use the Browser button to select) the address of the image to be used when the mouse is moved over the image but not clicked. This image typically appears right after the Up image when a visitor is exploring the site.
5. In the Down Image field, type in (or use the Browser button to select) the address of the image to be used when the mouse has clicked on an image and its page is loaded. This image is the one that lets visitors know exactly which page they are viewing within your site.
6. The Over While Down Image field should contain the address of the image to display when the mouse is moved over the image while the button is pressed. This image can be the same as the Over Image, or it can be separate, depending upon the effect you are creating.
7. The When Clicked Go To URL field provides the address of the document to load when the navigation bar image is actually clicked. Provide the target frame, or window, in the In field to the right of the Go To URL field.
8. Other options available include the Preload Images check box, which when checked adds the Preload Images behavior to your navigation bar images, so they are all loaded prior to being needed by the Navigation Bar effect. The second option, Show "Down Image" Initially, allows you to show the Down images rather than the Up images when the document loads.
9. Once you have completed the options on the Basic tab, you need to take a look at the options on the Advanced tab shown in Figure B-18. In many cases, you will not need to use these options, but they are described here just in case.

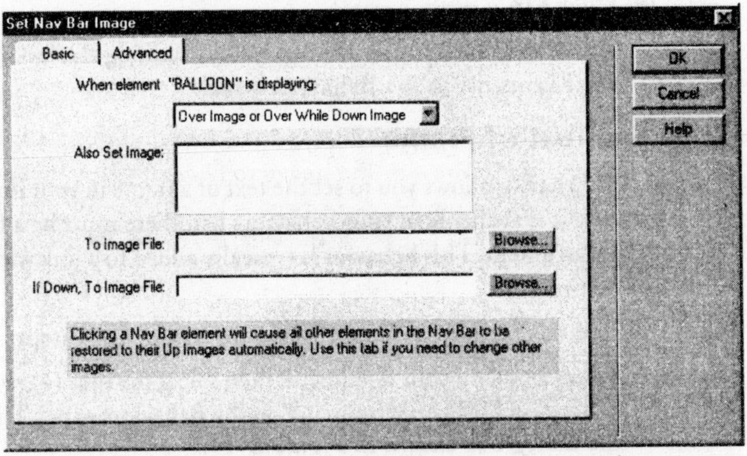

Figure B-18 The Advanced tab of the Set Nav Bar Image dialog box.

10. Click the Advanced tab of the Set Nav Bar Image dialog box. The options on this tab allow you to control other images while the Navigation bar image is being manipulated.
11. Select either Down Image or Over Image Or Over While Down Image from the When Element [name] Is Displaying drop-down list. This identifies the image state to which the other settings are being applied.
12. The Also Set Image field contains a list of the other images on the document. The image selected from this list will also be changed whenever the original image is manipulated by the mouse.
13. In the To Image File field, type the name of the secondary image to be loaded when the specified state is reached with the original navigation bar image. Alternatively, use the Browse button to select the image you wish to use.
14. In the To Image File field, type the name of the secondary image to be loaded when the specified state is reached with the original navigation bar image. Alternatively, use the Browse button to select the image you wish to use.
15. If you have selected Over Image Or Over While Down from the first drop-down list, then you will also need to specify the image to be displayed if the original navigation bar image is in the Down state, by providing a value in the If Down, To Image File field.

16. Click OK.
17. Select an event to use as the catalyst for running the function from the Events list in the Behaviors panel.

Set Text of Frame

This behavior allows you to set the text of a frame in your document. Before it is available in your behaviors list, there must be a frame on your document. This behavior is typically added to a link within your document.

To use the Set Text of Frame behavior, follow these steps:

1. Select a link on your document, then select the plus (+) →Set Text →Set Text Of Frame command on the Behaviors panel. This opens the dialog box shown in Figure B-19.

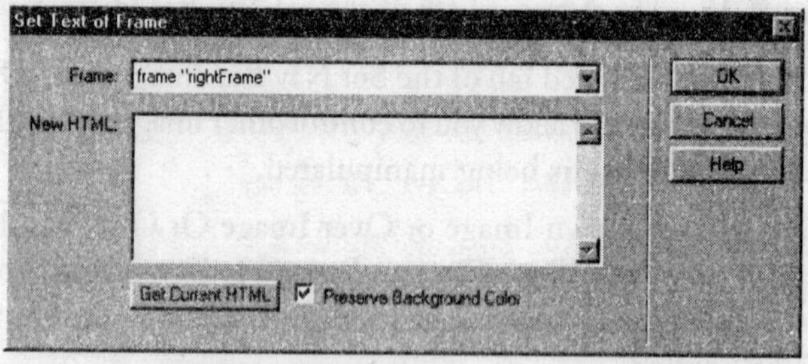

Figure B-19 The Set Text Of Frame dialog box.

2. Select the name of the frame in which you wish the text changed from the Frame field.
3. In the New HTML field, type the text you wish to place in this frame. You can use HTML codes in this field, but not the <head>, <html>, or <body> elements.
4. Click the Get Current HTML to get the HTML that is currently loaded into the frame. If you wish to be able to return the contents of the frame to its original state at some point, it is often easiest to do it first, before modifying the frame contents
5. Check the Preserve Background Color check box to preserve the background color settings of the original frame contents.
6. Click OK.
7. Select an event to use as the catalyst for running the function from the Events list in the Behaviors panel.

Set Text of Layer

The Set Text of Layer behavior allows you to alter the text contained within a specific layer on your document. Before this behavior is available, you must have at least one layer on your page.

To use the Set Text of Layer behavior, follow these steps:

1. Select a link on your document, then select the plus (+) →Set Text →Set Text Of Layer command on the Behaviors panel. This opens the dialog box shown in Figure B-20.

Figure B-20 The Set Text Of Layer dialog box.

2. Select the name of the layer in which you wish the text changed from the Layer field.
3. In the New HTML field, type the text you wish to place in this layer. You can use HTML codes in this field, but not the <head>, <html>, or <body> elements.
4. Click OK.
5. Select an event to use as the catalyst for running the function from the Events list in the Behaviors panel.

Set Text of Status Bar

The Set Text of Status Bar behavior allows you to modify the text contained within your web browser's status bar. This effect is often used to provide alternative information to the default link address placed in the status bar when your mouse is moved over a link.

To use the Set Text of Status Bar behavior, follow these steps:

1. Select a link on your document, then select the plus (+)→Set Text →Set Text Of Status Bar command on the Behaviors panel. This opens the dialog box shown in Figure B-21.

Figure B-21 The Set Text Of Status Bar dialog box.

2. Type the message to be displayed on the status bar in the Message field. This field can't contain HTML, but can contain some JavaScript commands formatted in the following fashion: {window.name}.
3. Click OK.
4. Select an event to use as the catalyst for running the function from the Events list in the Behaviors panel.

Set Text of Text Field

The Set Text of Text Field behavior requires the use of a form text field created with a textarea element. These form fields are added into your document using Insert→Form Objects→Text Area.

To use the Set Text of Text Field behavior, follow these steps:

1. Select a link on your document, then select the plus (+)→Set Text →Set Text Of Text Field command on the Behaviors panel. This opens the dialog box shown in Figure B-22.

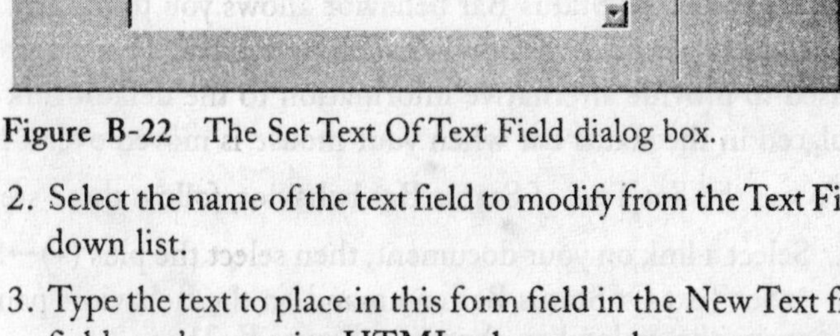

Figure B-22 The Set Text Of Text Field dialog box.

2. Select the name of the text field to modify from the Text Field drop-down list.
3. Type the text to place in this form field in the New Text field. This field can't contain HTML elements, but can contain some JavaScript commands formatted in the following fashion: {document.lastmodified}.

4. Click OK.
5. Select an event to use as the catalyst for running the function from the Events list in the Behaviors panel.

Show-Hide Layers

The Show-Hide Layers behavior is used to control the appearance, and disappearance, of the layers contained within your documents. You can use the Change Properties behavior to do this also, but this behavior is easier to use when you are adjusting layers.

To use the Show-Hide Layers behavior, follow these steps:

1. Select a link on your document, then select the plus (+)→Show Hide Layers command on the Behaviors panel. This opens the dialog box shown in Figure B-23.

Figure B-23 The Show-Hide Layers dialog box.

2. Select the name of the Layer whose visibility property needs set.
3. Select the Show, Hide, or Default button to control the visibility of the layer. Repeat steps 2 and 3 until you have set the visibility for all the layers in your document.
4. Click OK.
5. Select an event to use as the catalyst for running the function from the Events list in the Behaviors panel.

Swap Image

The Swap Image behavior allows you to control the swapping of images when you click on or move your mouse over an image in your document. You must have an image loaded in your document to have access to this behavior.

To use the Swap Image behavior, follow these steps:

1. Select a link on your document, then select the plus (+)→Swap Image command on the Behaviors panel. This opens the dialog box shown in Figure B-24.

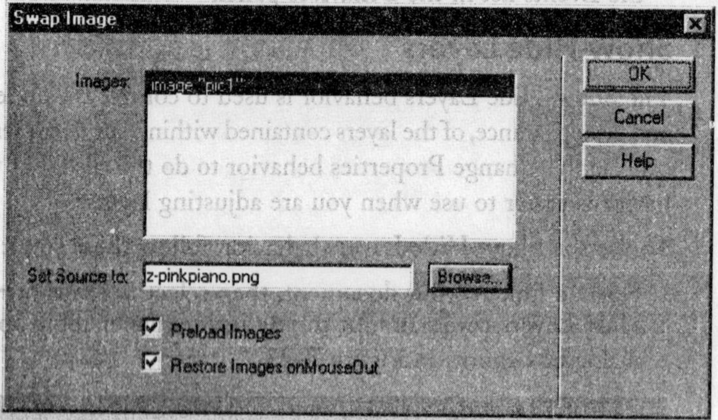

Figure B-24 The Swap Image dialog box.

2. Select the name of the image that needs to be swapped out from the Images list.
3. In the Set Source To field, either type the name of the file to be loaded or use the Browse button to select it from the list of files on your drive.
4. Check the Preload Images check box if you wish to have all the images used in the Swap Image behavior loaded before the behavior actually calls for them. This is the best option when creating an interactive site.
5. Check the Restore Images onMouseOut check box to force the automatic insertion of the Swap Image Restore behavior associated with the onMouseOut event associated with the element.
6. Click OK.
7. Select an event to use as the catalyst for running the function from the Events list in the Behaviors panel.

Swap Image Restore

The Swap Image Restore behavior allows you to restore images to their original state, if a Swap Image behavior has already been applied to them. You must apply the Swap Image behavior prior to the Swap Image Restore behavior.

To use the Swap Image Restore behavior, follow these steps:

1. Select a link on your document, then select the plus (+)→Swap Image Restore command on the Behaviors panel. This opens the dialog box shown in Figure B-25.

Figure B-25 The Swap Image Restore dialog box.

2. Click OK.
3. Select an event to use as the catalyst for running the function from the Events list in the Behaviors panel.

Go to Timeline Frame

The Go to Timeline Frame behavior is used to jump down a timeline to a specified point. Once at that point you can use the Play Timeline behavior to start the timeline running in normal mode again.

To use the Go to Timeline Frame behavior, follow these steps:

1. Select a link on your document, then select the plus (+)→Timeline→Go To Timelines Frame command on the Behaviors panel. This opens the dialog box shown in Figure B-26.

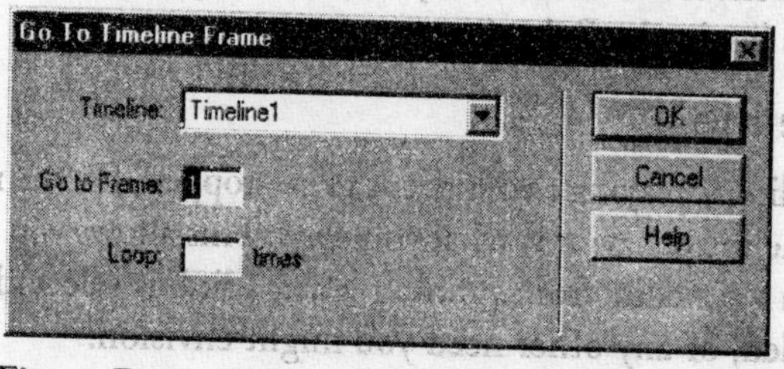

Figure B-26 The Go To Timeline Frame dialog box.

2. Select the name of the Timeline to maneuver from the Timeline drop-down list.
3. Provide a frame number to jump to in the Go To Frame text field.
4. Provide a number of times that the timeline should loop from that point in the Loop field.

5. Click OK.
6. Select an event to use as the catalyst for running the function from the Events list in the Behaviors panel.

Play Timeline

The Play Timeline behavior allows you to start a timeline from any event. By default a timeline starts when the document is opened, but you can also start it when a button is clicked or a value is selected in a form.

To use the Play Timeline behavior, follow these steps:

1. Select a link on your document, then select the plus (+)→Timeline→ Play Timeline command on the Behaviors panel. This opens the dialog box shown in Figure B-27.

Figure B-27 The Play Timeline dialog box.

2. Select the name of the timeline to start from the Play Timeline drop-down list.
3. Click OK.
4. Select an event to use as the catalyst for running the function from the Events list in the Behaviors panel.

Stop Timeline

When a timeline is playing and it needs to be stopped, for any reason, the Stop Timeline behavior is what you need. This allows you to stop the events on a timeline from running when a link is selected, or an image is loaded, or any other need you might envision.

To use the Stop Timeline behavior, follow these steps:

1. Select a link on your document, then select the plus (+)→Timeline→ Stop Timeline command on the Behaviors panel. This opens the dialog box shown in Figure B-28.

Figure B-28 The Stop Timeline dialog box.

2. Select the name of the timeline to be stopped from the Stop Timeline drop-down list. You can also select All Timelines if you wish to stop them all simultaneously
3. Click OK.
4. Select an event to use as the catalyst for running the function from the Events list in the Behaviors panel.

Validate Form

The Validate Form behavior allows you to check the values entered into forms on your Web pages before the information is processed. You can use this script to ensure that a visitor has entered a properly formatted e-mail address or date, if you want.

To use the Validate Form behavior, follow these steps:

1. Select a link on your document, then select the plus (+)→Validate Form command on the Behaviors panel. This opens the dialog box shown in Figure B-29.

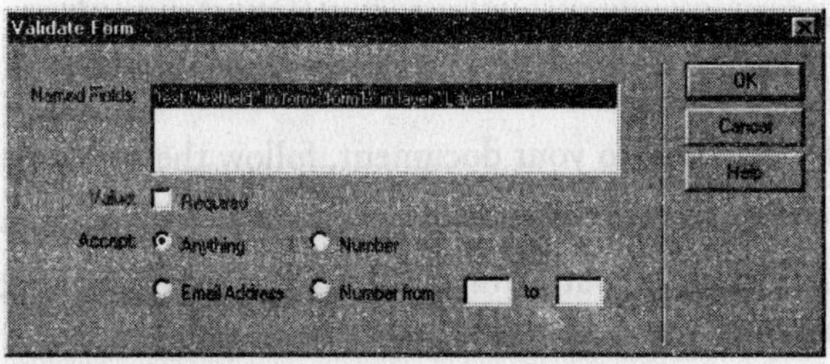

Figure B-29 The Validate Form dialog box.

2. Select the name of the field to be validated from the Named Fields list. Your fields must be named in order for the Validate Form dialog box to work.
3. Check the Value Required check box if you wish to force visitors to complete this field before the information can be processed.

4. Select one of the four options from the Accept radio buttons: Anything (literally, anything goes), Number (allows only numerical values, but any value will work), Email Address (allows only properly formatted e-mail addresses), or Number From _ To _ (allows only numbers between the given range).
5. Click OK.
6. Select an event to use as the catalyst for running the function from the Events list in the Behaviors panel.

Behaviors Panel

The Behaviors panel, shown in Figure B-30, provides access to all of the built-in Dreamweaver behaviors (customizable effects). These behaviors provide you with access to checking form contents, creating rollover images, and adjusting the content of individual pages, form fields, or even popup windows or status bar contents.

Figure B-30 The Behaviors panel.

To add a behavior to your document, follow these steps:

1. Select the object to which the behavior is to be applied.
2. Click the plus (+) button on the Behaviors panel and select the type of behavior you wish to use, as shown in Figure B-31.

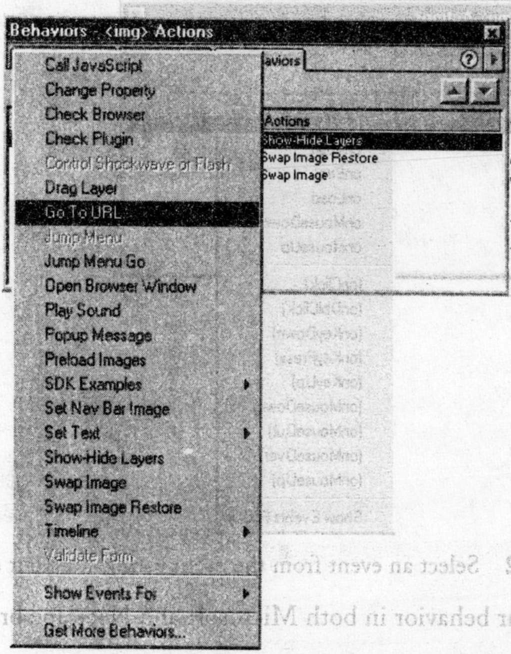

Figure B-31 Select from the available behaviors for your object.

NOTE *Some behaviors are only available when your document has specific items already added, for instance, you can only validate forms when a form and form fields have been previously added to your document.*

3. Complete the options listed in your chosen behavior's dialog box.
4. Select the event that will trigger your behavior from the Events list, as shown in Figure B-32.

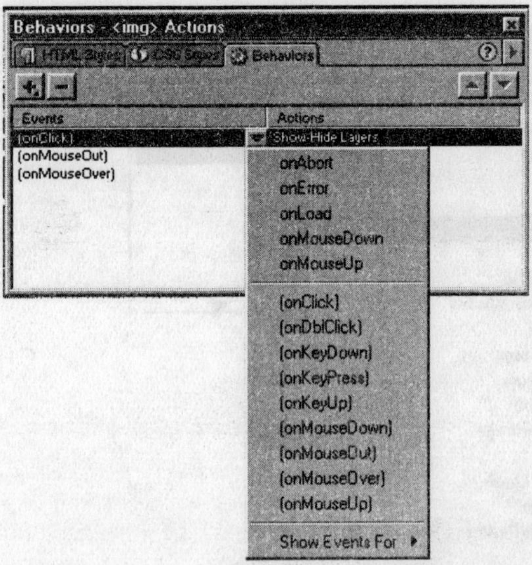

Figure B-32 Select an event from the event listings for your object.

5. Test your behavior in both Microsoft and Netscape browsers.

SEE ALSO *Behaviors, Events*

Borders

Many HTML elements can have a border applied to them. This border can be thick, thin, colorful, or just plain black. You can control the appearance of borders on images, tables, or frames by using their border attribute accessible from Dreamweaver's Properties inspector, shown in Figure B-33.

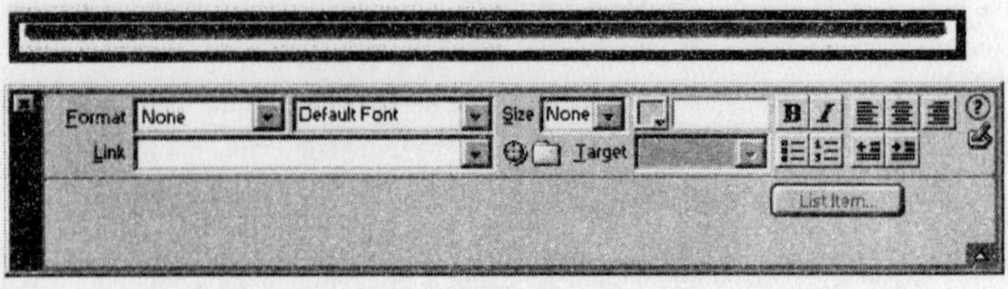

Figure B-33 Border options on an image's Properties inspector.

To add a border to one of these elements, make the border value greater than zero. You can adjust the color of the border by modifying that element's Cascading Style Sheet properties. You can also add borders to most other elements, such as layers and paragraphs, using Cascading Style Sheets.

SEE ALSO *Cascading Style Sheets, Colors*

Browser Checking see Behaviors

Browser Compatibility

Dreamweaver includes the ability to test for specific browser compatibility with the Web documents you create. To use this feature, select File→Check Target Browsers. This opens the Check Target Browsers dialog box shown in Figure B-34. In this dialog box, select all of the browser versions you wish to test. You can select more than one browser by holding down the Ctrl key while making your selection.

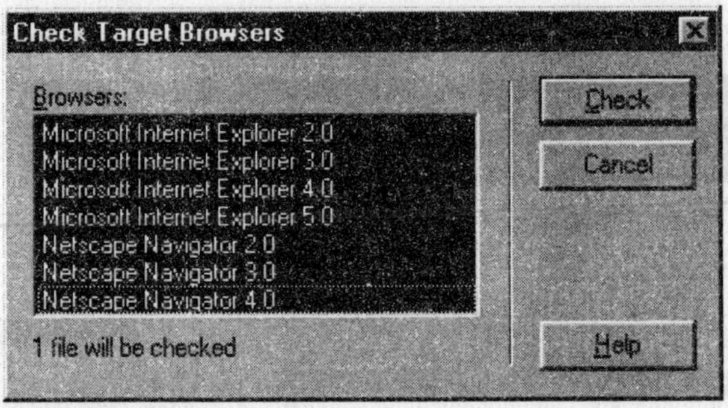

Figure B-34 The Check Target Browsers browser selection list.

Once you have chosen specific browsers, click the Check button. After a minute, or less, you will be greeted with the Dreamweaver Target BrowserCheck, as shown in Figure B-35. This report lists the individual browsers tested and the errors that were generated within each. Each of the individual error reports includes the type of error, the element it occurred in, and the line number the error occurred on.

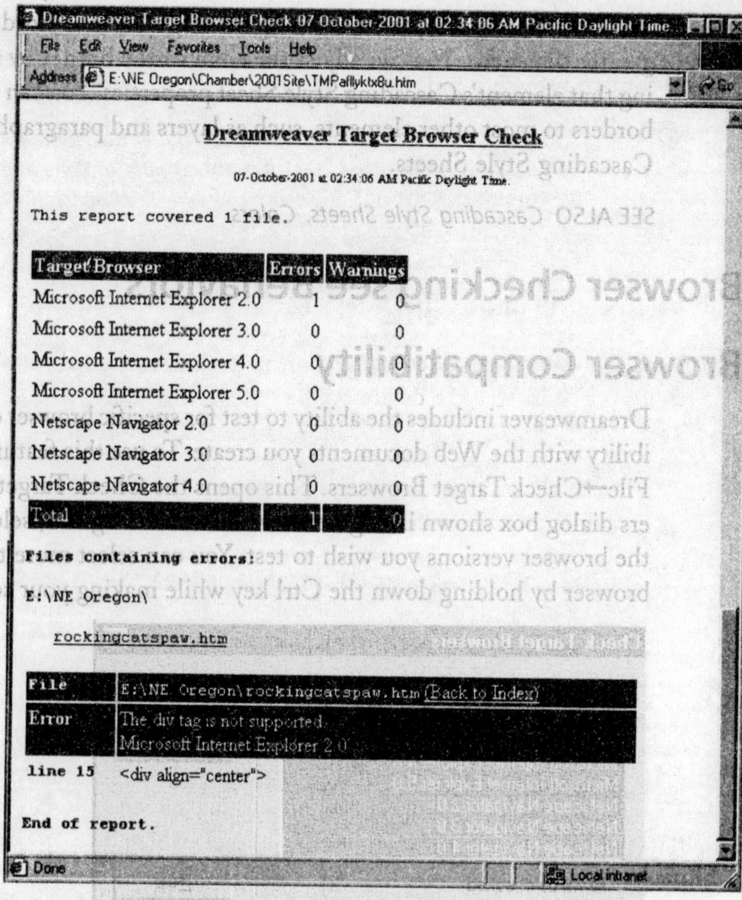

Figure B-35 Use the Dreamweaver Target Browser Check to find the errors in your document before visitors do.

Call JavaScript see Behaviors

Cascading Style Sheets

Cascading Style Sheets (CSS) enable document authors and users to control the presentation of document information. CSS separates the presentation elements of a document from its content, providing the formatting of information for HTML documents. CSS allows you to tailor the display of your document for visual applications, aural devices, print, Braille, TTY machines, or even television. Cascading Style

Sheets, level 2 (CSS2), the current version of CSS, built on the previous version, maintaining compatibility between currently conforming document browsers and their next generation.

NOTE *Cascading Style Sheets level 3 has been under development since 1999, but as of October 2001 it is not complete. You can follow the developments of CSS3 from the World Wide Web Consortium (W3C) Web site located at:* http://www.w3.org/Style/CSS/current-work.

Internal Style Sheets

Internal style sheets are contained within style elements at the top of your Web page. When a document has an internal style sheet, its code will appear similar to the following sample:

```
<html>

<head>

<style type="text/css" >

  p { color: red;

      font-face: Arial;

      background: grey; }

</style>

</head>

<body>

<p> This is a paragraph </p>

</body>

</html>
```

Internal style sheets are added to your document by clicking the New Style button on the CSS Styles panel (Window→CSS Style) and selecting Define In This Document Only from the resulting New Style dialog box.

External Style Sheets

External style sheets are linked to the current Web page with either the <link> element or the <style> @import </style> rules. These files typically have a css extension and are often located on the same computer hosting the original Web page. Dreamweaver stores the style sheet in the same directory as the document, although many servers will set up a special style sheet folder to contain all of the style sheet information for the entire Web site. They can be used by as many documents in your Web site, or others' Web sites, as needed.

To link to a previously created external style sheet, select Text→CSS Styles→Attach Style Sheet. Select the style sheet from the entries available from the Select Style Sheet File dialog box shown in Figure C-1.

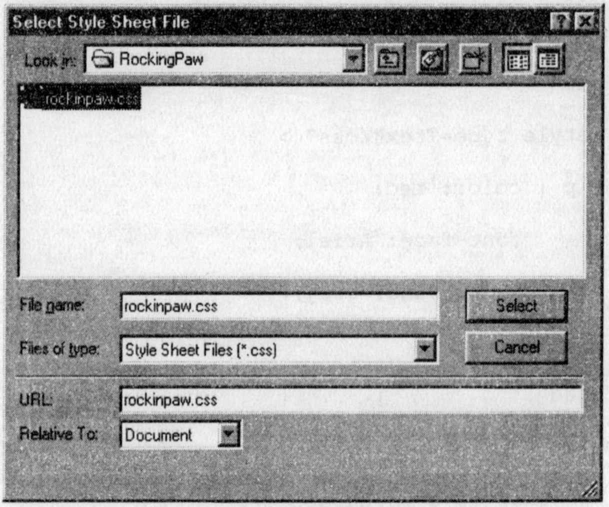

Figure C-1 The Select Style Sheet File dialog box, allowing you to select from style sheets available on your local computer or network.

When the style sheet has been added to your document, the following <link> element will be created.

```
<link rel="stylesheet" href="rockinpaw.css"
type="text/css">
```

A second alternative for adding an external style sheet is to use the Insert→Head Tags→Link command to open the Insert Link dialog box shown in Figure C-2.

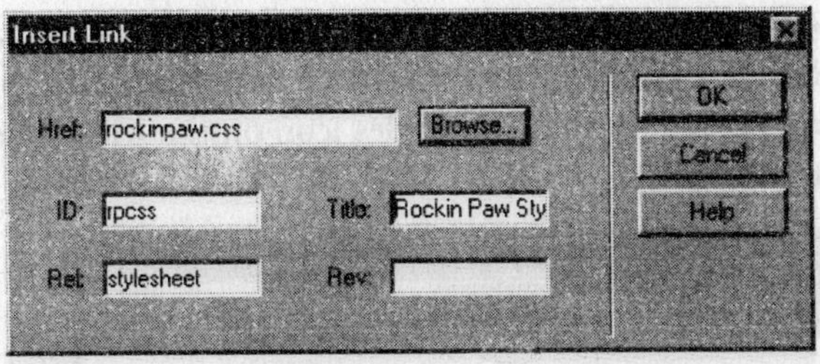

Figure C-2 The Insert Link dialog box, allowing you to specify a relationship between the style sheet you are adding and the current document.

This dialog box allows you to specify the ID and URL of the document, the relationship of the document (style sheet in this case), and a title for the style sheet. As you can see from the following code, by completing the Insert Link dialog box you provide more information for your style sheet, but the three main portions, the rel, href, and type attributes, are still provided.

```
<link href="rockinpaw.css" id="rpcss"

      rel="stylesheet" type="text/css"

      title="Rocking Paw Style Sheets">
```

Your third and last option to insert an external style sheet into your document can be done from the Attach Style Sheet button located on the CSS Styles panel. Open the CSS Styles panel by selecting Window→CSS Styles or by selecting Shift +F11. The CSS Styles panel allows you to create new internal or external style sheets and style sheet rules, attach previously created external style sheets, or edit an existing style sheet. This dialog box is discussed in more detail in the next section.

Creating Style Sheets

Internal style sheets are contained within your Web document. This allows them to work with only the document they are in. If you wish to create a single style sheet to be used in multiple documents, you will need to create an external style sheet.

To create an internal style sheet, follow these steps:

1. Select the Window→CSS Styles (Shift +F11) command to open the CSS Styles panel shown in Figure C-3. You may also open this panel by clicking on the CSS Styles icon on the Mini-Launcher on your status bar.

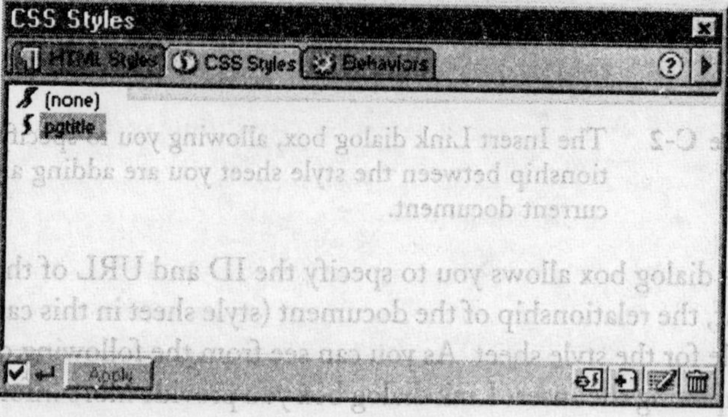

Figure C-3 The CSS Styles panel.

2. Click the New Style button (second of the four in the right bottom corner) to open the New Style dialog box shown in Figure C-4.

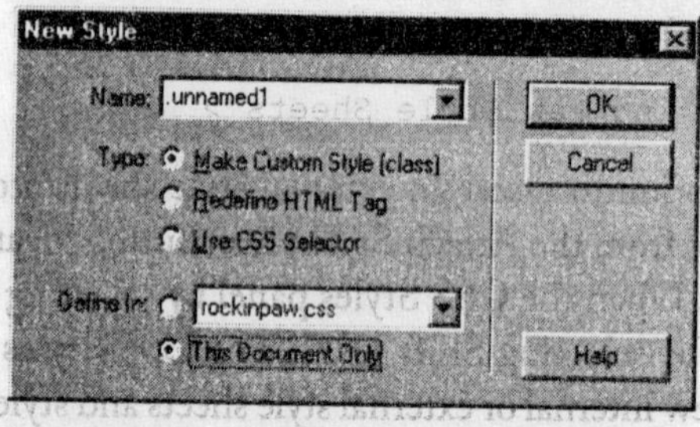

Figure C-4 The New Style dialog box.

3. In the New Style dialog box, you have a variety of options to control how the style sheet appears on your document. Although the following list doesn't appear in the order in which the options occur on your screen, you need to make your selections in this order:

- Type: Make Custom Style (class) - This option creates a custom CSS style that is associated with the class attribute of an element, not the element itself. This is typically how you will create styles for items that do not match with the other objects created using the same element. You will typically have a variety of styles created for formatting paragraphs, for instance, and you can't apply them all to the <p> tag. You get to provide a name for your own class in the Name field when this option is selected.
- Redefine HTML Tag - This option allows you to define all elements of a specific type to appear the same. In other words, all of the paragraphs (p) would look the same, whether they were used as headings, notes, quotes, or auxiliary information. The options available from the Tag field, when this option is selected, include all of the HTML elements used to create documents.
- Use CSS Selector - This option allows you to use one of the predefined CSS selectors that format the appearance of link text as your visitors interact with your Web pages. Options available to choose from the Selector field, when this section is chosen, include a:active, a:hover, a:link, and a:visited.

4. Make your selection in either the Tag or Selector fields, if you have chosen either the Redefine HTML Tag or the Use CSS Selector options from the Type list. If you chose Make Custom Style from the Type options, type in the name you wish to use to recognize this particular class of styles rules.
5. Select the Define In This Document Only option to create an internal style sheet, select Define In [New Style Sheet File] to create a new external style sheet document, or Define In [your filename] to add your new style to an existing style sheet document.

NOTE *If you are planning on using the same styles in multiple documents, create or update an external style sheet.*

6. Click OK when you are ready to start creating a new style rule. This will open the Style Definition For dialog box shown in Figure C-5.

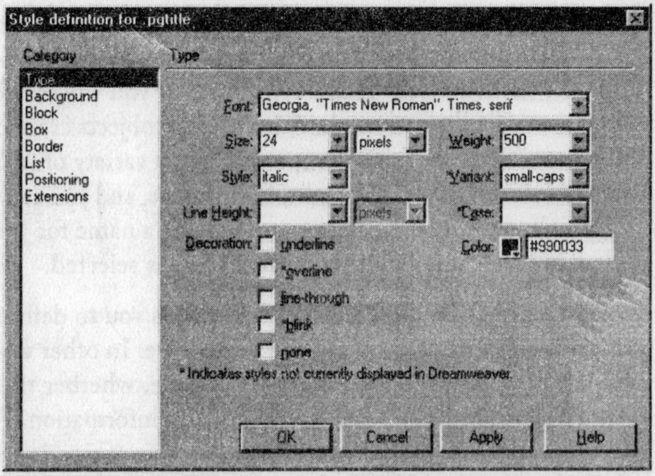

Figure C-5 The Style Definition For dialog box.

Within the Style Definition For dialog box there are a variety of options. Each of them affects some aspect of the display of your Web page objects. The following table shows the options available in each category of this dialog box.

CATEGORY	STYLE	DESCRIPTION
Type	Font	Specifies typeface.
	Size	Specifies typeface size as a measurement, such as points or pixels, or as a relative size, such as xx-large.
	Weight	Specifies the thickness of the characters as either bold, bolder, lighter, or a numerical value where 400 is equivalent to bold.
	Style	Specifies the visible type style, such as italic or oblique.

CATEGORY	STYLE	DESCRIPTION
Type	Variant	Specifies a typeface effect, such as small caps.
	Line Height	Specifies the height of an individual line.
	Case	Specifies the case of the letters, for example, all capitals or all lowercase.
	Decoration	Specifies the text effects you wish to be applied, including Underlines, Overlies, Line-Through, and Blink.
	Color	Specifies the color of the object you are creating.
Background	Background Color	Specifies the page or object background color.
	Background Image	Specifies the image to be used as a background.
	Repeat	Specifies how an image will be repeated in your background, whether never, horizontal (repeat-x), vertical (repeat-y), or tile (repeat).
	Attachment	Specifies whether the background image will be scrolled with a document or left static.

CATEGORY	STYLE	DESCRIPTION
Background	Horizontal Position	Controls the side margins around your background image.
	Vertical Position	Controls the vertical margins around your background image.
Block	Word Spacing	Spacing between individual words.
	Letter Spacing	Spacing between individual letters
	Vertical Alignment	Controls the vertical alignment of the object in reference to the text baseline applied.
	Text Align	Controls the horizontal alignment of the object: left, right, center, justify.
	Text Indent	Distance of the first line indent.
	Whitespace	Controls how white space should be treated, whether ignored (normal), preserved (pre), or prohibiting line wraps (nowrap).
Box	Width	Sets the width of the object box.
	Height	Sets the height of the object box.

CATEGORY	STYLE	DESCRIPTION
Box	Float	Controls the side that other objects can be located on.
	Clear	Controls the side that must be clear of other objects.
	Padding	Controls the top, bottom, left, and right distances around the outside of the object that are reserved from use by other objects.
	Margin	Controls the internal margins of the object box.
Border	Width	Controls the top, bottom, left, and right border line widths.
	Color	Controls the top, bottom, left, and right border colors.
	Style	Controls the appearance of the border. Options include, for example, dotted, dashed, double, groove, inset, outset, and ridge.

CATEGORY	STYLE	DESCRIPTION
List	Type	Controls the style of bullet/numeral to be used to set off each item of the list.
	Bullet Image	Specifies the URL of the image used as a bullet instead of the Type options.
	Position	Controls the position of the bullet, whether inside or outside of the list box.
Positioning	Type	Controls the style of positioning used to place an object: absolute, relative, or static.
	Visibility	Controls whether the object can be seen (visible) or is hidden.
	Z-Index	Specifies the vertical stacking order of positioned objects, such as layers.
	Overflow	Controls how content that is larger than the visible object should be treated.

CATEGORY	STYLE	DESCRIPTION
Extensions	Page Break Before	Controls the placement, or allowance, of page breaks when printing the document.
	Page Break After	Controls the placement, or allowance, of page breaks occurring with printing the document.
	Cursor	Specifies the mouse cursor to display when the mouse is over this object.
	Filter	Specifies one of the Microsoft filters to apply to the object.

After you have made your style sheet selections, click OK in the Style Definition For dialog box to save them to your style sheet document or your internal style sheet.

Once applied, your style sheets can create the effects shown in Figure C-6 without the use of any graphics. As you can see, Netscape Navigator 4.6 and Internet Explorer 5 display the document differently. Netscape Navigator 6 displays the information in a fashion closer to Internet Explorer, yet still somewhat different. When using CSS to control the appearance of your information, you may find that objects on your pages will look the same to everyone viewing them. You may have to modify your style sheet to make it work acceptably for all viewers.

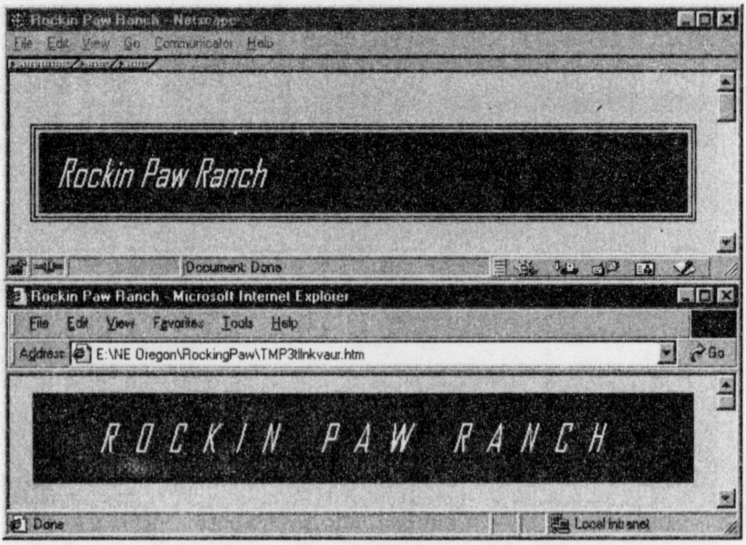

Figure C-6 Applied style sheet effects to the title of this document as displayed in Internet Explorer and Netscape Navigator.

The effects shown in this example were created with the following internal style sheet rules:

```
<style type="text/css">
<!-- .pgtitle {  font-family: "Agency FB";
      font-size: 24pt;  font-style: italic;
      font-weight: 500; font-variant: small-caps;
      color: #FFFFFF; background-color: #993333;
      letter-spacing: 1em; word-spacing: 5em;
      margin-top: 10px; margin-right: 10px;
      margin-bottom: 10px; margin-left: 10px;
      border: 4px #000000 double; clip: rect(   );
      padding-top: 15px; padding-right: 15px;
      padding-bottom: 15px; padding-left: 15px}-->
</style>
```

Editing Styles

You can edit, or modify, a style that has already been created by either editing the style sheet rule directly or by using Dreamweaver's tools. Although Dreamweaver doesn't have the best CSS tools on the market, they are a vast improvement over trying to modify the style sheets yourself.

To edit an existing style sheet rule, follow these steps:

1. Open the Edit Style Sheet window by selecting Text→CSS Styles→Edit Style Sheet or by right-clicking on the document object with the CSS style applied and selecting CSS Styles→Edit Style Sheet from the contextual menu. If the CSS Styles panel is still open, you can edit the style sheet entries by double-clicking their names as they appear in that panel.
2. In the Edit Style Sheet dialog box, shown in Figure C-7, select the style sheet document (external) or style sheet rule (internal) that you wish to modify. If you need to modify the style sheet options in a document, you will then be taken to a matching screen listing the styles available on that style sheet alone.

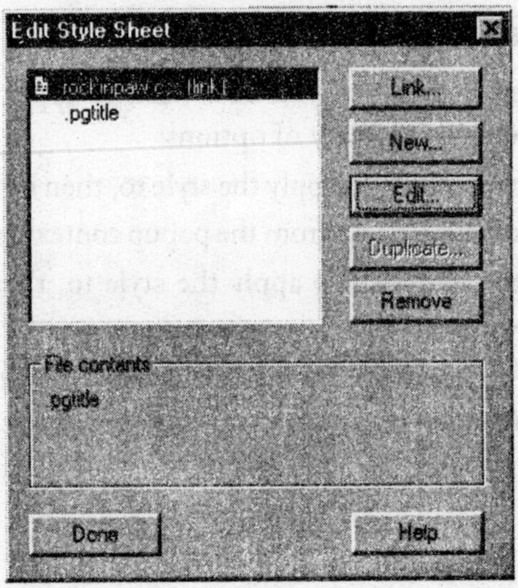

Figure C-7 The Edit Style Sheet dialog box.

3. Click the Edit button to start modifying your style sheet rule.

NOTE *If you wish to create a duplicate of your style sheet rule before modifying it, click the Duplicate button.*

4. The Style Definition For dialog box will open, containing all of the settings that were originally defined for the selected style. You can adjust the options provided to account for changes in browsers, upgraded software, new style sheet rules being provided, or any other reason, including a simple facelift on your site.
5. Once your adjustments are made, click the Apply button and view your changes in your Dreamweaver document. If you are satisfied with your changes, click OK and preview the documents in all the Web browsers you expect your visitors to use.

NOTE *By modifying the styles on an external style sheet, you will modify all of the items using that style for your entire Web site. If you modify a style on an internal style sheet, you will then need to make changes to all other documents that use that style. If you use multiple documents in your site, it is always best to use external style sheets.*

Applying and Removing Styles

After you have created a style that you now want to apply to your document objects, you have a variety of options:

- Highlight the object you wish to apply the style to, then right-click and select CSS Styles→stylename from the popup contextual menu.
- Highlight the object you wish to apply the style to, then select Text→CSS Styles→stylename.
- Select the name of the element from your Tag selector at the bottom left of your status bar, right-click on its name, and select Set Class→stylename, as shown in Figure C-8.

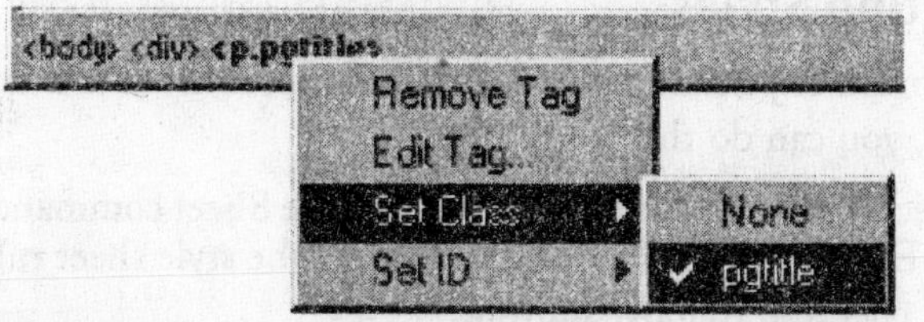

Figure C-8 Use the Tag selector on the status bar to apply a style.

Removing a style once it has been applied to objects in your document is just as easy. These steps simply unapply the style, they do not delete it from the complete style sheet.

- Highlight the object you wish to remove the style from, then right-click and select CSS Styles→None from the popup contextual menu.
- Highlight the object you wish to remove the style from, then select Text→CSS Styles→None.
- Open the CSS Styles panel by selecting the Window→CSS Styles command (Shift+F11), or clicking on the CSS Styles icon on the Mini-Launcher. In the CSS Styles panel, select the name of the style and click the Delete Style button.
- Select the name of the element from your Tag list at the bottom left of your status bar, right-click on its name, and select Set Class→None, as shown in Figure C-9.

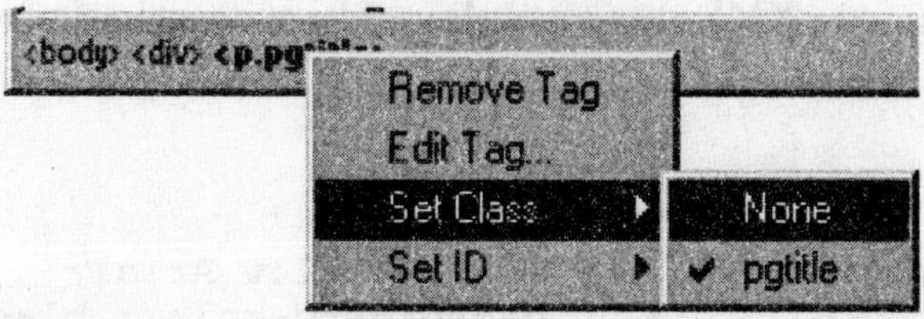

Figure C-9 Use the Tag selector on your status bar to remove a style.

NOTE *You can tell when a tag has a style applied, because it will appear in the form of <p.pgtitle> rather than just <p> in the Tag selector.*

Deleting Styles

To permanently delete a style from either your internal or external style sheets, you can do the following:

- Select the Text→CSS Styles→Edit Style Sheet command to open the Edit Styles dialog box. Then select the style sheet rule's name and click the Remove button.
- Right-click on the document screen, and select the CSS Styles→Edit Style Sheet command to open the Edit Styles dialog. Then select the style sheet rule's name and click the Remove button.
- Open the CSS Styles panel by selecting the Window→CSS Styles command (Shift+F11), or clicking on the CSS Styles icon on the Mini-Launcher. In the CSS Styles panel, select the name of the style and click the Delete Style button.

Once a style sheet item has been deleted, you can use the Undo button to recover it, before the document has been closed, or you can find an old copy of the style and copy it to your style sheet. In the event another copy of the style rule can't be found, you will have to re-create the style from scratch.

CSS Syntax

Cascading Style Sheets break individual style sheet rules into two parts: a selector and a declaration, as shown in Figure C-10. The selector identifies the XML element, such as order or itemname, to which the rule is applied.

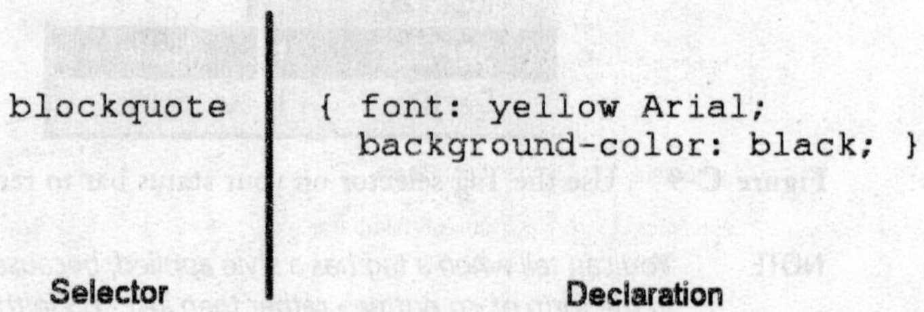

Figure C-10 The selector and two-part declaration of every CSS rule.

The declaration has two parts: the property name and the value. The property name, found to the left of the colon, identifies the aspect of the selector being set (for example, the font or background color of an itemname element). The value of the property, to the right of the colon, identifies the specific value used when adjusting the display of the element (for example, if the property is background color, a value of black would force the itemname element to display on a black background).

SEE ALSO *Assets Panel, Colors, Fonts, HTML Styles, HTML Styles Panel, Page Properties, Preferences, Properties Inspector, Reference Panel*

Change Property see Behaviors

Characters

Dreamweaver includes a variety of preinstalled characters (called character entities) that you can apply to your document, but can't actually type on the keyboard. These characters include such popular items as copyright symbols, pound signs, trademarks, and the Yen symbol.

The characters built into Dreamweaver are found either on the Character category of the Objects panel, shown in Figure C-11, or in the Insert→Special Characters menu. You can open the Characters category of the Objects panel by selecting it from the popup list at the top of the panel.

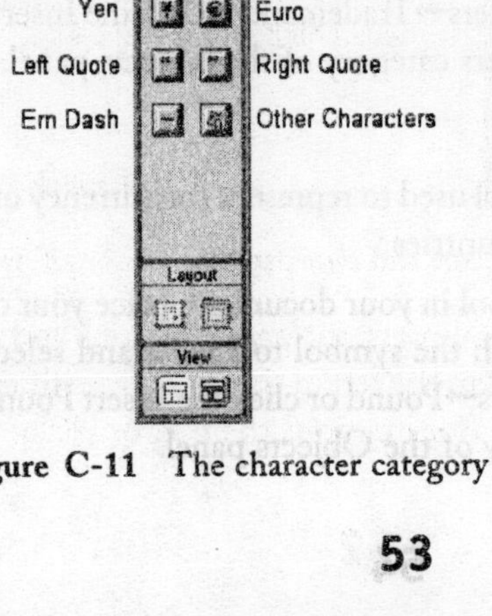

Figure C-11 The character category of the Objects panel.

Copyright

Copyright symbols represent material that legally belongs to the original creator. For instance, my Web site *wallowavalley.com* is copyrighted to myself and my company. I am the Web site's sole creator, as well as the creator of all of the graphics and text on that site. To protect my work, I put a copyright symbol and statement on the bottom of all the pages in the site.

To insert a copyright symbol in your document, place your cursor at the location where you wish the symbol to appear and select either Insert→Special Characters→Copyright or click the Insert Copyright button on the Characters category of the Objects panel.

Registered Trademark

Registered trademarks represent those items, such as logos, that have been registered and accepted with a U.S. or international trademark registering association, such as the U.S. Patents Office.

To insert a registered trademark symbol in your document, place your cursor at the location where you wish the symbol to appear and select either Insert→Special Characters→Registered Trademark or click the Insert Registered Trademark button on the Characters category of the Objects panel.

Trademark

The trademark symbol is used to note those items that have been registered, but not yet accepted, by a U.S. or international trademark registering association.

To insert a trademark symbol in your document, place your cursor at the location where you wish the symbol to appear and select either Insert→Special Characters→Trademark or click the Insert Trademark button on the Characters category of the Objects panel.

Pound

The Pound is the symbol used to represent the currency of the United Kingdom and other countries.

To insert a Pound symbol in your document, place your cursor at the location where you wish the symbol to appear and select either Insert→Special Characters→Pound or click the Insert Pound button on the Characters category of the Objects panel.

Yen

The Japanese Yen is the symbol representing the currency of Japan and other Asian countries.

To insert a Yen symbol in your document, place your cursor at the location where you wish the symbol to appear and select either Insert→Special Characters→Yen or click the Insert Yen button on the Characters category of the Objects panel.

Euro

The Euro symbol is generically used to represent many of the currencies of European and Asian countries.

To insert a Euro symbol in your document, place your cursor at the location where you wish the symbol to appear and select either Insert→Special Characters→Euro or click the Insert Euro button on the Characters category of the Objects panel.

Left and Right Quotes

Although you can type left and right quotes on your computer keyboard, those are straight quotes, not curly quotes. In order to use curly quotes, or quotes that curl into the text they surround, you have to use special character entities.

To insert a left quote in your document, place your cursor at the location where you wish the symbol to appear and select either Insert→Special Characters→Left Quote or click the Insert Left Quote button on the Characters category of the Objects panel.

To insert a curly right quote in your document, place your cursor at its intended location and select either Insert→Special Characters→Right Quote or click the Insert Right Quote button on the Characters category of the Objects panel.

Em-Dash

The em-dash character is an elongated dash used to provide additional space between statements.

To insert an em-dash in your document, place your cursor at its intended location and select either Insert→Special Characters→Em Dash or click the Insert Em-Dash button on the Characters category of the Objects panel.

Non-Breaking Space

A non-breaking space is one that can't be ignored, or allows a line of characters to wrap at that point. Non-breaking spaces are commonly used to add a few extra white spaces between images or indent text (when a style sheet is not used).

To insert a non-breaking space in your document, place your cursor at its intended location and select either Insert→Special Characters→Non-Breaking Space or click the Insert Non-Breaking Space button on the Characters category of the Objects panel.

Line Break

The line break character inserts an actual line break in your Web page. A line break doesn't insert additional white space around your text. It is a way to make text appear as in the following, rather than as normal paragraphs:

```
Myname MyLastName
My Address Is Here
My City, MyState MyZip
```

To insert a line break in your document, place your cursor at its intended location and select either Insert→Special Characters→Line Break, press Shift+Enter (Return on the Macintosh), or click the Insert Line Break button on the Characters category of the Objects panel.

Other Characters

There are many other characters that can be used in your Web pages that are accessible through the Insert Other Characters button on the Objects panel or by selecting Insert→Special Characters→Other. This will open the Insert Other Character dialog box shown in Figure C-12.

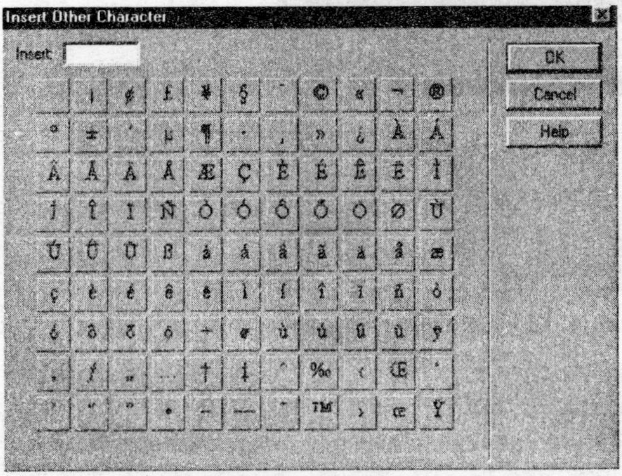

Figure C-12 The Insert Other Character dialog box.

To use these characters, select a character from the dialog box and click OK. You can see the actual character entity code being inserted in your document by looking at the contents of the Insert field, after selecting a character.

Check Browser see Behaviors

Check In

Dreamweaver includes a Check-In and Check-Out process, allowing teams of developers to work in conjunction without inadvertently overwriting the work of others. This system requires each person to check out a file before it can be edited. The file must then be checked back in before other members of the team can work with it. If someone has a file checked out, a team member can write the person, using the associated e-mail address, and ask them about the status of the file.

To use the Check-In feature, you need to turn it on in the Site Definition dialog box for each site being shared with multiple developers:

1. Open the Site Definition dialog box by selecting Site→Define Sites.
2. In the Define Sites dialog box, shown in Figure C-13, select the site you wish to add, or ensure, Check-In and Check Out is working for, then click the Edit button.

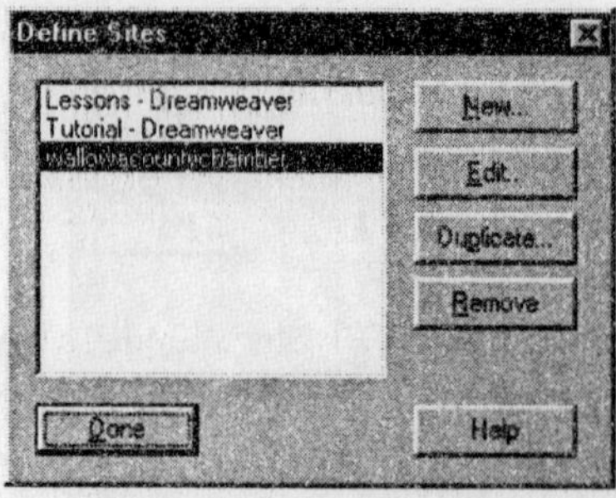

Figure C-13 The Define Sites dialog box lists all of your defined sites on the local computer.

3. In the Site Definition dialog box, shown in Figure C-14, select the Remote Info entry from the Category list.

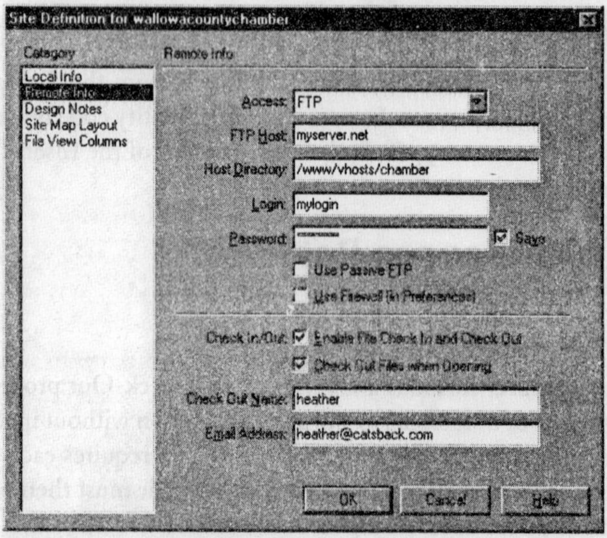

Figure C-14 The Site Definitions dialog box showing the Check In/Out options.

4. At the bottom of this screen are Check In/Out options. To turn on this feature, check the Enable File Check In And Check Out check box. This allows other options to appear.
5. Check the Check Out Files When Opening option to ensure that whenever you open a file, whether you check it out properly or not, Dreamweaver will mark that the file is checked out to you.

6. Type in your name, nickname, or other name that people will recognize you by in the Check Out Name field. If you are modifying the same site from multiple locations, you can use names such as Fred-Office and Fred-Home to help you keep track of where you were last working on the file.
7. Type your e-mail address in the Email Address field. Other people will be able to reach you through e-mail using this address.
8. Click OK to save your changes in the Site Definitions dialog box.
9. Click Done in the Define Sites dialog box to return to your document.

Now that you have turned on the Check In/Check Out features, you can check in your files by selecting Site→Check In from the Site window (in Windows) or the Site menu (Macintosh). You can also press Ctrl+Alt+Shift+D (Windows) or Cmd+Opt+Shift+D (Macintosh) to check in your files.

SEE ALSO *Check Out, Defining Sites, Site Window*

Checking Links

Dreamweaver provides a variety of tools, both internal and downloadable, that will allow you to check the links and files in your site. The easiest way to check the links in your files is to do the entire site at once. In your Site window, select Site→Check Links Sitewide. This opens the Link Checker dialog box shown in Figure C-15.

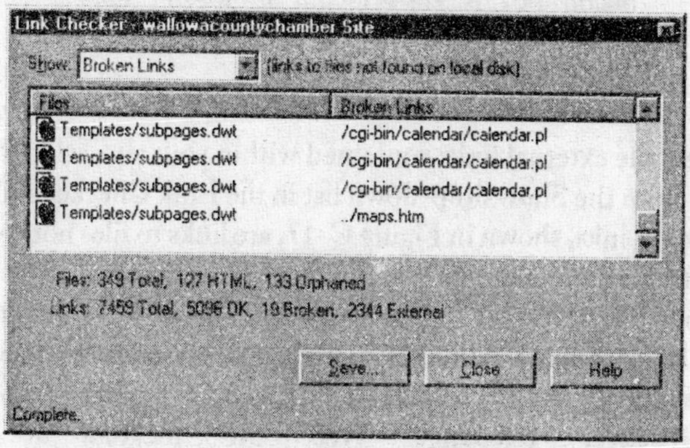

Figure C-15 The Link Checker dialog box lists the total number of files, broken links, orphaned files, and external links found in your Web site.

Broken Links

When the Link Checker dialog box opens it automatically displays the list of broken links in the Web site, as shown in Figure C-15. These links can be modified directly on screen by clicking on the link address in the Broken Link column, as shown in Figure C-16.

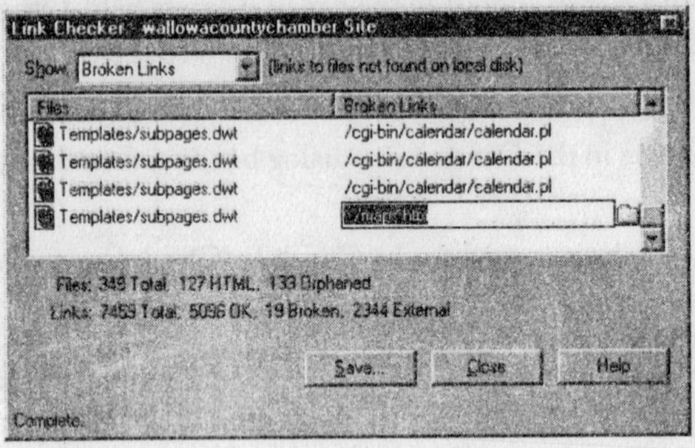

Figure C-16 Use the Broken Links column to fix links without leaving the Link Checker dialog box.

Once you have fixed a link, you will be asked if you wish to modify all other links to the same document that were found broken. If you are confident that this won't create any other problems, click Yes. If you wish to fix only this one instance, then click No.

NOTE *Not all links displayed in this dialog box may actually be broken. For instance, the reference to the CGI program at the top of this dialog box is correct, but it doesn't appear correct to Dreamweaver, so it marks it as a broken link.*

External Links

To view the external links contained within your site, select External Links from the Show drop-down list in the Link Checker dialog box. External Links, shown in Figure C-17, are links to files not contained on your local computer. These links may be correct, or may be broken, but Dreamweaver is unable to check them. If you wish to check the validity of external links from within Dreamweaver, you will need to download the External Link Checker extension from the Dreamweaver Exchange Web site located at *http://www.macromedia.com/exchange/dreamweaver*. Search for "external link" and you should be taken to the list of link checkers that are available for download.

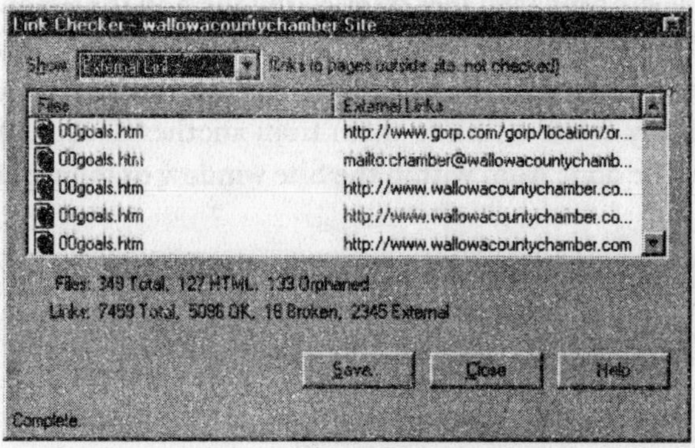

Figure C-17 The Link Checker dialog box lists, but doesn't validate, external links.

You can modify the addresses of external links by clicking on the Link's address in the External Link column and making your changes. You will be asked to modify all other matching links in your site. If you select Yes, all links to the previous address will be updated with the new address you provided.

Orphaned Files

Orphaned files are files that are not referenced anywhere in your Web site. You could have a long list of orphaned files in a Web site for a variety of reasons, including old files that you haven't deleted or production files that you were using to test information. The orphaned files are listed in the Link Checker, as shown in Figure C-18.

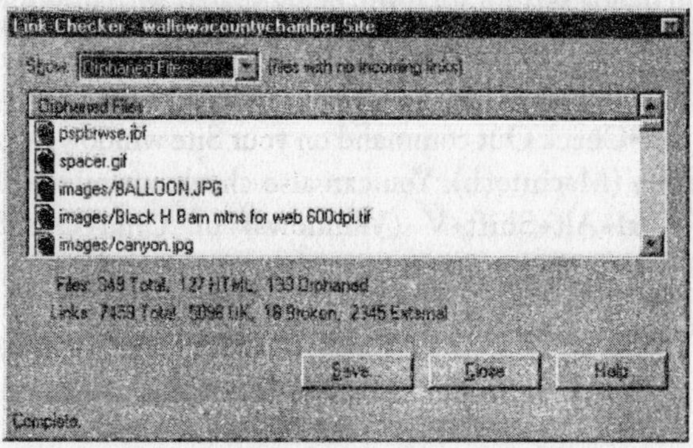

Figure C-18 Orphaned files contained within the site directory structure.

You can delete orphaned files by selecting them in the list and pressing Del on your keyboard. You will be prompted to verify your action, as shown in Figure C-19. You can't move files to new locations or automatically create a link to them from another document. Those tasks must be done from within the Site window or individual documents.

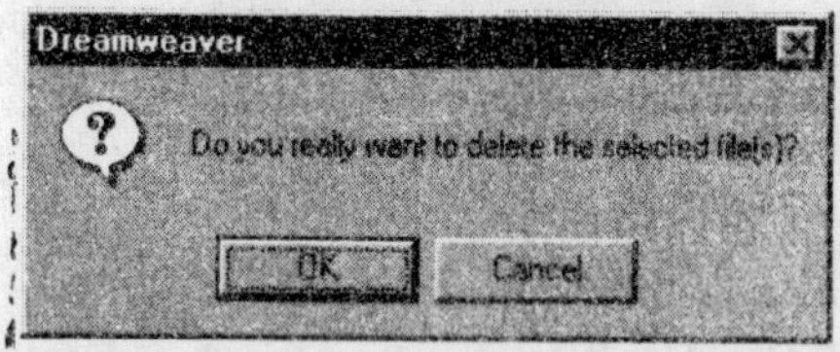

Figure C-19 You can delete orphaned files from the Link Checker dialog box.

SEE ALSO *Absolute Links, Dreamweaver Exchange, Email Links, FTP Links, Hyperlinks, Relative Links*

Check Out

Dreamweaver includes a Check-In and Check-Out process, allowing teams of developers to work together on a site without overwriting each other's work. This system requires each person to check out a file before it can be edited and then check it back in before other teammates can edit it.

To use the Check-Out feature, be sure it is turned on in the Site Definition dialog box for each site being shared with multiple developers. This process is explained in the Check In entry.

Once you are sure that Check In/Out feature is working for your site, use the Site→Check Out command on your Site window (Windows) or Site menu (Macintosh). You can also check out selected files by pressing Ctrl+Alt+Shift+V (Windows) or Cmd+Opt+Shift+V (Macintosh).

SEE ALSO *Check In, Defining Sites, Site Window*

Check Plugins see Behaviors

Checking Spelling

Dreamweaver allows you to check the spelling on your documents, something you should do every time you work on them, before saving them and especially before uploading them to your Web server. Nothing is more embarrassing than your client noticing that you had spelled "happening" as "happenng."

To start the Spelling Checker, select Text→Check Spelling or press Shift+F7. This opens the Check Spelling dialog box shown in Figure C-20.

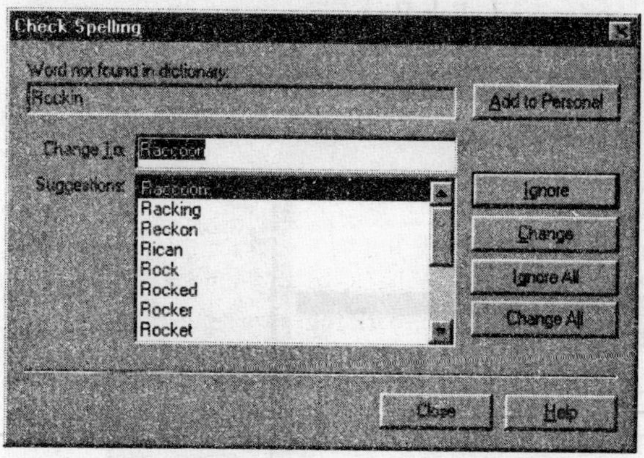

Figure C-20 The Check Spelling dialog box.

In this dialog box, you have a variety of options for each word that is found misspelled:

- Add To Personal - This option adds the current word to your personal dictionaries. This is great for adding place names, personal names, and other terms that aren't found in any dictionary.
- Ignore - This option allows you to ignore just this instance of the misspelled word.
- Change - This option changes the misspelled word to the word that you have selected in the Suggestions list or typed in the Change To field.
- Ignore All - This option ignores all instances of the misspelled word in your document.
- Change All - This option changes all of the misspelled words in your document to the word visible in the Change To Field.

Clean Up FrontPage HTML

The Clean Up FrontPage HTML feature is downloadable from the Dreamweaver Exchange located at *http://www.macromedia.com/exchange/dreamweaver*, and it allows you to evaluate the HTML code within a document that was created using Microsoft FrontPage. FrontPage is notorious for inserting its own code, comments, and propriety tags into HTML documents that create an infinite number of potential problems for Web visitors. To run the Clean Up FrontPage HTML extension after it is installed, select Commands→Clean Up FrontPage HTML Sitewide. This opens the Reports dialog box shown in Figure C-21. Check the Clean Up FrontPage HTML option and click Run.

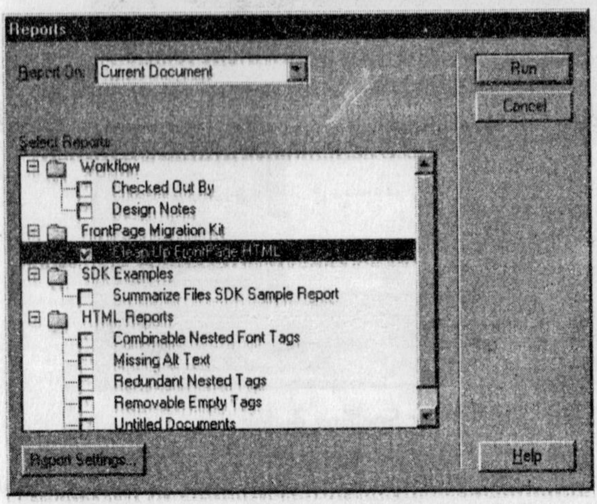

Figure C-21 The Reports dialog box.

The options that run with the Clean Up FrontPage HTML extension include the following:

- Report On - Selects either the current document or the entire site.
- Apply Source Formatting - Formats your code in a fashion similar to Dreamweaver's built-in Apply Source Formatting option.
- Show Log On Completion - Shows a list of the items that were altered once the process has completed.
- Set Background Color - Sets the background color for all pages on your site.

- Remove FrontPage Specific Meta Tags From <head> - Removes all FrontPage-specific meta tags, typically related to Navigation and Themes information, from your document.
- Remove FrontPage Specific WEBBOTs - Removes all <!-- WEBBOTs --> comments.
- Remove FrontPage Specific MSNavigation Comments - Removes all <!-- MSNavigation --> comments.
- Remove FrontPage Specific Themes Comments - Removes all <!--themes --> comments.
- Remove All Unused Style Definitions - Removes any CSS style definitions that aren't used in the document.
- Remove Empty Style Definitions - Removes all empty CSS style definitions.

These options work on all FrontPage documents and should help you convert your FrontPage Web site into a Dreamweaver Web site with a minimum amount of manual effort. When the report is done running, you will receive a list of the items that were altered. This list appears in the Results dialog box, as shown in Figure C-22.

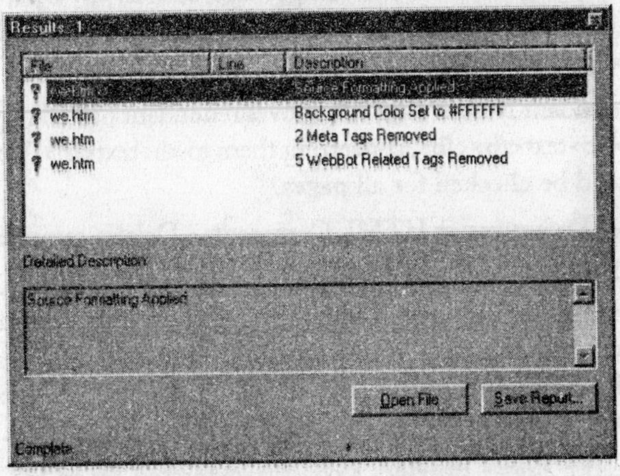

Figure C-22 The Results report delivered after running the Clean Up FrontPage HTML Sitewide extension.

SEE ALSO *AutoFormat HTML, Clean Up HTML, Clean Up Word HTML*

Clean Up HTML

The Clean Up HTML feature allows you to evaluate the HTML code within a document as a means of ensuring that there are no superfluous empty tags, redundant tags, or misplaced comments. To open the Clean Up HTML dialog box shown in Figure C-23, select Commands→Clean Up HTML.

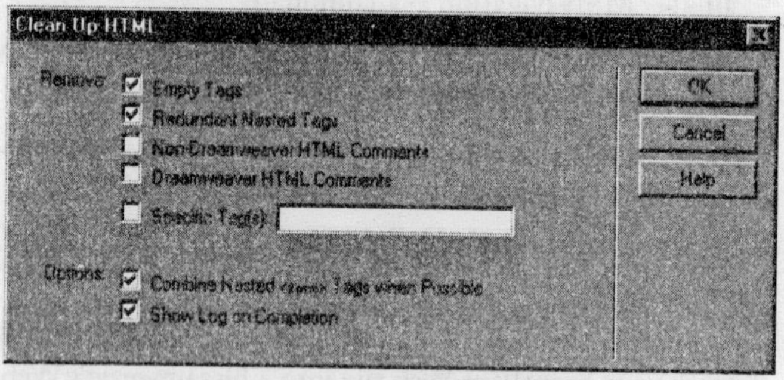

Figure C-23 The Clean Up HTML dialog box.

Options in the Clean Up HTML dialog box include the following:

- Empty Tags - Removes all empty tags, such as <p></p>, that have no content. This will not remove tags with attributes such as <img src="mygraphic.gif">. This option is typically checked for all pages.
- Redundant Nested Tags - Removes redundant nested tags, such as <b><b>text</b></b>, converting them to <b>text</b>. This option should be checked for all pages.
- Non-Dreamweaver HTML Comments – Deletes comments added by programs other than Dreamweaver.
- Dreamweaver HTML Comments – Removes all comments, including those added by Dreamweaver to mark the beginning and end of Library items and template editable regions. This check box should typically not be checked without specific reason.
- Specific Tags - Provides a comma-separated list of HTML elements that should be removed if they are found, for instance, the annoying small element used by FrontPage.
- Combine Nested <font> Tags When Possible - Combines font tags where possible. Font tags can easily take over a Web page; each setting exactly one font setting for your text.

- Show Log On Completion - Shows a list of all the changes made once the Clean Up HTML process has been completed.

Once you have checked your options, click OK. If Show Log On Completion was selected, a final dialog box will appear listing the changes that were made.

SEE ALSO *AutoFormat HTML, Clean Up FrontPage HTML, Clean Up Word HTML*

Clean Up Word HTML

Microsoft Word creates HTML documents with superfluous information just as Microsoft FrontPage does. To use these documents in Dreamweaver, you must clean them as you would your FrontPage documents. To open the Clean Up Word HTML dialog box, shown in Figure C-24, select Commands→Clean Up Word HTML.

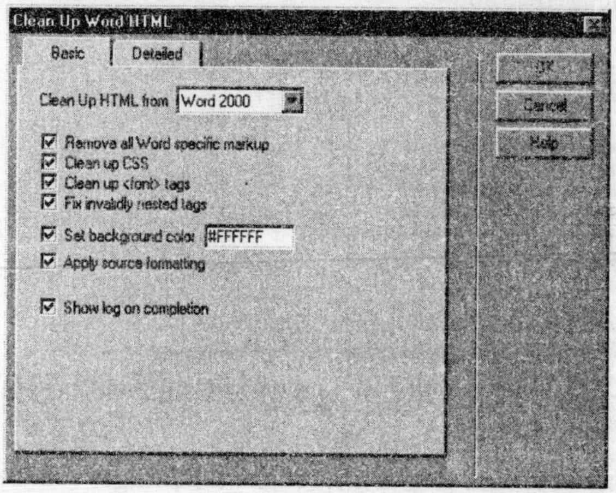

Figure C-24 The Basic tab in the Clean Up Word HTML dialog box.

The options available on the Basic tab include the following:

- Remove All Word Specific Markup - Removes all Word tags, including the combination of XML and HTML tags that are created.
- Clean Up CSS - Removes all the Word-specific style sheet rules included in the document.
- Clean Up <font> Tags - Clears out all extraneous <font> tags in the document.

- Fix Invalidly Nested Tags - Rearranges all HTML elements that are nested in the wrong order, such as <p><b>text </p></b> rather than <p><b>text </b></p>.
- Set Background Color - Sets the background color for your page.
- Apply Source Formatting - Formats your code in a fashion similar to Dreamweaver's built-in Apply Source Formatting option.
- Show Log On Completion - Shows a list of the items that were altered once the process has completed.

To look at the remaining options, shown in Figure C-25, click on the Detailed tab.

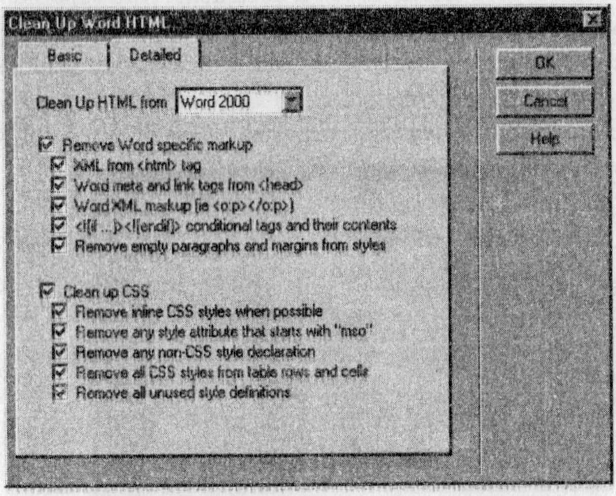

Figure C-25 The Detailed tab in the Clean Up Word HTML dialog box.

The options on this screen include the following:

- Remove Word Specific Markup - If Remove All Word Specific Markup was checked on the Basic tab, then you can specify the specific markup here.
- Clean Up CSS - If Clean Up CSS was checked on the Basic tab, then the options on the Detailed tab allow you to select the individual types of CSS statements that should be removed.

SEE ALSO *AutoFormat HTML, Clean Up FrontPage HTML, Clean Up HTML*

Clip Art

There are a variety of Web sites that provide clip-art services on the Internet. Many of these sites can be linked to from Web directories, such as Yahoo and About.com. Some of the best of these sites include the following:

- Clipart.com at *www.clipart.com*
- Barry's ClipArt server at *www.barrysclipart.com*
- Clip Art Center at *clip-art.easy-interactive.com*
- Free Clip Art Images at *www.free-clip-images.com*

Just because these sites are full of clip art doesn't mean that you can use the images they contain in your Web site. You need to read their copyright and fair-use statements carefully. Many of them allow use of their images only in nonprofit sites; some prohibit use for Web sites and allow only personal use.

Closing Dreamweaver

To close, or exit, Dreamweaver, choose the File→Exit command. Alternatively, click the program window's Close button.

NOTE *The program window's Close button is in the upper right corner of the program window and is marked with an "X."*

SEE ALSO *Opening Dreamweaver*

Code And Design View

Dreamweaver's Code And Design view, as shown in Figure C-26, allows you to view both your code and your visual page simultaneously. When using this document view, you can make changes to the document visually and see the changes take place in your code, or make changes to the code and see the changes occur in your document (after pressing F5). This is a great view to use if you want to learn HTML and actually see what effect all of your insertions and deletions have on your HTML code.

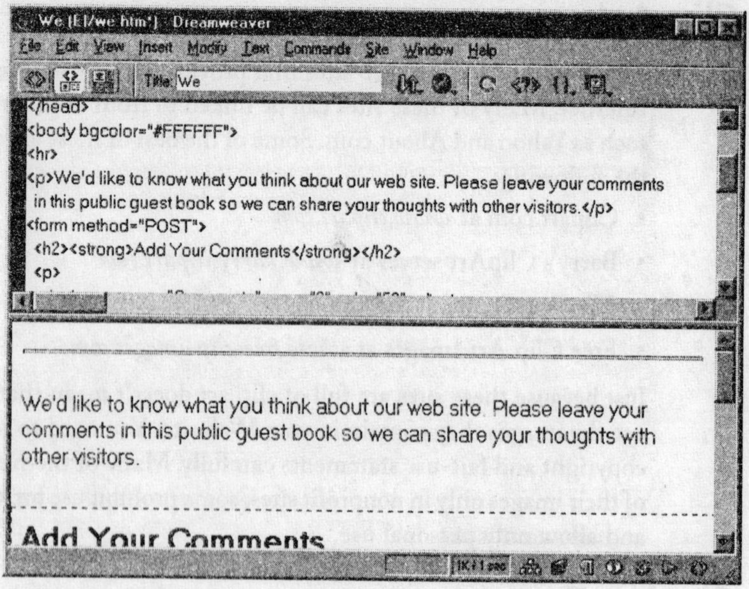

Figure C-26 Dreamweaver Code And Design view.

SEE ALSO *Code Inspector, Code View, Design View, Quick Tag Editor*

Code Inspector

The Dreamweaver Code inspector allows you to view your HTML code outside of the Dreamweaver document window. The Code inspector, although still available, has been superceded by the Code view of your document. Selecting Window→Code Inspector (F10) opens the Code inspector, as shown in Figure C-27. From here you can modify your HTML code directly, much as you would in any other text editor.

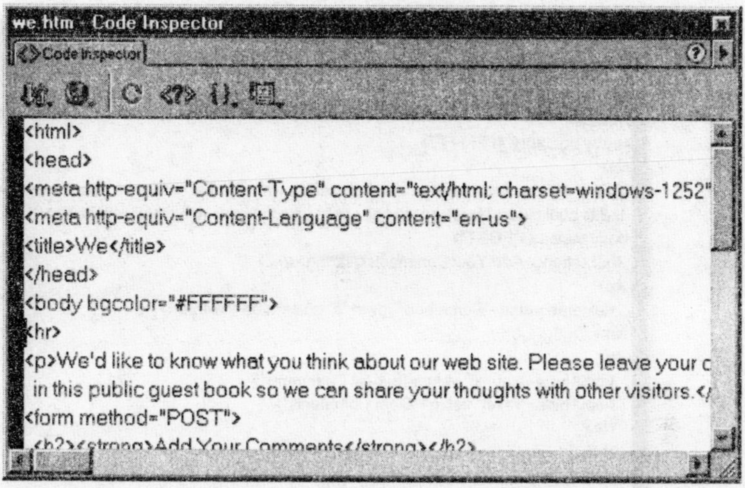

Figure C-27 The Code Inspector dialog box is redundant in view of the new Dreamweaver 4 Code view.

SEE ALSO *Code View, Quick Tag Editor*

Code View

Code view, new in Dreamweaver 4, provides direct access to the HTML code used to create your HTML document. To open Code view, select View→Code View. When opened, as shown in Figure C-28, you can directly modify the code, as well as view line numbers, view the tag layouts, and manipulate your document as necessary.

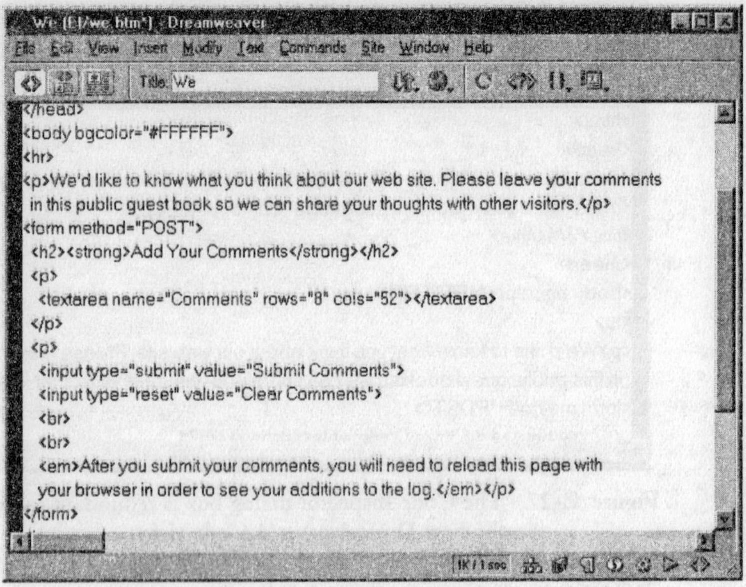

Figure C-28 Dreamweaver Code view.

SEE ALSO *Code And Design View, Code Inspector, Design View, Quick Tag Editor*

Cold Fusion

Cold Fusion is a server-side scripting language supported by Dreamweaver. This language can be used to automate the creation of Web pages based on information stored in databases. Cold Fusion is a simple language, using a structure similar to HTML. To learn more about Cold Fusion, visit *http://www.coldfusion.com.*

Colors

You can add color or change the color of most parts of an HTML document in Dreamweaver. Dreamweaver even includes a selection of easy-to-see and read color schemes that can be applied to any document. These color schemes can be accessed by selecting Commands→Set Color Scheme. This opens the Set Color Scheme Command dialog box shown in Figure C-29. These schemes all contain background colors for documents, including standard text, link, visited link, and active link colors. You can overwrite all the colors on your document, other than those specified within style sheets.

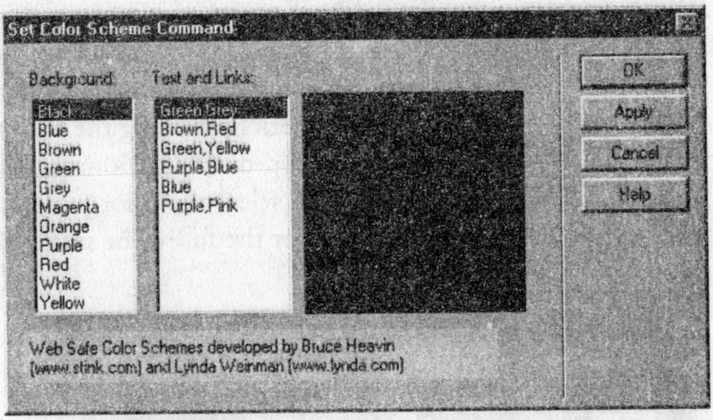

Figure C-29 The Dreamweaver Set Color Scheme Command dialog box.

To apply a color scheme to your document, select the base background color from the Background column, then the specific selection of text and links color from the Text And Links column. When your choice has been made, click OK.

You can specify your own color scheme in the Page Properties dialog box or as described in the following sections.

Coloring Text

To color the text on your document without using style sheets, highlight the text. Then click the Font Color control on the Properties inspector. The selector opens the color picker, shown in Figure C-30, from which you can select any of the 216 Web-safe colors. Simply click on a color and it will automatically be applied to your selected text.

Figure C-30 The Color Picker on the Properties inspector.

Alternatively, you can choose the Text →Color command to display the Color dialog box, shown in Figure C-31. This dialog box allows you access to the full range of colors available with your current screen settings. You can also reach this screen by clicking the System Color Picker icon on the Color Picker drop-down list from the Properties inspector. In the Color dialog box, select the color you wish to use from either the Basic Color chart or the full-color scale. Click OK when you are done.

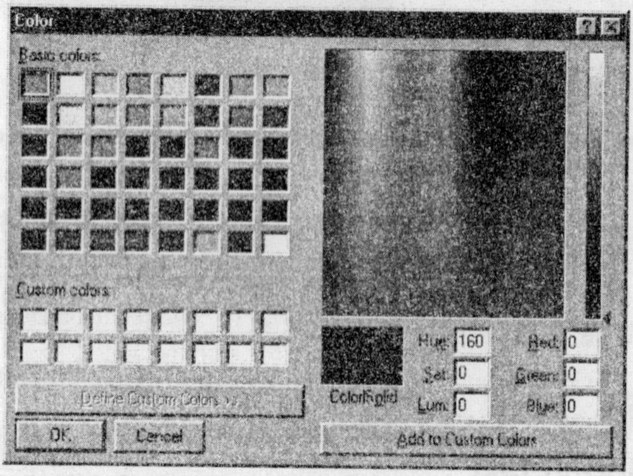

Figure C-31 The Color dialog box.

NOTE *The Color dialog box appears quite different on the Macintosh, although the functions available are the same.*

Coloring Borders

You can color the borders of images and other block objects using CSS Styles, as explained in the Cascading Style Sheets entry, but you can also do so by inserting a <font> tag directly around the image whose border you want to change. For instance, the following code changes the default black border to blue:

```
<font color="blue">

  <img src="myimg.gif">

</font>
```

You may have to do this manually in the Code View or with the Code inspector, as making these kinds of exact selections with a mouse in the Design view can be difficult.

Coloring Page Backgrounds

There are two ways to color the background of your pages: use the Page Properties dialog box or a CSS style. If your site is going to be viewed by people using current browsers, then CSS is the best way to go. Otherwise, you can use the Page Properties dialog box, which can be opened by selecting Modify→Page Properties.

Coloring Tables

There are a couple of ways that you can color a table in Dreamweaver. Individual cell backgrounds and borders can be adjusted, or you can treat the table as one complete unit. To adjust the background and border colors of a single table cell, select the cell with your mouse. Then click on the Bg Color selector in the Properties inspector, and select the background color from the list. To change the border color, select the Brdr Color selector and make a color choice.

These same options are also available on the Properties inspector for the entire table. When the whole table is selected, you will see a series of handles on the outside edge of the lower right corner of the table. At that point, your color selection choices will be applied to the entire table. The Bg and Brdr properties can be seen in Figure C-32.

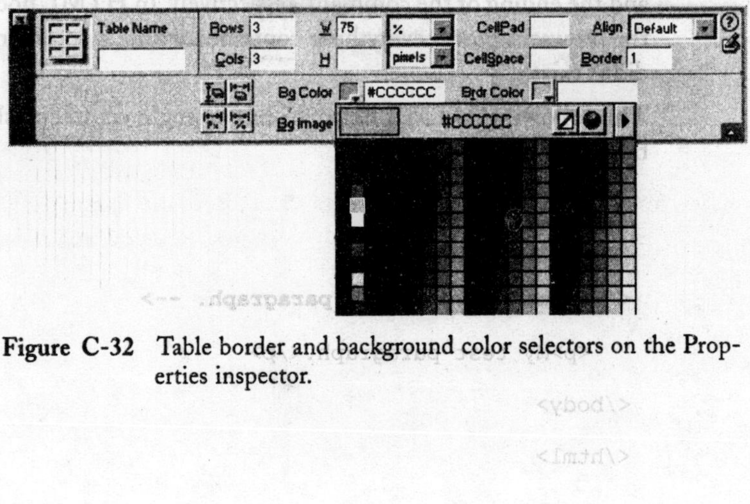

Figure C-32 Table border and background color selectors on the Properties inspector.

Coloring Layers

Layers can contain background colors. These are typically applied to a style sheet that is used to create the layer, although you can modify the background color without using the CSS Styles panel. Click on the Layer handle and then view the Properties inspector. Drop down the color selector for the Bg Color entry, as shown in Figure C-33. Select the color you want, and it will automatically be applied for you.

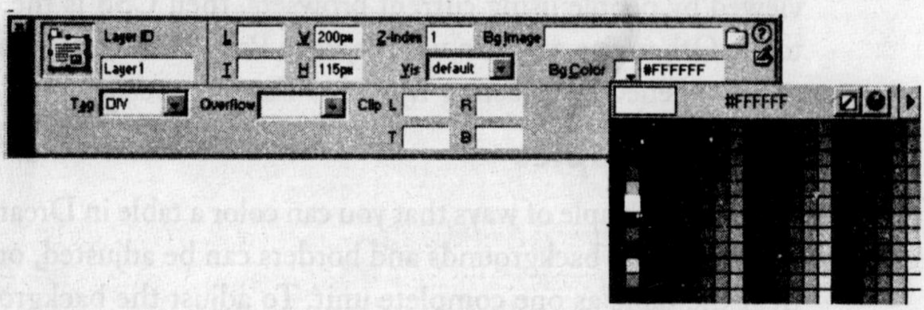

Figure C-33 Layer background color selector.

Comments

Comments within an HTML document serve as a means of interjecting a sideline thought or an instruction into the document at key points so that someone looking at the document would never find him- or herself lost.

Comments use the <!-- and the --> markers to identify the beginning and the ending of the comment, respectively. In HTML documents, the browser ignores everything contained within a comment as if it didn't exist.

The following HTML example has a single comment shown in boldfaced text:

```
<html>
<body>
<!-- The first sample paragraph. -->
   <p>My test paragraph.</p>
</body>
</html>
```

Comments can be added to your HTML document using the Insert→Invisible Tags→Comment command, which opens the Insert Comment dialog box shown in Figure C-34.

Figure C-34 The Insert Comment dialog box.

Type your comment in the Comment field, and click OK. The comment will automatically be added to your document at the current cursor location if possible. You can't see the comments on your screen, although you may be able to see a small yellow shield icon with a C in the middle of it. Your ability to see these hidden elements is controlled by your Dreamweaver Preferences.

Using Comments to Block Parts of Your Document

Comments can also be used to remove segments of your document that are not currently ready to be viewed, for example:

```
<html>

<head> <title> Sample 1 </title></head>

<body>

<!--

<div>

    <p>Still undergoing testing</p>

</div>

-->

</body>

</html>
```

In this code, the only statement that will be loaded into the Web browser is the document title.

Rules for Using Comments

Comments within HTML documents must follow these rules:

1. Comments can't appear before the <html> root element. For example, the following HTML document would create an error:

```
<!-- I have added a comment here. -->

<html>

</html>
```

2. Comments may not split HTML element tags. You cannot include the start tag of an element in a comment without including its ending element, or include an end tag without a start tag:

```
<!--

<div>

-->

   <p>Text</p>

</div>
```

3. You cannot include comments within HTML elements:

```
<div<!-- A comment is added here>>

   <p>Text</p>

</div>
```

4. Comments cannot include double hyphens within their text, unless those hyphens are part of either the opening or the closing tags. This prohibits the nesting of comments, as seen in the following example:

```
<!-- This is great <!-- I really liked it also.--> --
>
```

Contextual Menus

Contextual menus are popup menus that appear when you right-click on objects found within Dreamweaver. Contextual menus are also commonly called shortcut menus or right-click menus. Their contents vary depending upon the item being clicked on in the HTML document. For instance, Figure C-35 is the contextual menu created when you right-click on a horizontal rule element. Figure C-36 is the contextual menu that opens when you click on any other text element, in this case, paragraph text.

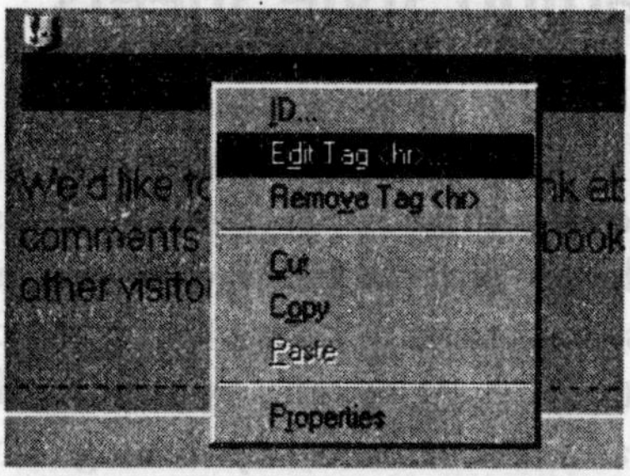

Figure C-35 A contextual menu created from a horizontal rule.

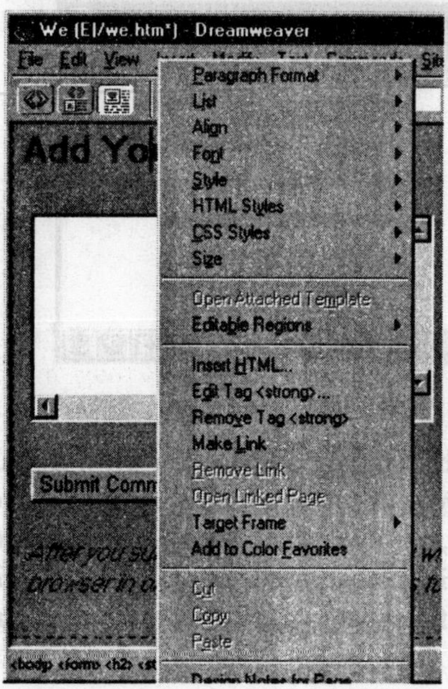

Figure C-36 A contextual menu created from paragraph text.

Control Shockwave or Flash see Behaviors

Copying Objects/Selections

To copy an object, such as a picture, click the object to select it. Click the Copy toolbar button. Click the location where the object should be copied. Click the Paste toolbar button.

SEE ALSO *Cutting Objects/Selections, Pasting Objects/Selections*

CSS Styles see Cascading Style Sheets

CSS Styles Panel

The CSS Styles panel, shown in Figure C-37, provides access to a list of the styles available with your current HTML document, as well as tools to create or delete styles, attach new style sheets, or edit existing styles. You can open the CSS Styles panel by selecting the Window→CSS Styles command (Shift+F11) or by clicking on the CSS Styles icon on the Mini-Launcher on your status bar.

Figure C-37 The CSS Styles panel.

This screen serves as the jumping off point for the manipulation of all the styles used on your document. The body of this screen only shows imbedded styles, but if you click the Edit Style Sheet button, located at the bottom right corner, one button in from the right, you will be able to view all of the styles sheet documents and internal styles that are applied to this document.

The buttons across the bottom of this dialog box are, in order:

- Auto Apply check box - Automatically applies a style that has been created to the currently selected text.
- Apply - Applies the selected style to the selected text or object in your document.
- Attach Style Sheet - Attaches a preexisting external style sheet to your document.
- New Style - Creates a new style sheet and stores it either on your current document or on an external style sheet. If the style sheet isn't already linked, this action will create a link for it.
- Edit Style Sheet - Opens the Edit Style sheet dialog box, allowing you to either edit an inline or externally linked style sheet rule.
- Delete Style - Deletes the selected style sheet rule from either the inline or the external style sheet.

SEE ALSO *Cascading Style Sheets*

Customizing Dreamweaver

Dreamweaver is made to be customized. This allows you to modify the menus, shortcut keys, default document templates, and even the appearance of the dialog boxes and objects used on the pages. All of these customizations are done using a collection of HTML documents, JavaScript, and a little ingenuity. To learn how to customize your Dreamweaver program and interface, visit the Dreamweaver Web site at *http://www.macromedia.com/resources* or read about customizing Dreamweaver in the Help files by selecting Help→Extending Dreamweaver.

SEE ALSO *Dreamweaver Extensions*

Cutting Objects/Selections

You use the Cut toolbar button and the Edit→Cut command to move text, tables, and objects.

SEE ALSO *Copying Objects/Selections, Pasting Objects/Selections*

Dates

Dreamweaver provides the ability to automatically insert the current date into your document. This is handy for updating Library items with the day when the site was last updated. To insert a date into your HTML document, select Insert→Date. This opens the Insert Date dialog box shown in Figure D-1.

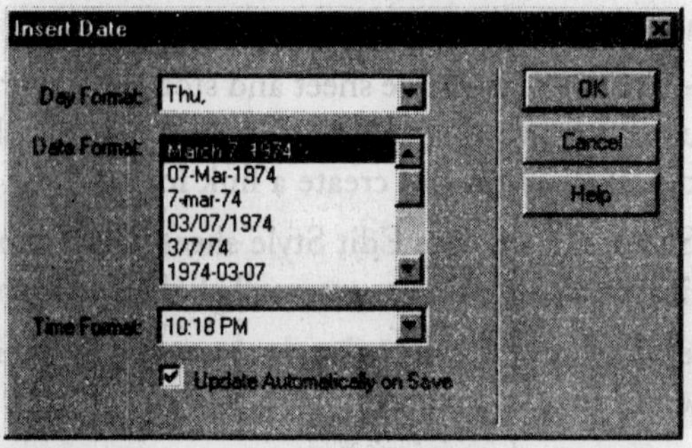

Figure D-1 The Insert Date dialog box.

From here, you can define how you want your date entered and updated.

- Day Format - Specifies the style used to display the name of the day of the week.
- Date Format - Specifies one of the available formats for entering the day of the month. You can select from 14 different formats of dates.
- Time Format - Specifies either the 24-hour format (22:54) or 12-hour format (10:54 PM) for entering time, or None if you don't want the time of day to be visible.
- Update Automatically On Save - Forces the value to automatically be updated in this field whenever the document is saved, whether any changes were made to it or not.

Once you have selected your date format, click OK, and you will see the date appear in your document.

NOTE *You can also insert a date in your document using JavaScript. For instance, the following example inserts the date when the document was last updated: {document.lastmodified}*

SEE ALSO *JavaScript*

Debugging JavaScript

When you create a lot of JavaScript, it is imperative to have a good debugging program. To run the JavaScript debugger:

1. Open a document containing JavaScript.
2. Select File→Debug In Browser→[browsername] (Alt+F12). This opens the JavaScript Debugger window, as well as the browser you had selected. If the document you chose has no JavaScript, you will not be able to run the debugger, and you will be notified that the document had no scripted content.
3. When the browser starts loading your document, answer the prompt to start debugging. Just click OK to continue.
4. At this point the JavaScript Debugger window will once again be on top of your screen, and you will be prompted to set breakpoints in the script, as shown in Figure D-2. Breakpoints allow you to move through your script without getting caught in infinite loops, or lose track of where in your code specific actions are taken.

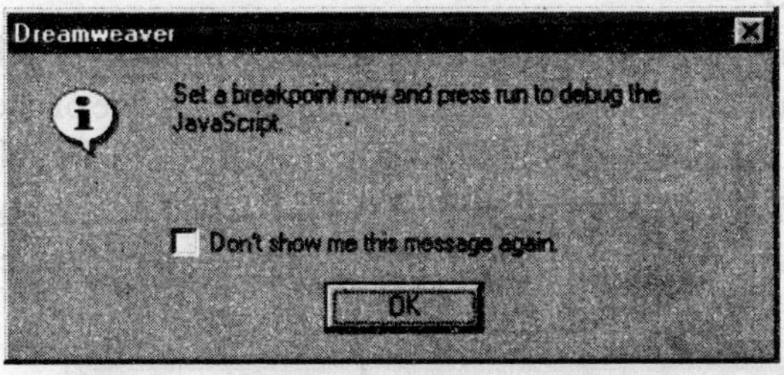

Figure D-2 Be sure to set breakpoints in your script so you can properly debug your code.

At this point, you have a variety of decisions to make.

Setting a Breakpoint

In the JavaScript Debugger, shown in Figure D-3, you can add your breakpoints by clicking on the line of code where the break should be located, and clicking the Insert Breakpoint icon on your icon bar. This icon, the pale red circle, forces the debugger to stop at that point when running through the script. This gives you a chance to evaluate the variables that you have set to be watched.

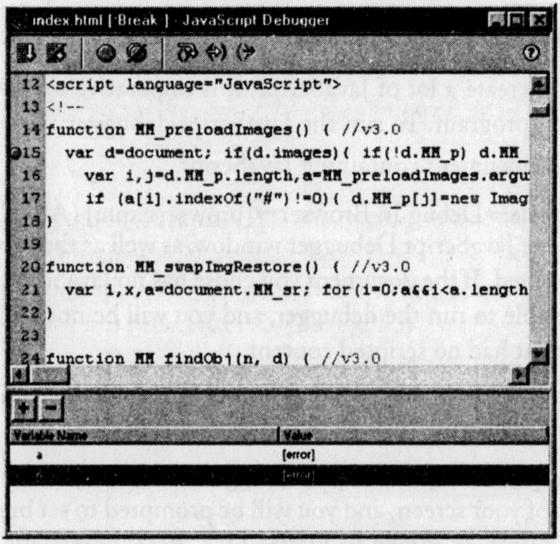

Figure D-3 The JavaScript debugger.

Defining Watch Variables

To define a JavaScript variable to be watched, or have the value of the variable tracked for you. You must highlight the name of the variable then click the plus (+) symbol to add it to the Variable Name list. Pressing the Enter key will officially add the variable to your watch list, and show the current value of the variable in the Value column. All of this is shown in Figure D-4.

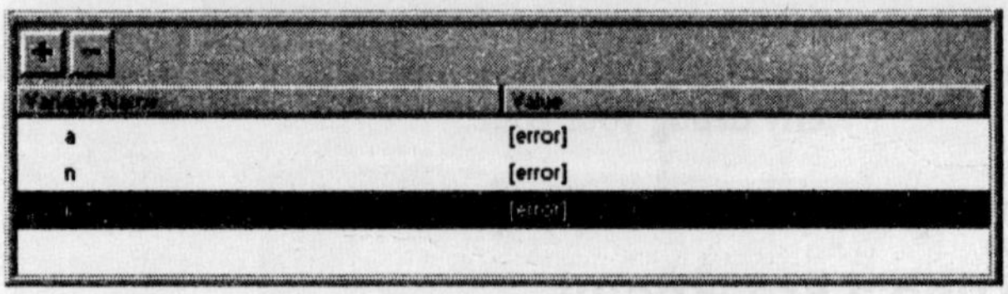

Figure D-4 The list of watch variables and values.

Stepping Through Script

To step through your script after all watch variables and breakpoints have been set, you have two options: stepping over a function or stepping into a function. Click the Step Over button to skip a function altogether. Click the Step Into button to process the information in the function itself. Both buttons are shown in Figure D-5.

Figure D-5 The Step Over and Step Into debugging buttons.

Running Script

You can run the script, or stop the script from running, whenever you wish by clicking on the Run Script button or pressing F8. You can stop the running, and therefore the debugging of a script, by clicking the Stop Debugging button. Figure D-6 shows both the Run Script and Stop Debugging buttons.

Figure D-6 The Run Script and Stop Debugging buttons.

Defining Sites

Dreamweaver uses site definitions to keep track of specific meaningful information about the individual assets associated with each Web site. In addition to tracking images and files used in the creation of the site, it also tracks the login information for the Web server, allowing you to easily update the information contained within the site

To define a site, select Site→New Site. This opens the Site Definition dialog box, as shown in Figure D-7. Multiple options must be completed for the definition of a site. Each of these options is discussed in the following sections.

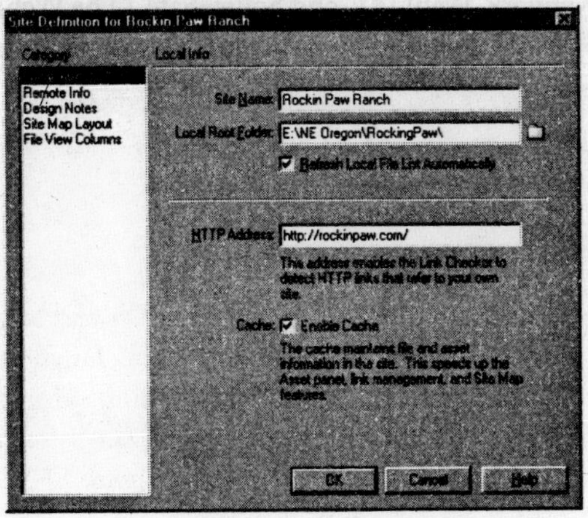

Figure D-7 The Site Definition dialog box.

Local Information

A variety of options must be completed in the Site Definition dialog box's Local Info category, shown in Figure D-7. The following options are available:

- Site Name - Defines the physical name of the site to be created. This site name will appear in the Define Sites list, and your list of Web sites on the local computer system.
- Local Root Folder - Identifies the address of the Web site as it is stored on your computer. You can use the yellow folder icon to browse your computer structure to find the site.
- Refresh Local File List Automatically - Allows your list of sites and files on the Web folder to be updated automatically.
- HTTP Address - Identifies the Web address of the Web site you are creating. For instance, *http://www.wallowavalley.com*.
- Cache: Enable Cache - Creates a Cache, which is a collection of information about the files and assets created in the Web site. Creating a cache allows you to effectively use the information contained within the Assets panel.

Remote Information

To set up the Remote information for the new Web site, click Remote Info in the Category list. The options available on this screen change based upon your selection in the Access drop-down list. This section discusses the FTP options, as shown in Figure D-8, but you can also select Local Network, WebDAV, and SourceSafe. (The WebDAV and SourceSafe options are discussed in separate entries in this book.)

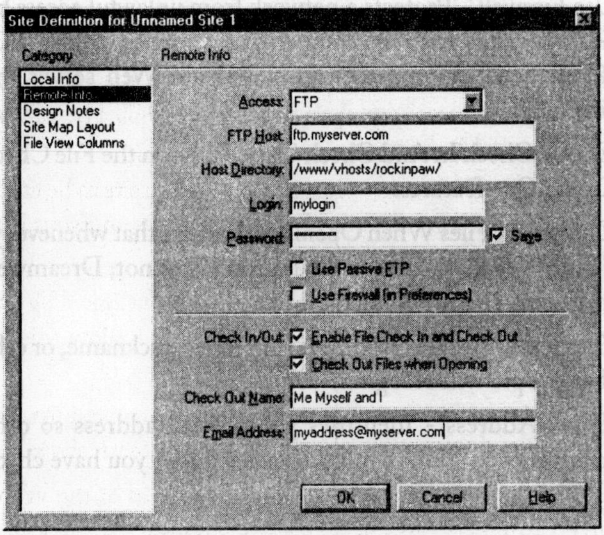

Figure D-8 FTP options for configuring access to your Web server.

The following options are available for FTP site access:

- Access - Uses the FTP protocol to send and receive files from your Web server when set to FTP. This is typically the system used when a dialup or other remote connection is used to connect to the Internet.
- FTP Host - Specifies the address of the FTP server used for storing the Web files.
- Host Directory - Specifies the specific folder structure referencing the location in which the FTO files will be stored.
- Login - Identifies the username, or login name, to access the FTP server.
- Password - Identifies the password used by the specified login name.
- Save - Saves the site password so you do not have to enter it each time you wish to upload information
- Use Passive FTP - Requires the use of Passive FTP to connect to the FTP server. Passive FTP is the process by which information is sent back and forth through a series of proxy servers to allow the exchange of information through a protected network.

- Use Firewall - Protects a network from unlawful access by people not associated with the company, or computer. Check this option if you need to communicate with your Web server through a firewall.
- Enable Check In And Check Out - Turns on the File Check In and Check Out features.
- Check Out Files When Opening - Ensures that whenever you open a file, whether you check it out properly or not, Dreamweaver will mark that the file is checked out to you.
- Check Out Name - Identifies your name, nickname, or other name that people will recognize you by.
- Email Address - Identifies your e-mail address so other team members can contact you if they need files you have checked out.

Design Notes

Design Notes allow you to maintain a log of the changes that each team member has made to the files in your Web site. Design Notes are effective only if all the team members use them. The Design Notes settings for your site are shown in Figure D-9.

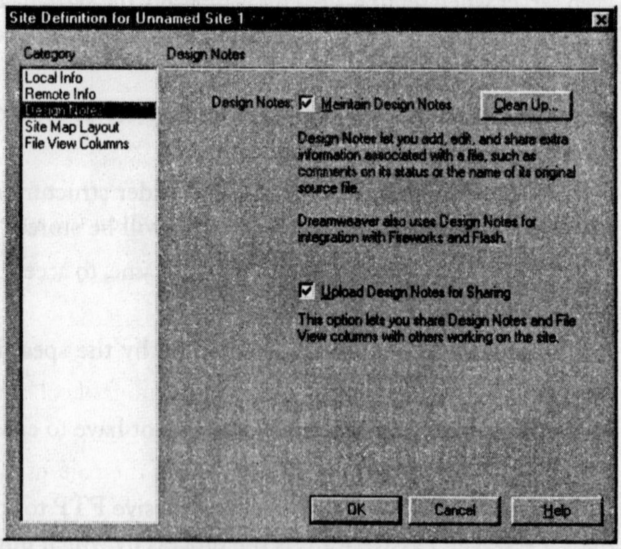

Figure D-9 Site Design Notes allow you to track information on all files in your site, as well as provide integration with Fireworks and Flash.

Select from the following settings:

- Maintain Design Notes - Enables design notes for your site. The Clean Up button allows you to clean up notes created for nonexistent pages
- Upload Design Notes For Sharing - Uploads Design Notes to your Web server. For Design Notes to work in a team situation, you must have the notes available to everyone on the team.

Site Map Layout

The Site Map Layout screen, shown in Figure D-10, defines the appearance of the site in the Site Map window.

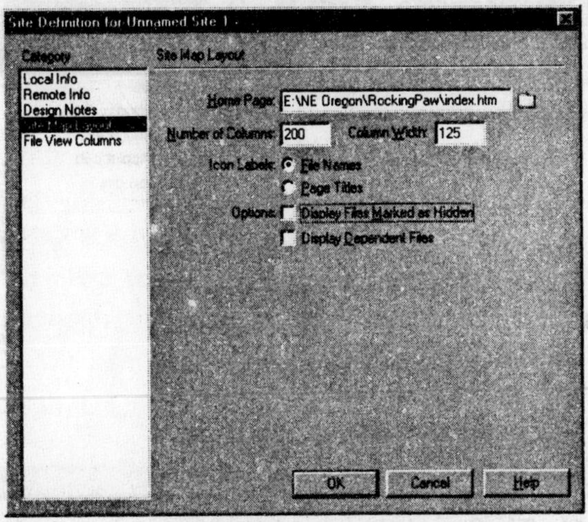

Figure D-10 The Site Map Layout options control the appearance of the site when in Map view.

Choose from the following options:

- Home Page - Specifies the name of the main page of the Web site.
- Number Of Columns - Identifies the number of columns that can be visible in the Site Map view of your site.
- Column Width - Controls the width of the columns in the Site Map view, in a measurement of pixels.
- Icon Labels - Specifies either File Names or Page Titles to control the appearance.

- Display Files Marked As Hidden - Forces all hidden files in the site, such as .dll files or others, to be visible in the Site Map.
- Display Dependent Files - Shows all dependent files, such as linked script files or style sheets.

Finalizing the Site Definition

Once all of the categories have been defined, click OK to finalize the creation of your site definition. This will return you to the Site window, as shown in Figure D-11.

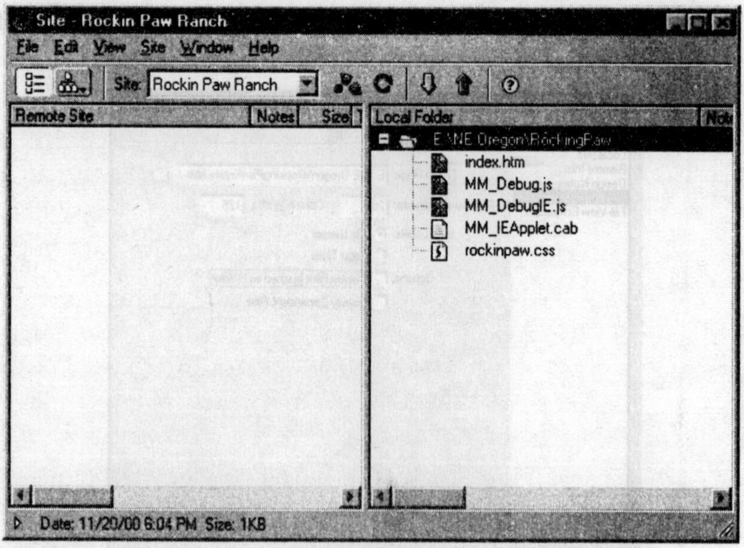

Figure D-11 The Site window showing your recently created site.

Design Notes

Design Notes allow you to store notes about the creation of each document in your Web site. Design Notes must be turned on in the Site Definition to be active. To add a note to a document, select the page in your Site window and select File→Design Notes. You can also select File→Design Notes from within the document window. The Design Notes dialog box is shown in Figure D-12.

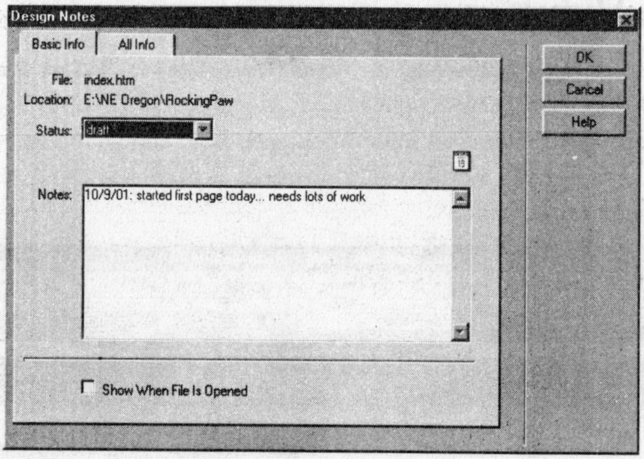

Figure D-12 The Design Notes dialog box tracks information about the changes made on each page in your site.

On the Basic Info tab, you can add a series of notes and change the current status of the file. Use the Date icon to add the date to all of your notes. The All Info tab, shown in Figure D-13, provides access to a variety of other pieces of information, which you can configure. One option is to insert the name of the developer working on the document.

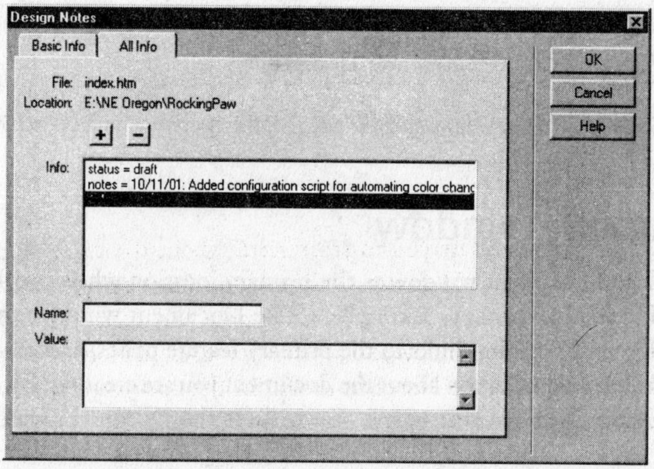

Figure D-13 The All Info tab in the Design Notes dialog box allows you to create your own information to track.

SEE ALSO *Defining Sites*

Design View

Design view provides a What You See Is What You Get (WYSIWYG) view of your HTML document. To open Design view, select View→Design View. When opened, as shown in Figure D-14, you can directly modify your document as necessary using the actual objects in the page.

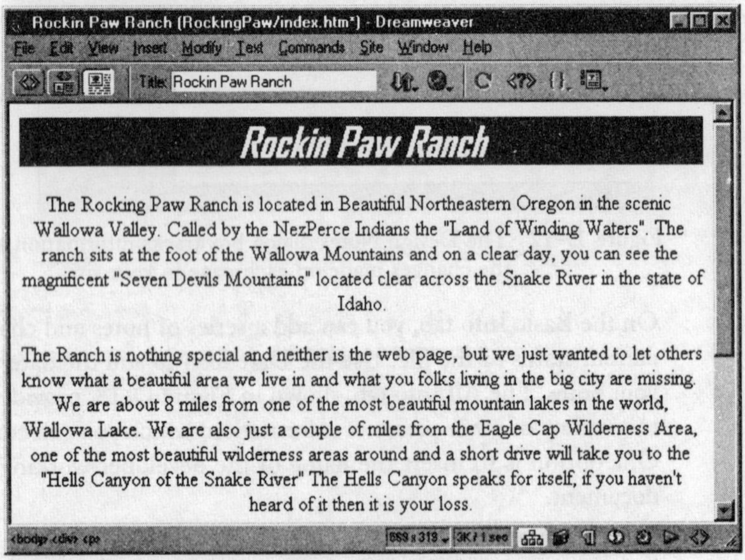

Figure D-14 Dreamweaver Design view.

SEE ALSO *Code And Design View, Code Inspector, Code View, Quick Tag Editor*

Document Window

The Document window is the primary location where work on all HTML documents takes place. The Document window, shown in Figure D-15, has links to the primary feature panes, as well as some helpful information about the document you are creating. By default, when Dreamweaver opens, you will see the Document window.

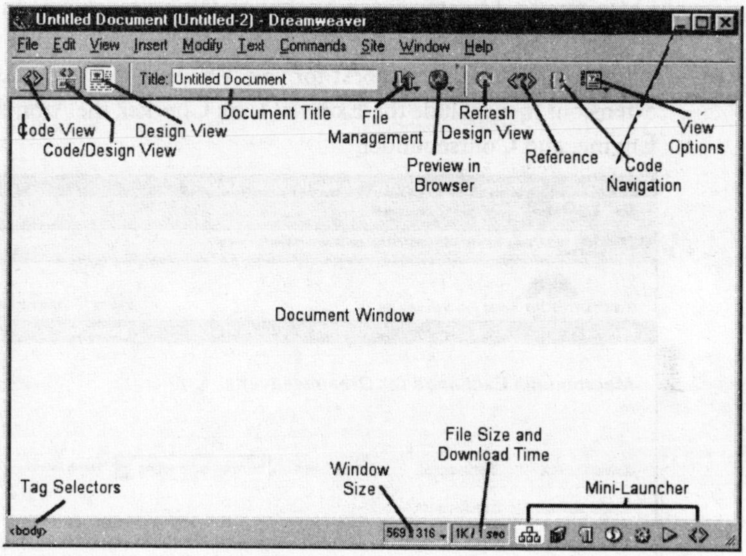

Figure D-15 Dreamweaver Document window and major features.

SEE ALSO *Code And Design View, Code View, Design View, Site Window*

Drag and Drop

Drag and drop refers to copying or moving items with your mouse. For example, if you select an item, you can move the selection by dragging it to a new location. And if you select an item and hold down the Ctrl key, you can copy the selection by dragging it to a new location.

Drag Layer see Behaviors

Dreamweaver Exchange

The core of Dreamweaver is extensible. This means that you can add as many new features to the program as you can find or create for yourself. If you don't have the time, interest, or know-how to write your own Dreamweaver extensions, then you can download any or all of the approximately 500 extensions currently available at the Dreamweaver Exchange (*http://www.macromedia.com/exchange/dreamweaver/*).

Once on the Dreamweaver Exchange Web site, shown in Figure D-16, use the Category drop-down list or the Search field to find the extensions that will work best for you. I have found the most usable extensions may include the External Link Checker, the Atomz Search Engine, and Coursebuilder.

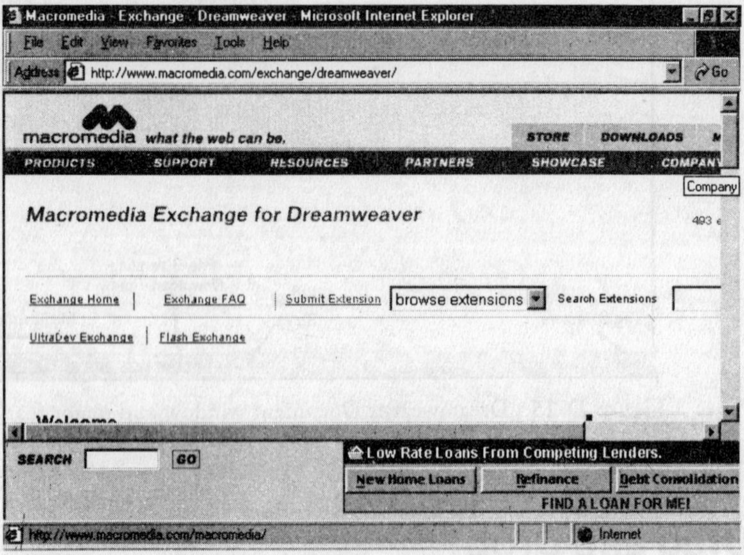

Figure D-16 Macromedia Dreamweaver Exchange Web site.

SEE ALSO *Customizing Dreamweaver, Extensions*

Dreamweaver Fireworks Studio

The Dreamweaver Fireworks Studio is the merging of the Dreamweaver 4 and Fireworks 4 packages into a single shrink-wrapped box. But the merging is more than just the external packaging. When you use the Dreamweaver Fireworks studio, you get a good Web graphic development package as well as a great Web document package. Fireworks works in conjunction with Dreamweaver to create page layouts, Web photo albums, enact Roundtrip Graphics editing, and many other features of Dreamweaver.

SEE ALSO *Fireworks, Roundtrip Graphics Editing, Web Photo Album*

ECMAScript

The European Computer Manufacturers Association (ECMA), with the help of companies such as Netscape and Macromedia, developed the ECMA-262 standard, which creates an international standard for the development of the JavaScript language. Prior to the development of this standard, JavaScript "belonged" to Netscape and JScript "belonged" to Microsoft. Although JavaScript and JScript are similar, and both languages use enough of the same functions and keywords that many scripts will function properly, there are enough variances that it is difficult, at best, to create any complex scripts that run well on both browsers.

SEE ALSO *Behaviors, JavaScript, JScript, Scripts*

Email Links

Dreamweaver allows you to create a link directly from your Web page to someone's e-mail address without you having to remember whether the prefix is email:, or email//, or mailto:. (It's mailto: by the way.) To insert an Email link, select Insert→Email Link. In the Insert Email Link dialog box, shown in Figure E-1, type the e-mail address into the Email field. The address needs to be complete, for instance, george@windingrivers.com rather than just George. Click OK when you are done. Be sure to test all your Email links when testing the rest of the links on your Web site.

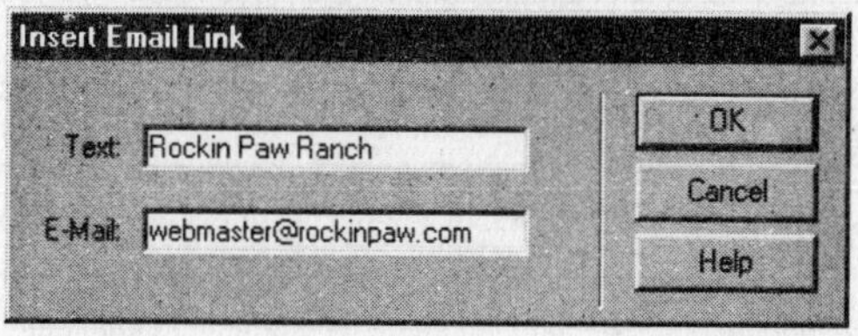

Figure E-1 The Insert Email Link dialog box.

SEE ALSO *Checking Links, FTP Links, Hypertext, Links, Named Anchors*

Embed

HTML requires that some items, such as sound files, be embedded into your document to work. For instance, the <embed> element allows you to add Java applets using the Insert→Media→Applet command. The <embed> element is also used to add sound files using the Play Sound behavior.

Events

Dreamweaver uses events, or actions that take place on your Web page when a visitor is looking at it, to control the automation of your page. For instance, whenever a visitor clicks on a link, they have enacted an onClick event. When your mouse moves over an image, an onMouseOver event occurs; when the mouse moves off an image, the onMouseOut event occurs. Dreamweaver can use the Behaviors panel to insert effects into your Web pages. Each of these effects is associated with one of the events in the following table that are available in all version 4.0 and newer browsers. If you are attempting to support only one of the browsers, your list of possible events will be more extensive.

ACTION	EVENT
on	Click
on	DblClick
on	Blur
on	MouseDown
on	MouseUp
on	MouseOver
on	MouseOut
on	KeyPress
on	KeyDown
on	KeyUp
on	Error
on	Focus
on	Load
on	Unload
on	Resize

If you specify a browser to use, then you will have a wider list of events available. This list shows only those events that are available for both Internet Explorer and Netscape Navigator 4 and later.

SEE ALSO *Behaviors, JavaScript, Scripting*

Extending Dreamweaver see Extensions

Extension Manager

The Dreamweaver Extension Manager, called the Package Manager in Dreamweaver's printed documentation but the Extension Manager in its online documentation, controls the installation and use of the different extensions that have been added to your copy of Dreamweaver. The Extension Manager is opened by selecting Help→Manage Extensions from within the Dreamweaver document window. It can also be opened from the Site window or by clicking on the Extension Manager icon in the Start menu, or the Finder on the Macintosh.

To use the Extension Manager, shown in Figure E-2, you will need to have downloaded an extension from the Dreamweaver Exchange Web site (*http://www.macromedia.com/exchange/dreamweaver*) or create your own extension.

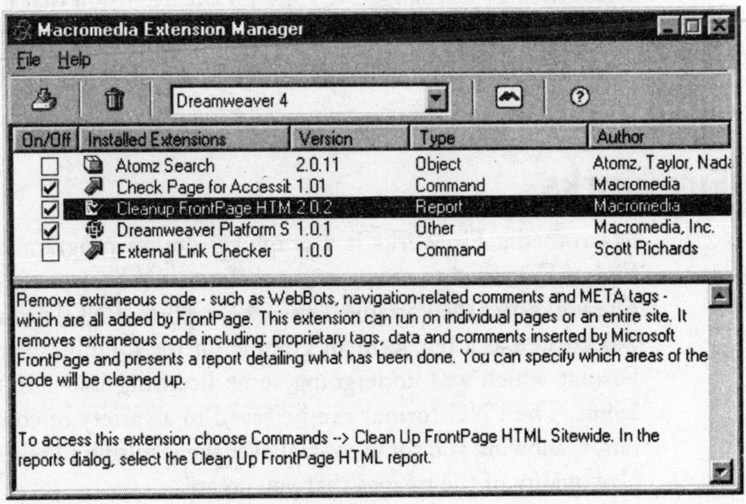

Figure E-2 The Extension Manager.

To install an extension, select File→Install Extension or click the Install button on the toolbar. You will be asked to agree to the extensions licensing agreement, and then the files associated with the extension will be copied to the appropriate places in your Dreamweaver installation's file structure. Once the extension is installed, you may be asked to restart Dreamweaver. I typically don't have Dreamweaver running when I install extensions for just this reason.

Once installed, and Dreamweaver is restarted, if necessary, you will be able to access your extension from within Dreamweaver's menu system or from the Objects panel. The location of the command is dependent upon the extension itself. If you can't find the command's placement, check the description of the extension as it is displayed in the Extension Manager screen.

SEE ALSO *Dreamweaver Exchange, Extensions*

Extensions

You can extend the capabilities of Dreamweaver by using Dreamweaver Extensions. Using Extensions, you can add features and functions to your program that you may use frequently, but that aren't included in Dreamweaver's original installed feature set. Search the Dreamweaver Exchange Web site for the extension that meets your needs, or write your own extensions. To learn more about writing your own extensions, see the Help→Extending Dreamweaver command.

SEE ALSO *Customizing Dreamweaver, Dreamweaver Exchange*

Fireworks

Macromedia Fireworks is a graphical design program, shown in Figure F-1, used to create many different Web-oriented graphics. Fireworks uses the Portable Network Graphics (PNG) format, which was created as a replacement graphic for the Graphics Interchange Format which was undergoing some licensing issues in the mid-1990s. The PNG format can be saved in a variety of compression ratios, allowing you some control over the resulting file size and display quality of the images that you create.

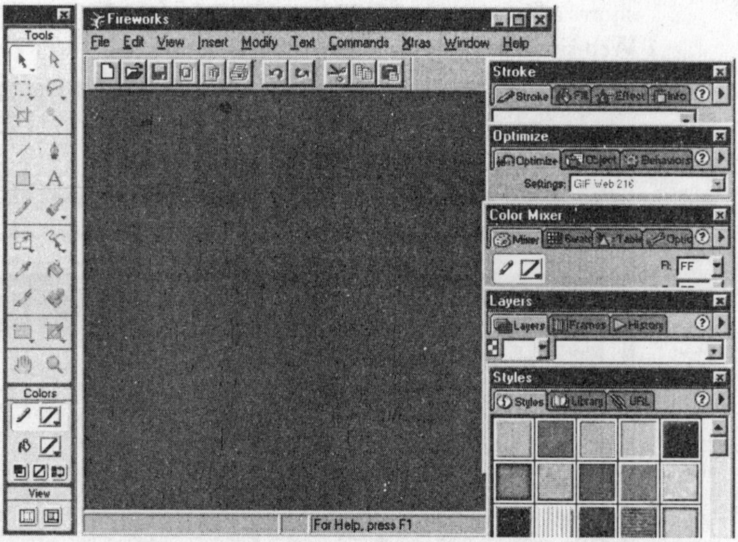

Figure F-1 Macromedia Fireworks creates graphics as well as exports the HTML code to control the layout of those graphics.

Fireworks is closely related to Dreamweaver and is shipped with it as part of the Dreamweaver/Fireworks Studio. A few features of Dreamweaver can't be used without the presence of Fireworks. These include the Web Photo Album, Insert Fire Works HTML, and Roundtrip Graphics editing.

Image Creation

All of the images created in Fireworks can be used within your Dreamweaver documents through either the Insert→Image option or by dragging and dropping the image into your document. Fireworks can be used to create complete page layouts, including menu bars, image rollovers, navigation bars, and animations.

HTML Creation

In addition to creating images, Fireworks can be used to create HTML pages. These pages are typically based on graphics and use Fireworks Export option to export the information contained within the PNG file into an HTML file and its associated individual graphics elements. HTML files created by Fireworks will contain a <!— Created by Fireworks → style comment at the top of the document. Figure F-2

shows a Fireworks image being used as the foundation of a complete Web site layout.

Figure F-2 A Fireworks image used to create a complete document layout.

SEE ALSO *Dreamweaver Fireworks Studio, GIF, JPG, PNG*

Flash

Flash is a Macromedia program that creates compact interactive multimedia presentations that can be added to Web pages. Flash requires a plug-in so that everyone wishing to view Flash media, whether a movie, button, or text object, must have that plug-in. Luckily almost 80 percent of Internet users have at least one version of the Flash plug-in for either Netscape Navigator or Internet Explorer. This plug-in ships with both Windows Professional and Windows XP to make the lives of Flash developers even easier.

Within Dreamweaver you have three options for using Flash: movies, buttons, or text objects. Each of these options is discussed in the following sections.

Flash Movies

Flash movies are presentations that have been created in the Macromedia Flash program, not in Dreamweaver. Movies typically have multiple objects, effects, and animations that interact together to create a complete interactive experience on your Web site. To insert a Flash movie into your Web document, select Insert→Media→Flash. This will open the Insert Flash Movie dialog box from which you can select the Flash presentation to add to your document. Select the movie file and click OK. With the Flash movie installed on your page, you will see a large gray block representing the Flash media. To play the movie, as shown in Figure F-3, through Dreamweaver click the Play button on the Flash media Properties inspector.

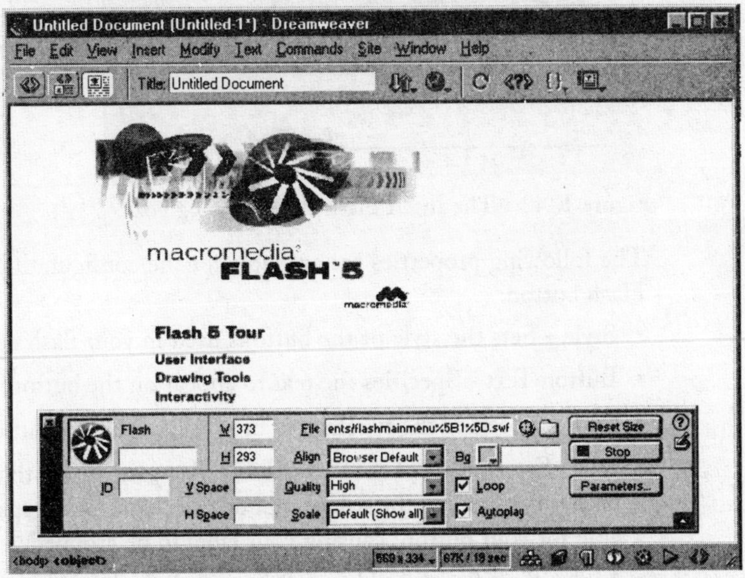

Figure F-3 A Flash movie in Dreamweaver.

Flash Buttons

Flash buttons are small Flash movies that can be automatically configured by Dreamweaver to serve as buttons on your Web sites. Flash buttons automatically have multiple states that work like rollover effects when the mouse moves over them. To insert a Flash button into your Web page, select Insert→Interactive Images→Flash Button or click on the Flash Button icon in the Common category of the Objects panel. This opens the Insert Flash Button dialog box shown in Figure F-4.

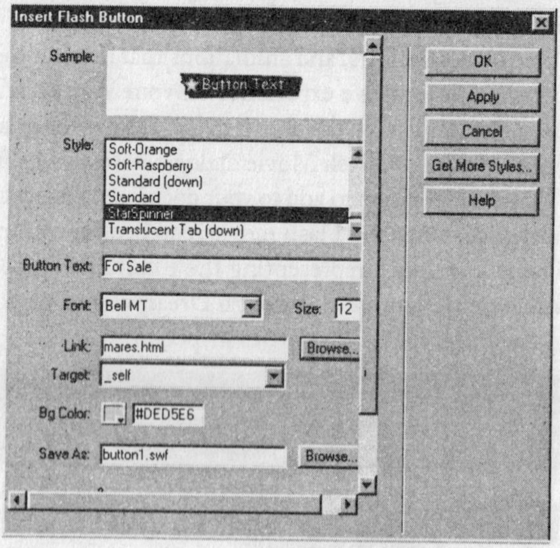

Figure F-4 The Insert Flash Button dialog box.

The following properties are available for the configuration of your Flash button:

- Style - Sets the style of the buttons used in your flash effect.
- Button Text - Specifies the text to appear on the button.
- Font - Specifies the typeface to use for labeling the button.
- Size - Sets the size of the button label. Test your button thoroughly, because you can set the size of your text too large for the space available for your button, causing your label to be cropped.
- Link - Specifies the address of the page linked to this text, if it is to serve as a link.
- Target - Specifies the target frame or window of the linked page.
- Bg Color - Sets the background color of your text item.
- Save As - Specifies the file where your Flash effect configuration instructions will be stored.

Once added to your document, your Flash buttons will look like those shown in Figure F-5.

Figure F-5 A selection of Flash buttons serving as a navigational bar for the Web site being created.

SEE ALSO *Images, Navigation Bars, Rollover Images*

Flash Text

Flash Text objects create Flash-enabled text so that you can use any font you want with a rollover effect without forcing your visitors to download additional fonts just to view your pages. Of course, this only works well for headings and other small sections of text. Flash text can't be indexed by search engines, so if you use Flash text for too much information, your document will receive poor placement in the very sources of the majority of your visitors. Don't use Flash text for document body text, and if you use it for headings, you should ensure that the same text is also used in other areas of your document.

To add Flash text to your document, select Insert→Interactive Images→Flash Text or select the Flash Text icon from the Common category of the Objects panel. This opens the Insert Flash Text dialog box, shown in Figure F-6.

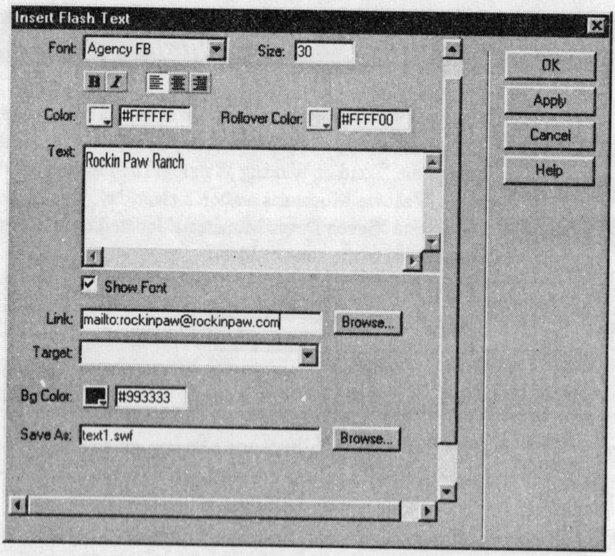

Figure F-6 The Insert Flash Text dialog box.

In the Insert Flash Text dialog box, configure your Flash Text object using the following settings:

- Font - Specifies the font face, any one located on your computer, for your base text.
- Size - Controls the point size of the text.
- Bold/Italic - Sets the bold or italic character of the font.
- Alignment - Controls the alignment of text: left, center, right, or justified.
- Color - Sets the color of your text.
- Rollover Color - Sets the color of your text when a rollover effect is occurring.
- Text - Allows you to select the text that you want to use. Typically, this should be a heading rather than a complete paragraph, although you can use paragraphs.
- Show Font - Allows you to see your text in your selected font while you are configuring your Flash effect.
- Link - Specifies the address of the page linked to this text, if it is to serve as a link.
- Target - Specifies the target frame or window of the linked page.

- Bg Color - Sets the background color of your text item.
- Save As - Specifies the file where your Flash effect configuration instructions will be stored.

Once added to your document, your Flash text statements will look like those shown in Figure F-7.

Figure F-7 The Rockin Paw title replaced with Flash text.

SEE ALSO *Cascading Style Sheets, Fonts*

Fonts

If "content is king," and the fastest way to get content to your visitors is by using text with a few well-placed images, then you must have text that is both informative and pleasing to the eye. There are two ways that you can use fonts to format the text on your page: by using style sheets or by using the HTML font properties.

NOTE *Dreamweaver doesn't use Cascading Style Sheets (CSS) to configure the appearance of fonts, although the use of font properties are no longer a part of the HTML specification. Dreamweaver only uses these deprecated font properties.*

CSS Font Settings

Cascading Style Sheets (CSS) properties can be used to configure the appearance of the text on your HTML pages by applying style sheet rules to types of elements, classes of elements, or even individual identified elements. To use style sheets to format the appearance of your text, select the element or item that you wish to format, and select Window→CSS Styles. This opens the CSS Styles dialog box from which you can create a new set of style rules for your text. Click the New Style button to open the New Styles dialog box from which you can create your font style.

Font Properties

Dreamweaver uses the properties associated with the HTML <font> element to control the appearance of text on your document unless you purposefully use a style sheet. If you are going to be developing sites strictly for users of the 4.0 browsers, then you will be best served to take the extra time to use style sheet properties in your document. If you wish to support even the low percentage of users using browsers that don't support style sheets, then you will want to use the <font> properties available on the Properties inspector.

To format text using the properties available on the Properties inspector, shown in Figure F-8, highlight the text you wish to format and then make your adjustments on the Properties inspector.

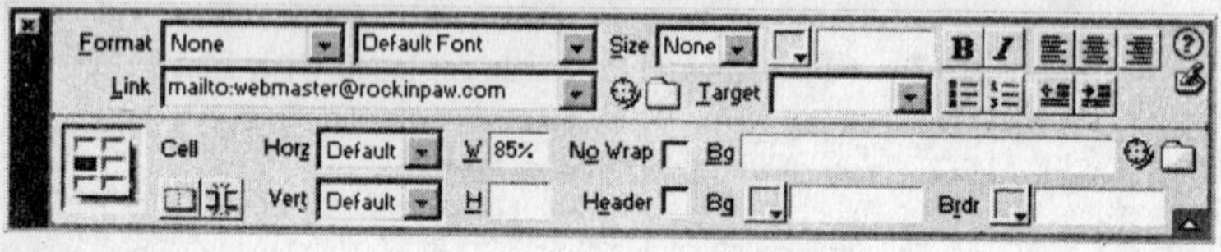

Figure F-8 Font Properties on the Properties inspector.

The following options are available:

- Format - Specifies six heading styles, paragraph (p), or preformatted text (pre).
- Font - Controls the typeface used in the text. You can select from one of the typefaces that are defined by default, and available on every operating system, or you can add your own by selecting the Edit Font List option at the end of your default font list.
- Size - Controls the appearance of the text.
- Color - Sets the color of the text characters.
- Bold / Italic - Sets the bold and italic properties on your text.
- Left / Center / Right - Controls the alignment of your text.
- Bulleted List - Turns the current text into a bulleted list.
- Numbered List - Turns the current text into a numbered list.
- Indent / Outdent - Indents, or removes the indentation, of text.

In addition to setting these properties on the Properties inspector, you can set them directly from the Text menu, as shown in Figure F-9.

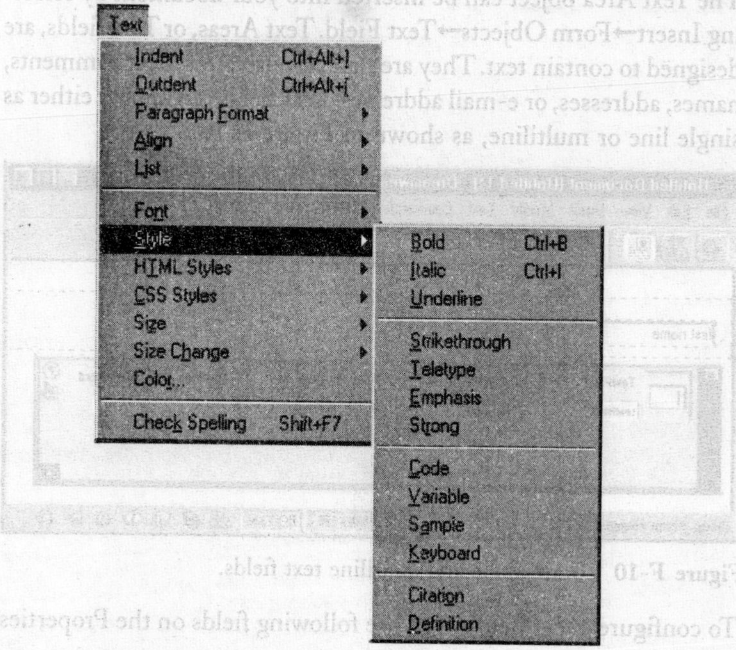

Figure F-9 Text menu options.

Be sure to have the text you want to format selected before making your formatting choices. If you do not, then your choices will be applied to the next text typed.

SEE ALSO *HTML Styles, Properties Inspector*

Form Objects

Forms, which allow people to provide Web site owners with information in addition to what a Web server's log files provide, have a variety of options available on them. These options are described in the following sections. All of these options are available from the Insert→Form Objects menu or from the Form category of the Objects panel. Each of these form controls is discussed in the following sections.

Text Area

The Text Area object can be inserted into your document by selecting Insert→Form Objects→Text Field. Text Areas, or Text fields, are designed to contain text. They are typically used to collect comments, names, addresses, or e-mail addresses. Text fields can appear either as single line or multiline, as shown in Figure F-10.

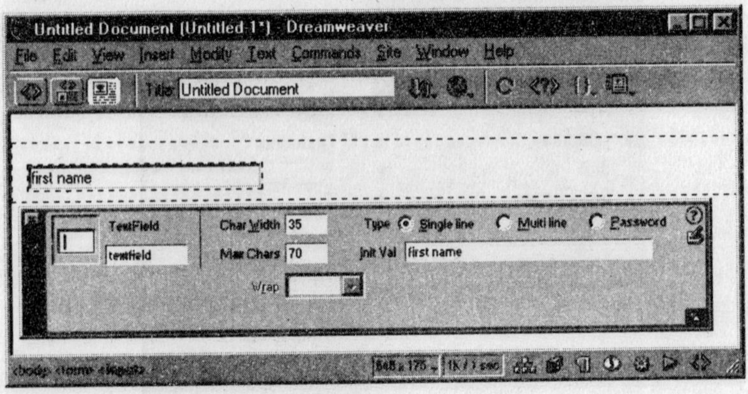

Figure F-10 Both single and multiline text fields.

To configure a text field, fill in the following fields on the Properties inspector:

- Name - Identifies a unique name for the field. This name can't have a space in it, but you can use an underscore.
- Char Width - Sets up the width of the character field. This is the number of characters across, not the number of pixels across.
- Max Chars - Specifies the maximum number of characters that can be contained within this field. Leaving it blank allows as much information typed in as the site visitor wishes.
- Type - Specifies a single line, password, or multiline field. If you select single line, then your field will appear as only one line on your screen. Selecting Password disguises the content typed into the field, but does nothing for the information as it is passed through the Internet. Multiline allows you to display multiple lines of text in the field.
- Init Value - Sets the default value of the form field.
- Num Lines - Sets the total number of lines you want to have displayed, if you have selected a multiline type.

List/Menu

Forms allow you to create a list of options from which visitors must make selections. The biggest use of the List/Menu field is to list a variety of options from which a visitor can select one or more answers, as shown in Figure F-11. You can insert a List/Menu field into your form by selecting Insert→Form Objects→List/Menu Field.

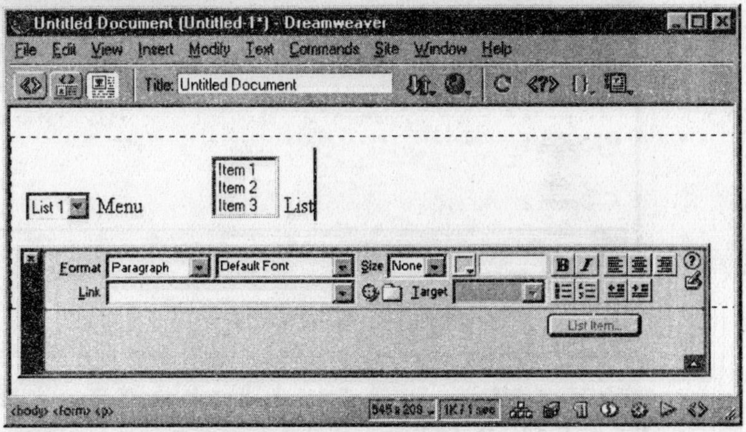

Figure F-11 A List/Menu field and its configurable fields on the Properties inspector.

List/Menu fields have the following options:

- ID - Identifies the name of the field.
- List Value - Specifies the list of values that can be contained within the field.
- Height - Specifies the number of lines to display if this is a list entry.
- Type - Specifies the type of list/menu item being created. Lists show multiple values at once, while a menu shows only one value at a time.
- Allow Multiple - Allows multiple selections to be made.
- Initially Selected - Selects the list item that you want to be selected when the document first loads.

Radio

Radio buttons allow you to make a single selection from a group of objects, as shown in Figure F-12. Radio buttons are commonly used to request that a visitor makes an income range selection on forms. You can insert a radio button into your form by selecting Insert→Form Objects→Radio Button.

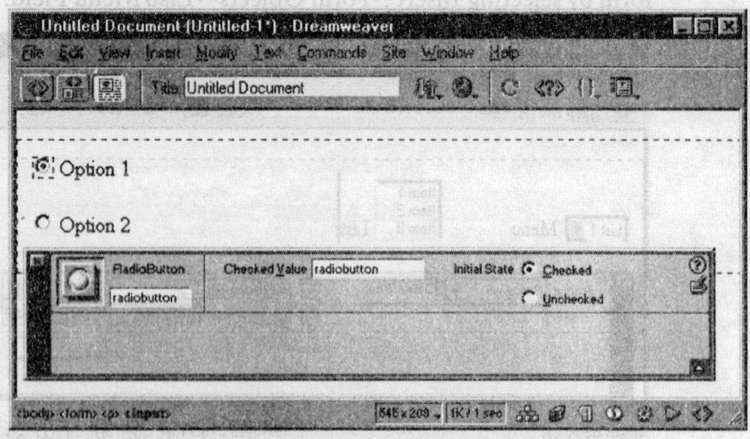

Figure F-12 Radio buttons and their properties.

The properties associated with a radio button are shown in the following list:

- Name - Identifies the name for the complete group of radio buttons.
- Checked Value - Specifies the value of the radio button that is sent to the server when the button is checked.
- Initial State - If set to Checked, this is the default setting for this group of radio buttons.

Check Box

Check boxes allow you to make a multiple selections from a group of objects, as shown in Figure F-13. Check boxes are commonly used to request that a visitor make a series of selections, often about e-zines that they would like to receive. You can insert a check box into your form by selecting Insert→Form Objects→Check Box.

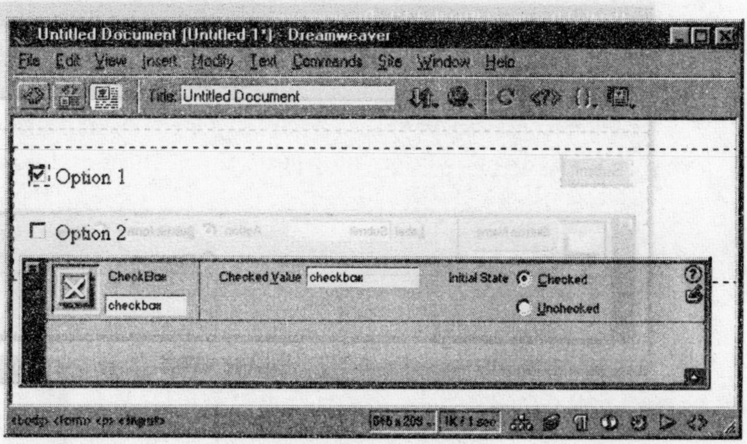

Figure F-13 Check boxes and their properties.

The properties associated with a check box are shown in the following list:

- Name - Identifies the name for the check box.
- Checked Value - Specifies the value of the check box that is sent to the server when the button is checked.
- Initial State - If set to Checked, this is the default setting for this check box.

Button

Buttons have a variety of use in forms. They can reset form fields, submit the information, as shown in Figure F-14, or simply serve any other task that you want. To insert a button into your HTML document select Insert→Form Objects→Button.

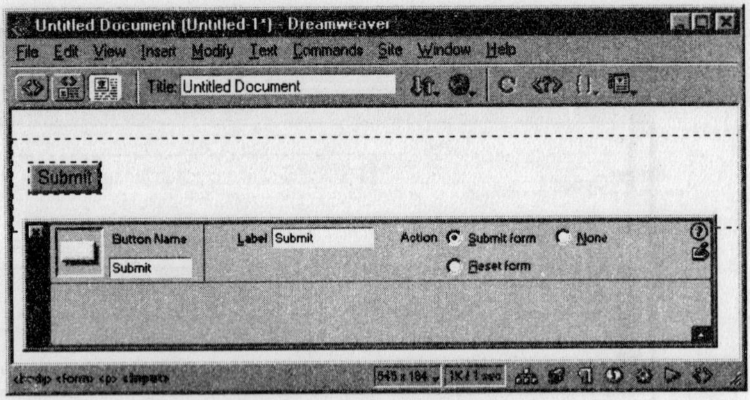

Figure F-14 Form button objects properties.

The following properties are associated with a button:

- Name - Identifies the button name. This can't be Submit or Reset unless you want the button to have the traditional purpose of these buttons.
- Label - Specifies the text to appear on the face of the button.
- Action - Specifies an action to take when the button is pressed. Submit sends the form information to the server. Reset returns all the values of the form back to their defaults. None leaves the processing of the form information up to the processing script.

File

File fields allow your visitors to upload files to you, if your server is set up to allow anonymous FTP and the Form field's method attribute is set to POST. To set up a file field, as shown in Figure F-15, insert the field by selecting Insert→Form Objects→File Field.

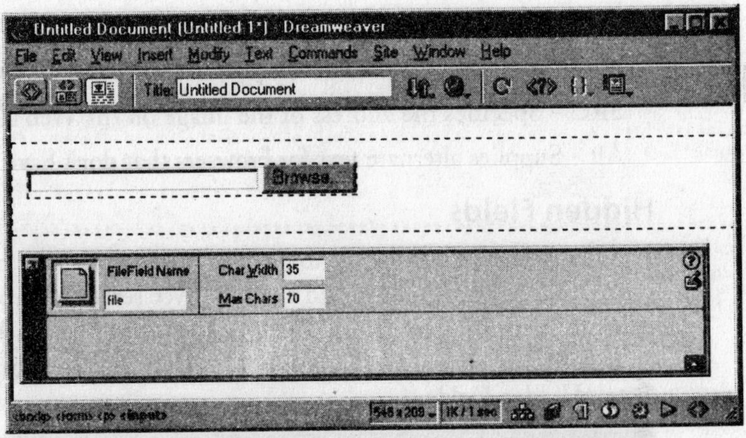

Figure F-15 File fields in forms.

The following properties are available on the Properties inspector:

- Name - Identifies a name for the file field object.
- Char Width - Specifies the width of the field based upon the number of visible characters it can display.
- Max Chars - Specifies the maximum number of characters the field can contain. If left blank, there is no maximum applied.

Image

Images can serve as submit buttons for forms. To insert an image into your HTML document, as shown in Figure F-16, select Insert→Form Objects→Image Field.

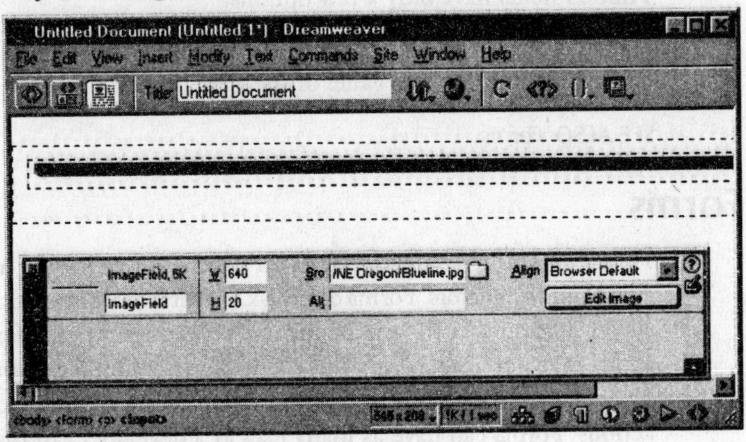

Figure F-16 Form image objects properties.

The following properties are associated with an image:

- Name - Identifies the image name.
- SRC - Specifies the address of the image on the Web server.
- Alt - Supplies alternate text for browsers that don't have an exit.

Hidden Fields

Hidden fields are not visible to anyone viewing the site, but they contain information to be passed on to the Web server and from there either to an e-mail address or a database. To insert a Hidden field into your form, as shown in Figure F-17, select Insert→Form Objects→Hidden Field.

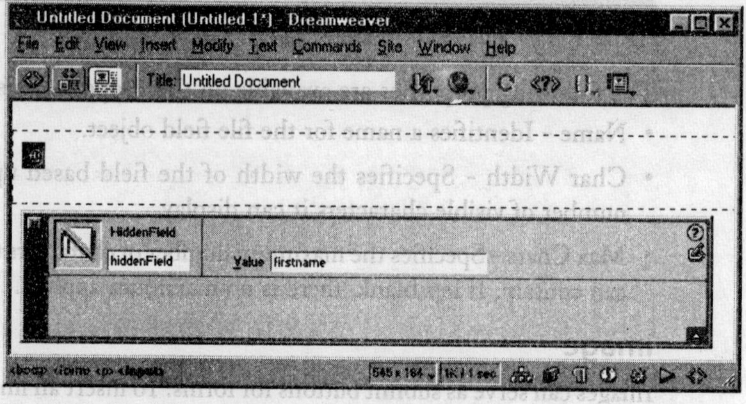

Figure F-17 The properties for Hidden field elements.

Hidden fields have only a few options:

- ID - Identifies the name of the field.
- Value - Specifies the value of the field.

SEE ALSO *Forms*

Forms

Forms provide Web developers with a means of collecting information from site visitors. Forms often ask for personal information about the visitors so that the site owner can send them more information about their services. Forms will collect information for guest books. Forms are used to collect information to complete e-commerce transactions. Forms can have as many uses as a developer can think of.

Forms are created with two different parts: the HTML source code, which you create in Dreamweaver, and the processing script or application, which is often a CGI script or a Java application. The HTML page collects the information from site visitors, while the processing application does something with it so that the information is returned to the site owner in a meaningful way.

Dreamweaver uses a selection of Form Objects to collect the information in a style that best fits the information trying to be collected. For instance, Text fields are used to collect names, while a List field might be used to provide a list of states as part of an address.

Forms can be entered into your document by selecting Insert→Forms. This adds an empty form field to your document, as shown in Figure F-18.

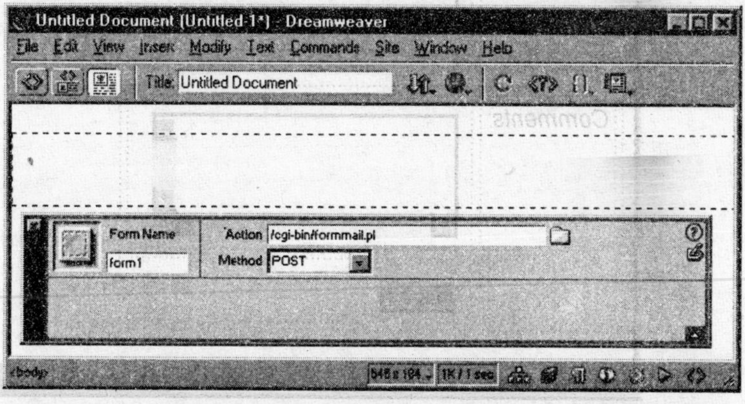

Figure F-18 The dashed line shows the outlines of the current empty form field.

NOTE *If you can't see the form outline on your screen, ensure that View→Visual Aids →Invisible Elements is checked.*

The form itself has a variety of options, as listed below:

- Name - Identifies a unique name for this form.
- Action - Specifies the URL for the processing script or application.

- Method - Sets the method used to handle the form data. If GET, then the information is sent to the processing application with all of the form values appended to the URL. If POST, then the form information is sent to the processing application in the body of a message.

Once you start adding form objects to your form field, as shown in Figure F-19, you can expand your form to contain the fields needed to collect your data.

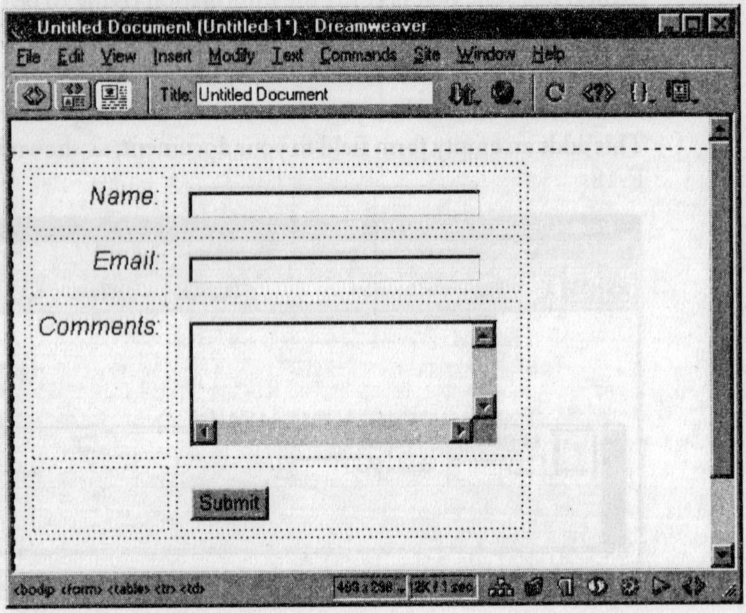

Figure F-19 Form field collecting information for a Guest book.

SEE ALSO *Behaviors, Form Objects*

Frame Layouts

Frames provide a way of creating multiple windows out of your Web browser. Frames allow you to load more than one document at a time, with each document being loaded into its own frame or window. Dreamweaver provides a lot of preconfigured frames configurations, all of which are available from the Insert→Frames→[frame options].

Figure F-20 shows an example of all the frameset layouts built into Dreamweaver.

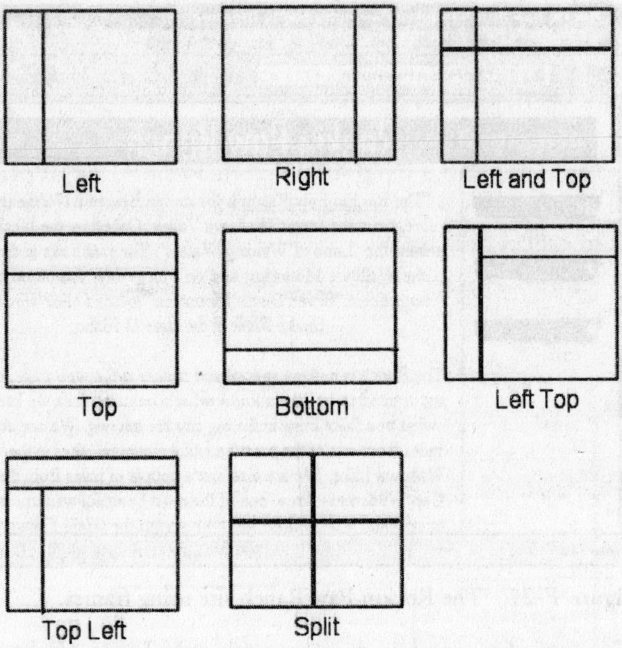

Figure F-20 Dreamweaver Frameset configurations.

SEE ALSO *Frames*

Frames

Frames break your Document window into multiple panes, allowing you to load multiple documents simultaneously. Figure F-21 shows a common use of frames. The top frame loads the site's logo. The frame on the left lists the site's table of contents. The bottom right frame is the only frame whose contents will change as the site is navigated.

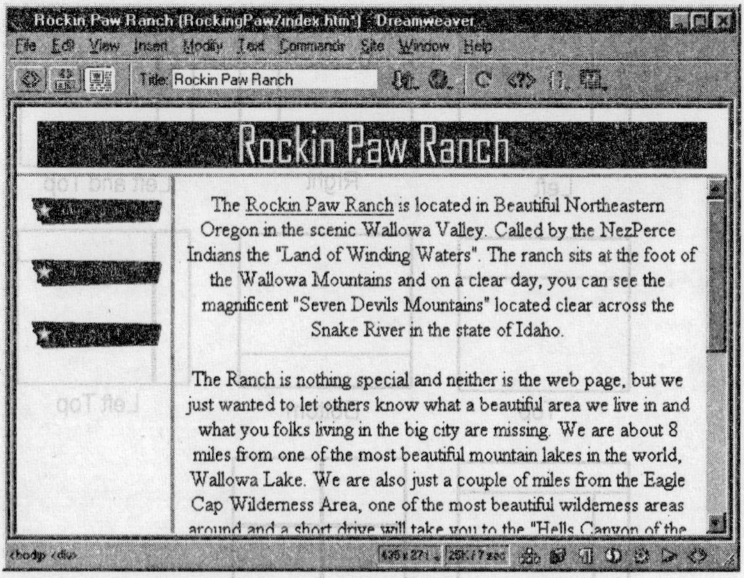

Figure F-21 The Rockin Paw Ranch site using frames.

To create a frame in your document, select the Insert→Frames→[frame options] command. The Rockin Paw site, shown in Figure F-21, uses the Left and Top frameset configuration.

Frames are often touted as being downright evil, because they can make the navigation of a Web site difficult or hard to understand. If you have no more than three frames in your document, then there should be no problem with people finding their way around. Like anything else, frames need to be used judiciously.

Once you have added your frames layout to your document, you need to decide how you are going to format each of the individual frames. You have two choices. You can either format each frame from the document window or you can use the Frames panel to link an existing document to the frame, thus avoiding re-creating document formats that you have already completed.

To add information to a frame, you can modify the objects in the document just like you would any other document. If you wish to insert a preexisting document into a frame, open the Frames panel by selecting Window→Frames or by pressing Ctrl+F10 (Windows) or Cmd+f10 (Macintosh). In the Frames panel, shown in Figure F-22, select the frame you wish to modify by clicking the frame title. This will updated your Properties inspector, shown in Figure F-23, to reflect the information referencing the current frame.

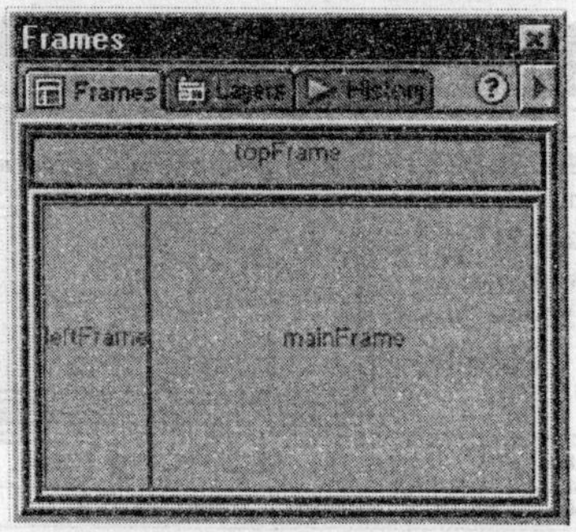

Figure F-22 The Frames panel.

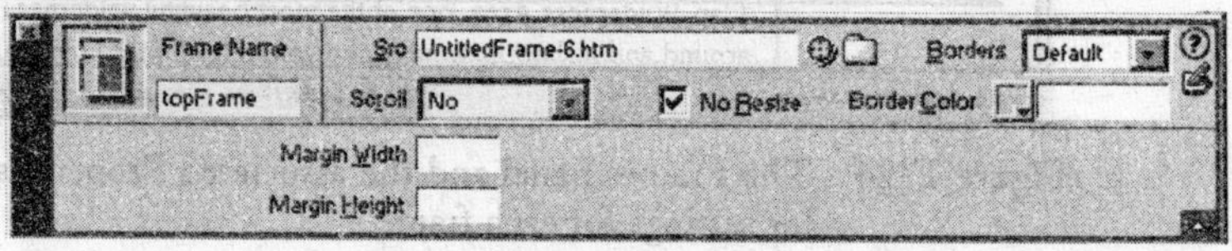

Figure F-23 The Frames Properties inspector.

The Frame Name field will allow you to provide each frame in the document with a unique name. The Src field allows you to update the URL of the document to reflect the page you intend to show in that frame. If you have created the content from within the frames file, then you will need to save the frame with your changes. This is done by selecting the frame and using the File→Save command. You can use File→Save Frameset to save the main document containing the frames information. Use File→Save All to save the all of the files in the frames based document included the frameset and all three documents visible through the frames.

SEE ALSO *Frame Layouts, Frames Panel*

Frames Panel

The Frames panel, shown in Figure F-24, provides access to the frames properties for each frame individually. Essentially all you can do from here is to select individual frames and then updated their information in the Properties inspector.

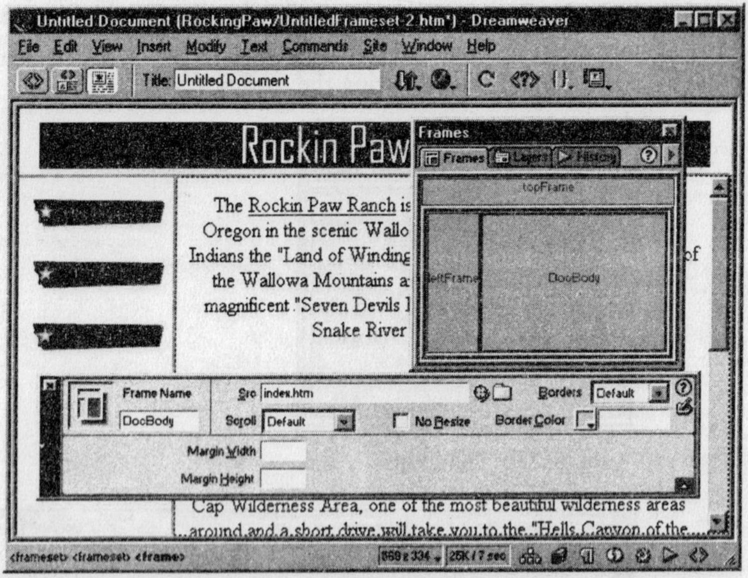

Figure F-24 The Frames panel and the associated Properties inspector settings for each frame.

SEE ALSO *Frame Layouts, Frames*

FTP

The File Transfer Protocol (FTP) is the set of rules that were defined strictly to facilitate the exchange of files between your computer and a Web server, or to make any other networked computer simpler and easier to work with. FTP is the primary system used by people with dialup or DSL connections to put files onto and takes files off of Web servers. FTP is also the system that Dreamweaver uses to put files onto a Web server, unless that server uses either a WebDAV or Visual SourceSafe or is part of a local area network.

SEE ALSO *Defining Sites, Visual SourceSafe, WebDAV*

FTP Links

Dreamweaver allows you to link to files using FTP as well as http Web links. In order to create an FTP link to a file highlight the text you wish to use, and then place your cursor in the Link field of the

Properties inspector and type the URL, prefaced by ftp:// as shown in the Properties inspector shown in Figure F-25.

Figure F-25 FTP Link format.

SEE ALSO *Email Links, Hypertext*

Generator

Macromedia Generator is a program created to serve dynamic Web content. Generator files can be created using either Flash or one of the Generator templates.

To insert a Macromedia Generator program, select Insert→ Media→Generator or click the Generator icon in the Objects panel. Select a Generator template (*.swt). Generator files will often require that additional parameters be set. To set a parameter, select the Plus button to add the parameter as a set of name="value" pairs of information. When finished, click OK and the Generator object will be inserted into your document.

SEE ALSO *Fireworks, Flash, Shockwave/Director*

GET

There are two methods for sending information to a Web server using Forms: GET and POST. The GET method appends all of the forms content to the URL of the application processing the form information.

SEE ALSO *Forms, POST*

GIF

GIF images are one of the three types of image formats available for use on the Internet. GIFs are best used for simple graphics with smooth lines and under 256 colors. GIFs can contain animations and transparent portions, which are unavailable with JPEG images.

SEE ALSO *Images, JPG, PNG*

Go to Timeline Frames see Behaviors

Go to URL see Behaviors

Headings

HTML has six elements that provide default formatting for document headings. These elements can be inserted using the Text→Paragraph Format→Heading *x* command to select your document heading size. Figure H-1 displays the size of the headings available with all HTML documents. Heading 1 is the largest heading size. You can use font-formatting elements to make normal text appear like a Heading 1 element, or to change the appearance of the default Heading 1 formatting, but you should still use the headings to describe the content of your document.

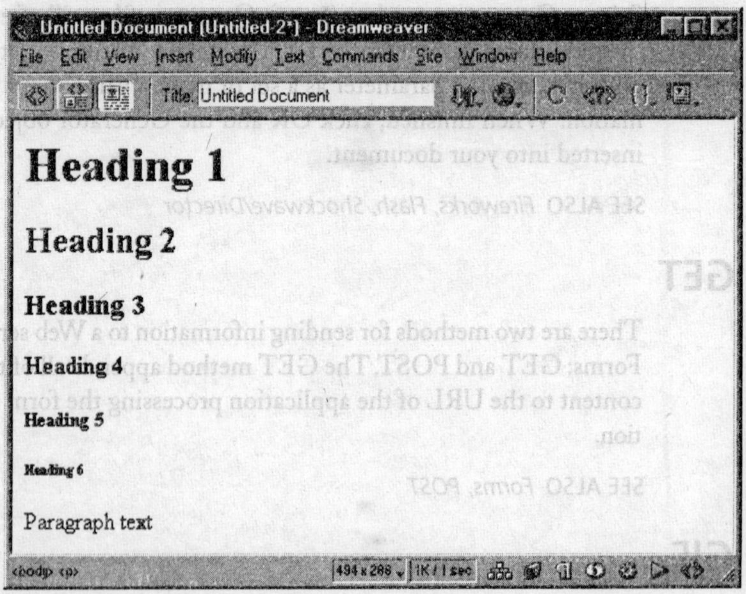

Figure H-1 HTML headings.

SEE ALSO *Fonts*

Help Files

Dreamweaver includes a variety of help files, all of which are available through the Help menu. These help files include assistance for all aspects of Dreamweaver. The help menus include the following:

- Using Dreamweaver
- Reference Information
- Dreamweaver Exchange
- Managing Extensions
- Macromedia Support Center
- Extending Dreamweaver
- Creating and Submitting Extensions

History Panel

The History panel keeps track of all the steps taken within Dreamweaver between the time a document was opened and closed. The History panel provides you with the ability to backtrack your steps either singly, or in groups. You can also copy a series of steps into a macrolike command that can be reused. You can open the History panel, shown in Figure H-2, by selecting Window→History.

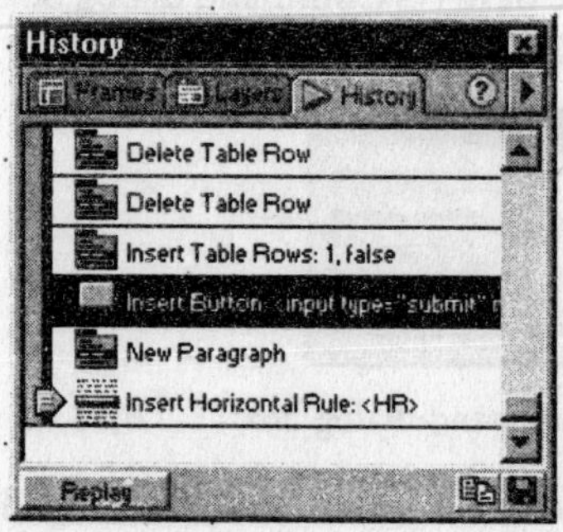

Figure H-2 The History panel.

Undoing Steps

The History panel allows you to undo any steps that you have taken by moving the slider up a step. Every step that you move the slider up works like pressing Ctrl +Z (Windows) or Cmd+Z (Macintosh). You may also move to a particular step in the History by clicking on the slider bar to the left of that step itself. This will automatically move the slider and undo all of the steps back to that point.

NOTE *If you undo some steps and then make a change to the document, you can't redo your previous steps. You will have to recreate them by hand.*

Recording Commands

Because you can repeat steps that have been stored in your History file, you can record them and save them for future use. You can both replay steps that you have recently performed on this one document, or save those steps and replay them on multiple documents.

To replay steps that you have recently completed, highlight them in the History panel, and then click the Replay button. To select more than one step, click on the first step you wish to play, then drag your mouse down through the text of the step labels until you have reached the step that you wish to end with. The alternative is to click on the first step you wish to repeat, press the Shift key, and then click on the step that you wish to end with.

To record your steps, select your range of steps as previously shown, and then click the Save As Command button, or choose the Save As Command option on the History panel's contextual menu. Enter the name for the command in the Save As Command dialog box, shown in Figure H-3, and click OK.

Figure H-3 The Save As Command dialog box.

This will force your command to be stored on the Commands menu, as shown in Figure H-4. Once on the Commands menu, you can use this entry to run it from any other document or site.

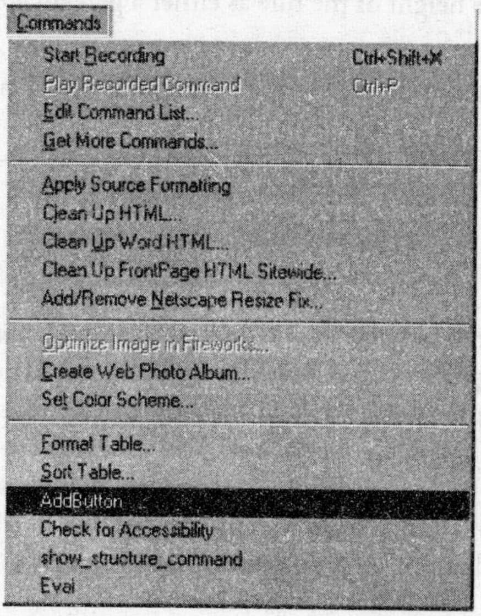

Figure H-4 The Dreamweaver Commands menu.

SEE ALSO *Customizing Dreamweaver*

Horizontal Rules

Horizontal rules are lines across your Web pages that serve as visual breaks in the text. To insert a horizontal rule into your document, select Insert→Horizontal Rule or click the Insert Horizontal Rule button on the Objects panel. This inserts the horizontal rule and opens the horizontal rule Properties inspector, as shown in Figure H-5.

Figure H-5 The Horizontal Rule Properties inspector.

On the Properties inspector you can modify the following properties:

- Width - Sets the width of the rule as either a percentage or pixel width.

- Height - Sets the height of the rule as either a percentage or pixel width.
- Shading - Configures the rule to have the appearance of a shadow.
- Align - Sets the alignment of the rule.

SEE ALSO *Images*

HTML

The Hypertext Markup Language (HTML) is the foundation of Web page design and implementation. HTML can be displayed by all Web browsers. HTML provides its own formatting and content descriptions. HTML is a derivative of the Standard Generalized Markup Language (SGML) and uses a series of elements, attributes, character references, and comments to identify and define portions of a document. A standard HTML document would appear as follows:

```
<html>

  <head>

    <title> document title </title>

  </head>

  <body>

    Elements and text content goes here.

  </body>

</html>
```

As you can see, a HTML document is broken into two sections, the head and the body. XML documents may be configured this way, but generally aren't.

SEE ALSO *Cascading Style Sheets*

HTML Styles

Dreamweaver has a unique feature called HTML Styles that allows you to control the formatting of the information on your Web site using HTML codes rather than Cascading Style Sheets (CSS). HTML Styles add preformatted HTML codes to your text so that you can format all of your paragraphs, headings, and document objects in the same manner. A wider range of Web browsers supports HTML Styles, but they take longer to load than CSS Styles. You can view the HTML Styles panel, shown in Figure H-6, by selecting Window→HTML Styles or clicking the HTML Styles button on either the Launcher or the Mini-Launcher.

Figure H-6 The HTML Styles panel.

When opened, the HTML Styles panel allows you to see a list of all the HTML Styles that have already been created. You will notice that one of two icons is in front of the style name. The underscored icon represents a character style that can be applied to any set of selected characters. The Paragraph mark represents a style that must be applied to whole paragraphs.

NOTE *Dreamweaver has two built-in styles: Clear Selection Style and Clear Paragraph Style. Both of these styles allow you to remove existing styles from your document, and neither of them can be removed from your Dreamweaver installation.*

Creating HTML Styles

You have two options when creating an HTML Style. You can base it on existing text, or you can base it on an existing HTML Style.

To create an HTML Style based upon existing text, either select text that has the formatting you want or create and format your own text. Then click the New Style icon (the plus sign [+]) in the HTML Styles panel. In the Define HTML Style dialog box, shown in Figure H-7, use the following options to format the style to fit your needs:

- Apply To Selection - Forces the style to be applied to a selection of characters.
- Apply To Paragraph - Forces the style to be applied to a complete element.
- When Applying, Add To Existing Style - Adds these new controls to the existing formatting controls.
- When Applying, Clear Existing Style - Overwrites all other formatting applied to the selected text.
- Font - Sets the typeface.
- Size - Sets the typeface size.
- Color - Controls the color of the text.
- Style - Specifies either bold or italic text.
- Paragraph Attributes: Format - Controls the format of the text (paragraph, heading, or preformatted text) for paragraph styles.
- Paragraph Attributes: Alignment - Controls the alignment of the paragraph for paragraph styles.

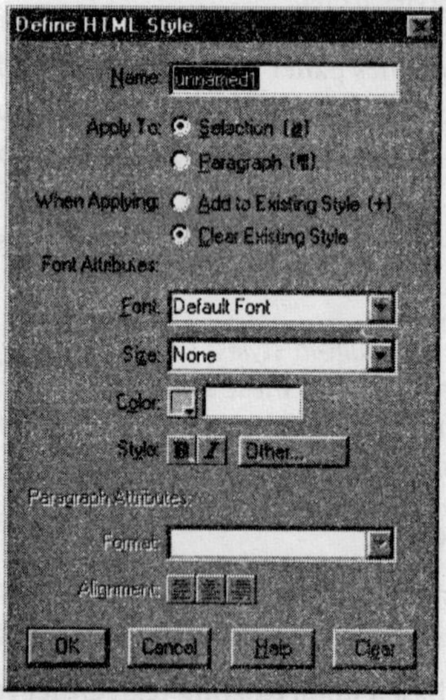

Figure H-7 The Define HTML Style dialog box.

Once done, click OK.

Modifying Styles

To modify an existing HTML Style, select the style from the HTML Styles panel (with Auto Apply unchecked so you don't apply the style). Right-click (Windows) or Ctrl+Click (Macintosh) on the name of the style and select Edit from the contextual menu. This opens the Define HTML Style dialog box shown previously in Figure H-7. To reset the contents of this dialog box to its default values, click the Clear button; otherwise, adjust the properties listed in this screen to control the formatting of your information. Once done, click OK.

NOTE *Dreamweaver doesn't automatically update the information that was previously formatted by this modified style. If you wish to do that, either create a Library item or put that information on a template. You can update the format of your data by reapplying the style.*

Removing Styles

To remove a style from the HTML Styles panel, select the style and click the Delete Style icon (the trashcan) on the panel. This will remove a style, but not remove the formatting from elements to which it has previously been applied.

Applying Styles

To apply an HTML Style to a selection of text in your document, select the portion of the document that you wish to be formatted using this style. If the Auto Apply check box is already selected, then selecting the style in the Define HTML Style dialog box will automatically apply it. If Auto Apply is not checked, then select the style and click the Apply button.

SEE ALSO *Cascading Style Sheets*

HTML Styles Panel

The HTML Styles panel provides a list of the entire programmed HTML-based styles in your document. Figure H-8 shows all of the parts of the HTML Styles panel labeled for your convenience. HTML Styles are a feature of convenience, which has been integrated into Dreamweaver. It is Dreamweaver's own special tool and not available in other programs.

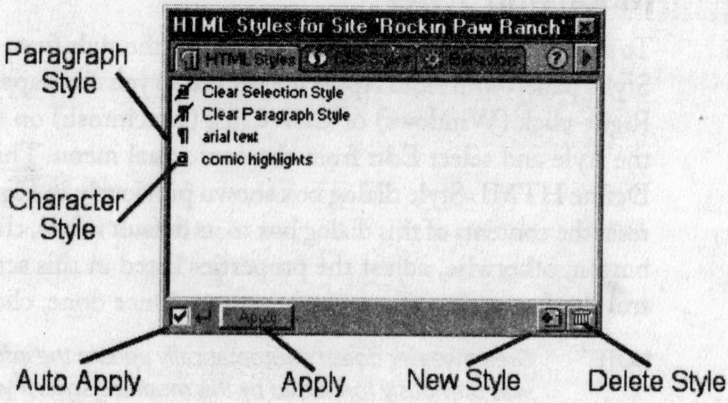

Figure H-8 The HTML Styles panel.

With the HTML Styles panel, you can create, modify, and apply different predefined HTML codes to your text.

SEE ALSO *CSS Styles Panel, HTML Styles*

Hyperlinks see Hypertext

Hypertext

Hypertext references the application of specific markup code, which allows for the linking of multiple documents. These links, also called hyperlinks, provide a document reader with the ability to quickly jump from one document to another at a click of the mouse. Links in HTML documents are created using the <a> tag.

SEE ALSO *HTML, Links*

Hypertext Markup Language see HTML

Image Maps

An image map is a combination of an image and a mapped-out collection of links. HTML uses the <img>, <map>, and <area> elements to create an image map.

You can create an image map by following these steps:

1. Select an image.
2. In the lower half of the Properties inspector, as shown in Figure I-1, you will be able to see the Map options. If these options are not visible, click on the expander arrow located in the lower right corner of the Properties inspector. Type a name for the map in the Map Name field.

Figure I-1 The Image/Image Map Properties inspector.

3. Use one of the Hotspot drawing tools to describe the areas of the image that will serve as links. The Circle tool creates circles, the Rectangle tool can create either rectangles or squares, and the Polygon tool can create irregular multisided shapes, such as starbursts. Once the hotspot is defined, then the Hotspot Properties panel will appear, as shown in Figure I-2.

Figure I-2 Hotspot Properties panel for controlling hotspots on image maps.

4. Set the value of the Link field to the name of the file, which serves as the destination of the link.
5. In the Target field, specify the ultimate target of the link. This could be a frame, another new window, or even the current window.
6. In the Alt field, specify the alternate text to appear for this image in text-only browsers.

Your image map is now created. When you preview the document (choose FileÞPreview In Browser), you will be able to use the hotspots on your image map as a navigational tool.

NOTE *When creating your image map, you will want to move the map itself to an unobtrusive location, such as the end of your document. When the image map is located directly in your document layout, it will spread the layout of your information off the screen when you are in Dreamweaver, although it has no effect on the document layout when seen through the Web browser.*

Modifying Image Maps

To modify an existing image map, select the image with the map. You will then have access to all of the properties for the map and the individual hotspots. Modifications to your image map can include the following tasks:

- Move A Hotspot - To move a hotspot, select the hotspot in the image file. This will place handles on the hotspot itself and remove them from the image. You can then use your mouse to click and drag the hotspot to a new location.
- Resize A Hotspot - Select the hotspot and use the handles on the hotspot area to maneuver the size and shape of the hotspot.
- Change The Target - To change the target of the hotspot, click on the hotspot and select the Link field in the Properties inspector. From here, either type or use the Browse button to select the new destination file.

SEE ALSO *Hypertext, Images, Links*

Images

Images are pictures. They are the graphical elements that are associated with your HTML document. Images in HTML documents viewed through a Web browser can be of three types: GIF, PNG, and JPG.

You can insert an image into your HTML document by selecting Insert→Image. Select your image from the Insert Image dialog box. When applied to your document, as shown in Figure I-3, the Image Properties inspector appears. The Properties inspector lists all properties for the image, including those listed below:

- Image Name - Identifies the name of the image.
- Src - Sets the URL for the image.
- Link - Identifies the address of the link, if the image serves as a link to another document.
- Width (W) - Sets the width of the image.
- Height (H) - Sets the height of the image.
- Align - Controls the placement of an image on a horizontal line.
- Alt - Provides descriptive text about the image.
- Map - Identifies the name of the image map to associate with the image.
- VSpace - Controls the vertical space reserved around the image.

- HSpace - Controls the horizontal space reserved around the image.
- Target - Sets the destination of the link.
- Low Src - Loads this image for low-resolution monitors.

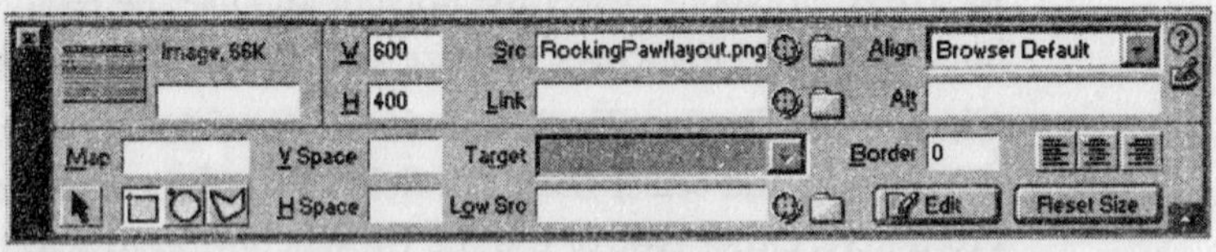

Figure I-3 The image and its associated Properties inspector properties.

Once these settings are set, or left blank, you are ready to preview your image in a Web browser.

SEE ALSO *GIF, Image Maps, JPG, PNG*

Importing Table Data

Dreamweaver can import delimited table data, such as comma-delimited Microsoft Excel files. You can use this tool to import any image that is delimited with a comma, colon, semicolon, tab, or other specified character. To import table data, select File→Import→Import Tabular Data or select Insert→Tabular Data. When either of these options are selected, the Import Table Data (alternatively called Insert Tabular Data) dialog box appears, as shown in Figure I-4.

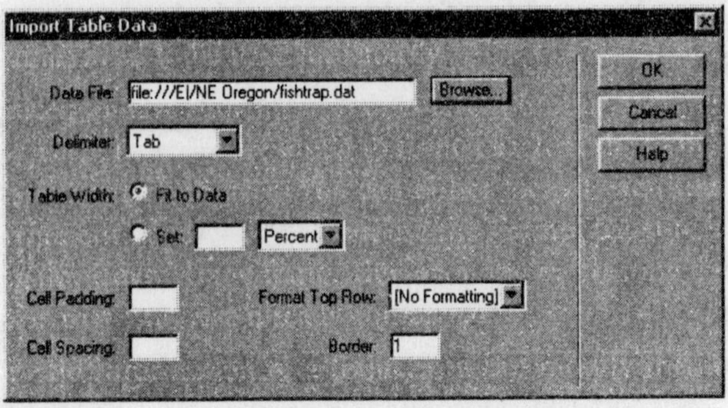

Figure I-4 The Import Table Data dialog box.

In this dialog box, you have the following options to set:

- Data File - Sets the URL of the file to be imported.
- Delimiter - Sets the character used to separate out different fields in the database.
- Table Width - Sets either the inherited width of the data or a preset width measured either as a percentage of the page width or as a preset measurement in pixels.
- Cell Padding - Controls the amount of reserved space between the cell border and the cell contents.
- Cell Spacing - Controls the amount of reserved space between the borders of two cells.
- Format Top Row - Controls the formatting of the top row of the table that is typically the header row.
- Border - Controls the width of the border of the table. If the border is set to 0, then no border is visible.

NOTE *Once imported, you can use the other table formatting options to further configure the appearance of your table.*

SEE ALSO *Importing Word Documents, Layout Tables, Tables*

Importing Word Documents

The Import Word Document function of Dreamweaver allows you to convert documents created in Microsoft Word into a more compliant format. Select File→Import→Import Word HTML to automatically start Clean Up Word HTML.

SEE ALSO *Clean Up Word HTML, Importing Table Data*

Internet Explorer

Internet Explorer is the most popular browser currently used on the Internet. By some estimates, it has over 85 percent of the browser market. There are currently four versions of Internet Explorer still being used: IE 3, IE 4, IE 5, and the newly released IE 6.

IE 3 Capabilities and Support

The following table summarizes the support for Dreamweaver's technologies in IE 3:

FEATURE	SUPPORT LEVEL
JavaScript	JavaScript 1
CSS 1	None
CSS 2	None
HTML	HTML 3.2
DOM	None

IE 4 Capabilities and Support

The following table summarizes the support for Dreamweaver's technologies in IE 4:

FEATURE	SUPPORT LEVEL
JavaScript	JavaScript 1.1
CSS 1	Partial
CSS 2	Partial
HTML	HTML 4
DOM	Partial Level 1

IE 5 Capabilities and Support

The following table summarizes the support for Dreamweaver's technologies in IE 5:

FEATURE	SUPPORT LEVEL
JavaScript	JavaScript 1.3 and JavaScript 1.5 (IE 5.5)
CSS 1	Partial
CSS 2	Partial
HTML	HTML 4 and XHTML
DOM	Partial Level 1

IE 6 Capabilities and Support

The following table summarizes the support for Dreamweaver's technologies in IE 6:

FEATURE	SUPPORT LEVEL
JavaScript	JavaScript 1.5
CSS 1	Full
CSS 2	Partial
HTML	HTML 4 and XHTML
DOM	Full Level 1, Partial Level 2

SEE ALSO *Netscape Navigator*

Java

Java was developed by programmers at Sun Microsystems as a way of controlling interactive televisions and VCRs and grew into a full-fledged programming language.

Java borrowed a lot of its syntax and structure from the C++ language. Unlike C++, Java is not compiled; it is interpreted. In other words, Java programs aren't converted to executable programs prior to its being run on your computer. There is one problem with interpreted programs, though, and that is they tend to run somewhat less efficiently than compiled programs. Although Java is touted as being able to run on any operating system, with no changes to the code, this happens only if your entire application uses only Java. Any introduction of other languages will most likely limit the use of your application to one operating system. One reason that many developers use external languages in addition to Java is that Java lacks some core features, such as its own ability to print. In order to get around obvious deficiencies such as this, many developers create their own core Java programs and then create a series of modules that can access the missing features for each operating system.

NOTE *Java is not related to JavaScript in any fashion, although there are some similarities in the syntax.*

SEE ALSO *JavaScript, JScript*

JavaScript

JavaScript, originally called LiveScript, was developed by the Netscape Communications Corporation as a means of adding some scripting ability to Web pages. JavaScript, related to Microsoft's JScript, can be used to send information to Java applets, alter the contents of documents, load information proactively, and even identify the Web browser that is viewing the document.

JavaScript is an interpreted scripting language. It was designed to be simple enough for anyone with some interest and time to learn. JavaScript's syntax is very similar to C, so anyone already familiar with that language can start using JavaScript quite quickly.

In the mid-1990s, Netscape began working with the European Computer Manufacturers Association (ECMA) to develop a standard scripting language for use in Web documents. The completed language is ECMA-262, or commonly called ECMAScript. ECMAScript is now the language referred to as JavaScript in the Netscape Navigator 6 browser.

SEE ALSO *Behaviors, ECMAScript, Java, JScript, Scripting*

JPG

JPG images contain up to 16 million images, no transparencies, and no animations, but they are one of the three types of images allowed on the Internet. JPG images display highly compressed, high-quality photographs.

SEE ALSO *GIF, Images, PNG*

JScript

JScript is Microsoft's version of JavaScript and ECMAScript. Microsoft's implementation of JScript 5.5 is a full implementation of the ECMAScript 3.0 specification, with some additional enhancements that work only with Internet Explorer.

JScript, in addition to providing basic scripting and automation services for Web pages, works with Microsoft ActiveX controls and Java applets.

SEE ALSO *Behaviors, ECMAScript, Java, JavaScript, Scripting*

Jump Menu Behaviors see Behaviors

Jump Menu Go see Behaviors

Jump Menus

Jump menus are form elements that allow you to create an interactive menu system. The options shown on the Jump menu provide a link directly to the page represented by the option list. For instance, if you were to select an item called Macromedia Dreamweaver, you would expect to be taken to the Macromedia Dreamweaver site, not the Microsoft FrontPage site.

To insert a Jump menu into your document, select Insert→Forms Objects→Jump Menu. This opens the Insert Jump Menu dialog box shown in Figure J-1.

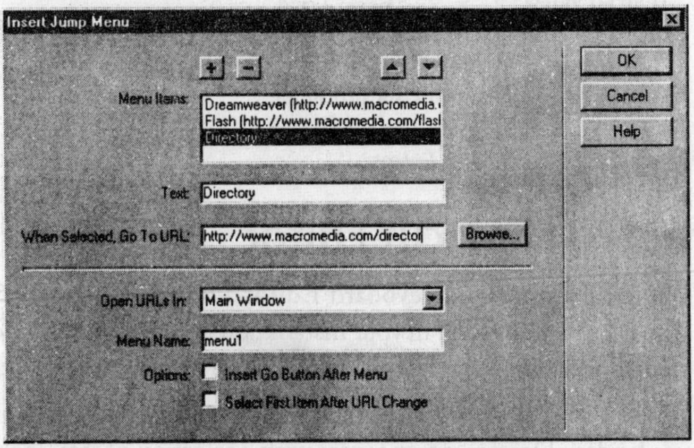

Figure J-1 The Insert Jump Menu dialog box.

NOTE *You can have as many Jump menus in your document as you wish.*

The options available on this screen include the following:

- Text - Provides the name appearing in the menu as the selection item.
- When Selected, Go To URL – Automatically opens a page (the visitor does not have to press the Go button).
- Open Urls In - Identifies the frame or window into which the linked documents will load.

- Options, Insert Go Button After Menu - Places a Go button after the menu that must be pressed before the link will be traveled.
- Options, Select First Item After URL Change - Automatically selects the first item in a page after the page URL has changed.

Once you have completed these options for your first item, click on the plus (+) sign to add your second menu item. Use the minus (-) button to remove a selected menu item. The Up and Down arrows can be used to control the order of the items in the menu. Once your menu is complete, click OK. Your completed Jump menu will appear similar to what is shown in Figure J-2.

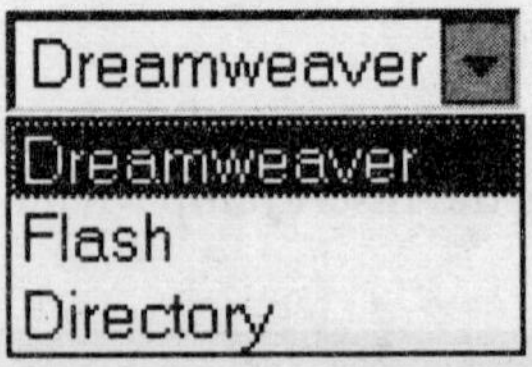

Figure J-2 A drop-down Jump menu listing links to other Macromedia products.

SEE ALSO *Behaviors, Forms*

Keyboard Shortcut Editor

The Dreamweaver Keyboard Editor allows you to modify the keyboard shortcuts used in your installation of Dreamweaver. To open the Keyboard Shortcut Editor, select Edit→Keyboard Shortcuts. .

On this editor you will find the current set of keyboard shortcuts that is loaded. Dreamweaver comes with a selection of sets, including that used with Dreamweaver 3 and the new Macromedia set used in Dreamweaver 4. Don't try to modify the existing keyboard shortcut files. If you need to create new shortcuts, create a duplicate copy of one of the existing sets and modify the copy.

To export a copy of the shortcut keys that you are currently using, select the Export Set As HTML button. This will give you an HTML version of all of your keyboard shortcuts.

NOTE *In the Press Key field, don't try to type in the command to use; press the key combination.*

SEE ALSO *Keyboard Shortcuts*

Keyboard Shortcuts

Keyboard shortcuts provide a way to control the features of Dreamweaver using your keyboard. This is the easiest way to work for some people, while others prefer using the mouse and finding the proper menu options and icons. To view all of the keyboard shortcuts used in your installation of Dreamweaver, select Edit→Keyboard Shortcuts and click the Export Set As HTML button. This will make a copy of your keyboard shortcuts in an HTML file that you can place anywhere on your computer. View this file with your Web browser, and print it to have an easily accessible reference for all keyboard shortcuts.

SEE ALSO *Keyboard Editor*

Launcher Bar

Dreamweaver uses a moveable panel, called the Launcher, to contain links to the other primary panels. These links, as shown in Figure L-1, include Site Window, Assets panel, HTML Styles, CSS Styles, Behaviors panel, Show History, and Code inspector. The Launcher can be opened by selecting Window→Launcher.

Figure L-1 The Dreamweaver Launcher.

To open one of the other panels available from the Launcher, click on that icon.

In addition to the Launcher, a Mini-Launcher is permanently available at the bottom of the document window. This Mini-Launcher, shown in Figure L-2, provides access to the same panels of information available by the Launcher.

Figure L-2 The Mini-Launcher.

You can control the icons visible on both the Launcher and the Mini-Launcher by adjusting the settings in the Launcher Dreamweaver

Preferences dialog box, which is accessible by selecting Edit→Preferences and selecting the Panels category.

SEE ALSO *Pane, Panels*

Layers

Layers provide absolutely positioned elements on your Web pages. Because layers are viewable only by 4.0 versions of browsers, you should use layers only when you know that your visitors will be using somewhat current versions of Internet Explorer, Opera, and Netscape, which actually make up 95% of the Web browsing population. Layers can be used to create complex effects, as shown in Figure L-3, without using multitudes of graphics or tables of figures.

Figure L-3 A complete site created without the use of graphics, just layers and CSS styles.

Creating Layers

To create a layer, select the Layer tool on the Objects panel, or select the Insert→Layer command. If you use the Layer tool, you will need to draw the layer onto your document in the position and size that you wish it to appear. If you use the Insert→Layer menu option, then the layer will be added in conformance to the layer settings in the Layers Preferences dialog box, as shown in Figure L-4.

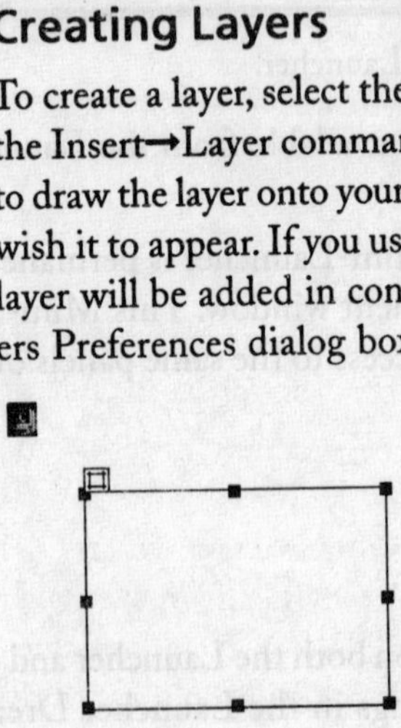

Figure L-4 A simple layer as shown in Dreamweaver.

Positioning Layers

Once you have added a layer to your document, you will need to adjust its positioning either by using the Layers Property inspector or by dragging it about your document.

The most precise method for adjusting the location of your layer is using the Properties inspector. The Left (L), Top (T), Width (W), and Height (H) settings on the Properties inspector, shown in Figure L-5, control the position and size of the layer. Each of these properties is controlled in a measurement of pixels, as you can see by the px unit of measurement notation to the right of the dimension. The Left (L) and Top (T) settings control the location of the top left corner of the layer in relationship to the top left corner of your document.

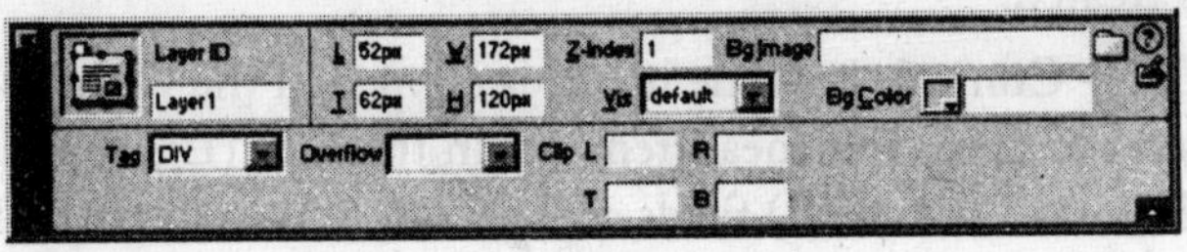

Figure L-5 Layers properties.

If exact precision is not required, you can use your mouse to click on the layer handle and drag the layer to a new position. You can resize a layer by clicking on the smaller size handles located around the edges of the layer. If you need to resize your layer with more precision, then use the Width (W) and Height (H) fields on the Properties inspector.

NOTE *If you are creating a fixed position layer, you then the Left and Top settings control the location of the layer in relation to the browser window.*

Formatting Layers

To format a layer, you can use the remaining options show in the Properties inspector in Figure L-5. These properties include the following:

- Z-Index - Controls the vertical stacking order of your layer. Because layers can be stacked on top of each other, as shown in Figure L-3, you must specify the order of your layers. Z-index values of 0 are level with the main HTML document, with values of 1 appearing over the HTML document. Z-index values of 2 appear over those with a 1, and so on. There is no limit to the number of layers you can create, although it is often best to keep under 10 levels of layers.

- Vis (Visibility) - Controls the default visibility of the layer. If set to Hidden, when the layer loads you won't be able to see it; it will be invisible.
- Bg Image - Controls the background image that appears in the layer. Just like your main document, you can type over this image.
- Bg Color - Controls the background color of the layer. This is the setting that was set to create the color blocks in Figure L-3.
- Tag - Specifies the HTML tag (DIV, SPAN, LAYER, ILAYER) to use to create the layer. For broadest compatibility between Web browsers, select DIV.
- OverFlow - Controls how information that is too large for the layer is treated.
- Clip - Controls how the image is clipped, if the Overflow setting is set to Clip. The measurements in the Left (L), Top (T), Right (R), and Bottom (B) fields are measured from the top left corner of the layer.

Layer Preferences

You can configure the preferences for layers by setting them in the Layers Preferences dialog box accessible from the Edit→Preferences command.

Converting Layers to Tables

To convert a series of layers to a table, select the Modify→Convert→Layers To Table command. This will convert the existing layers on your document to a table layout, with only the cells of the table filled where the layer content was located. The Convert Layers To Tables dialog box, shown in Figure L-6, allows you to set the options controlling the conversion. These options include the ability to use transparent GIF images, center the contents of the table on your page, and control the appearance of Dreamweaver's layout tools.

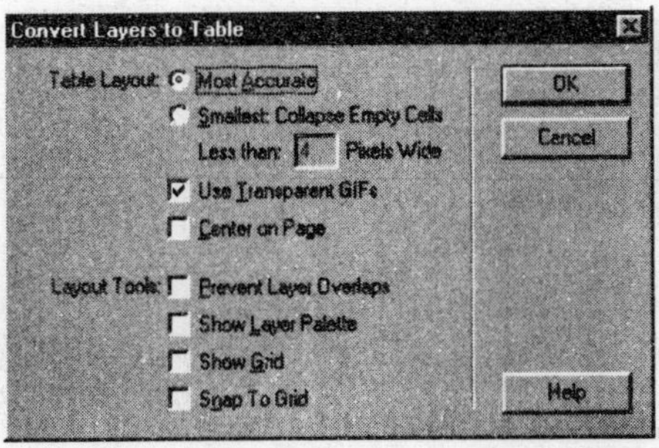

Figure L-6 The Convert Layers To Tables dialog box.

Figure L-7 shows our previous layer image converted to a table.

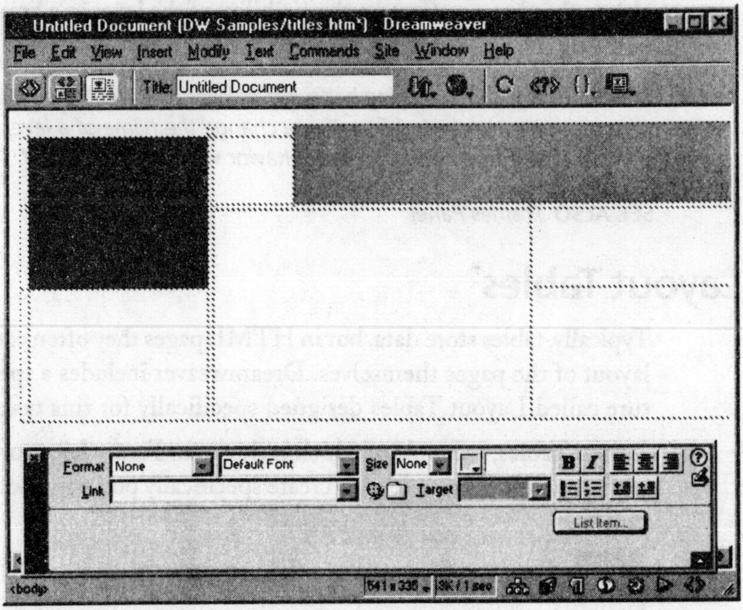

Figure L-7 Layers converted to a table layout

NOTE *This command does not function in Table Layout view.*

SEE ALSO *Frames, Layout Tables, Preferences, Tables*

Layers Panel

The Layers panel, shown in Figure L-8, provides access to the formatting options for each layer created on your page. You can open the Layers panel by selecting Window→ Layers or by pressing F2.

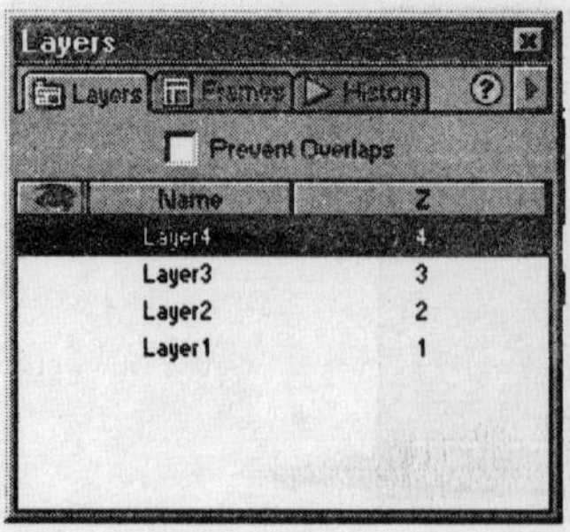

Figure L-8 The Layers panel.

On this panel, you can control the visibility of a layer in Dreamweaver, although it has no effect on the visibility of the layer in a browser, the name of the layer, and the Z-index value of the layer.

NOTE *If you are applying behaviors to layers, be sure to have your layer's name selected first. If you change the name of a layer after applying a behavior, the behavior will not be updated.*

SEE ALSO *Frames Panel*

Layout Tables

Typically, tables store data, but in HTML pages they often control the layout of the pages themselves. Dreamweaver includes a special feature called Layout Tables designed specifically for this task.

Layout Tables, a sample of which is shown in Figure L9, provides you with the controls you need to create specifically positioned document objects.

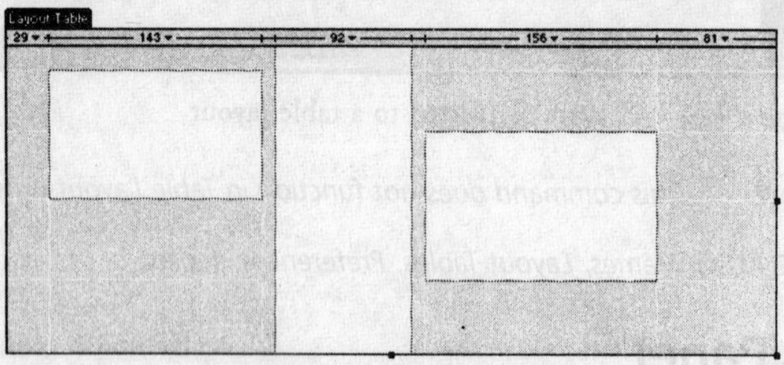

Figure L-9 The Layout Table feature controls the tight control of information placement within tables.

Inserting a Layout Table and Cells

To insert a layout table into your document, complete the following steps:

1. Click the Layout View icon on the Objects panel, as shown in Figure L-10. When clicked, a warning lets you know what can be expected when using the Layout View and tells you the order in which you must complete the tasks.

Figure L-10 Layout View controls on the Objects panel.

2. Once you have read this information, you can safely click the Don't Show Me This Message Again option at the bottom of the screen the next time it appears.
3. Click OK to continue.
4. If you do not already have a table on your screen, click the Draw Layout Table icon on the Objects panel and use your mouse to draw the outside borders of your table.
5. Click on the Draw Layout Cell icon on the Objects panel. If you want to draw multiple cells, then hold the Ctrl key while clicking the Draw Layout Cell icon.
6. Use your mouse to draw the new cell within your layout table.
7. Repeat steps 5 and 6 until you have drawn on all the primary cells in your table that will have contents. As you can see, the remaining areas of the table are also turned into cells, but they are created based upon the positions of the primary areas you have drawn.

NOTE *You can draw a layout table inside of another layout table to create an embedded table if you wish. You must draw the nested table in an area without a layout cell identified. If at all possible, you should format your primary layout table to incorporate the columns of information included in the sub-table.*

Formatting Layout Tables

You can control most of the formatting of a layout table through the use of the Layout Table and Layout Cells Properties inspectors shown in Figure L-11 and L-12.

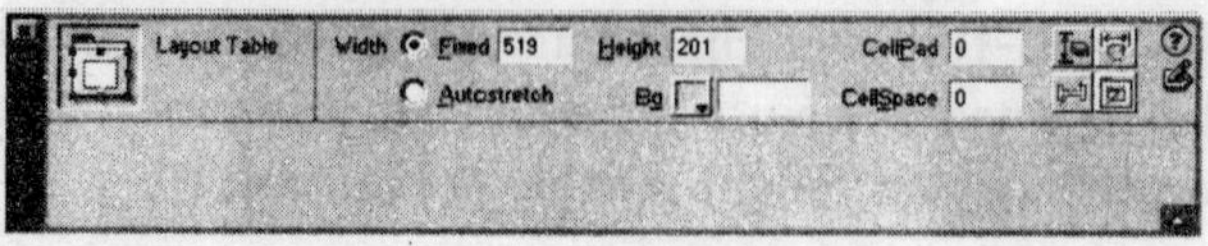

Figure L-11 The Layout Table Properties inspector.

The following list identifies all of the properties available for use with a layout table. You can select the table by clicking on one of its outside borders.

- Width: Fixed - Specifies a fixed width for the entire table.
- Width: Autostretch - Specifies a table with a single autostretched column, which can be stretched to contain all of the free space in the table. This area will vary depending upon the screen resolution settings of the page visitor. You can have only one Autostretch column in each table.
- Height - Specifies the height of the table in pixels.
- Bg - Specifies the background color of the table.
- CellPad - Controls the cell padding, or the space between the individual cells of a table. If your table contains images that have been cut from a single larger mural image, then this setting should be zero.
- CellSpace - Controls the cell spacing, or the space between the cell border and the cell contents.

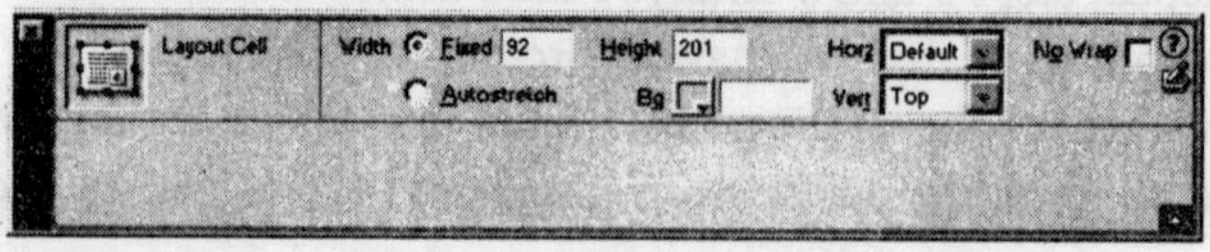

Figure L-12 The Layout Cell Properties inspector.

The following list identifies all of the properties available for use with layout cells. You can select a cell by clicking on one of the cell borders.

- Width: Fixed - Specifies a fixed width for the cell.

- Width: Autostretch - Sets the cell, and therefore its column, to Autostretch. In other words, this column will increase or decrease in size depending upon the size of the viewer's window.
- Height - Specifies the height of the cell in pixels.
- Bg - Specifies the background color of the cell.
- Horiz - Specifies the horizontal alignment of the cell contents.
- Vert - Specifies the vertical alignment of the cell contents.
- No Wrap - When checked, prohibits a cell's text content from wrapping.

Making a Column Autostretch

An Autostretch column will stretch and shrink based upon the width of the viewable area of a visitor's Web browser window. To create a stretchable column, either click your left mouse button on the width measurement for the column and select Make Column Autostretch from the contextual menu, shown in Figure L-13, or click the Autostretch check box in the Layout Table Cell Properties inspector.

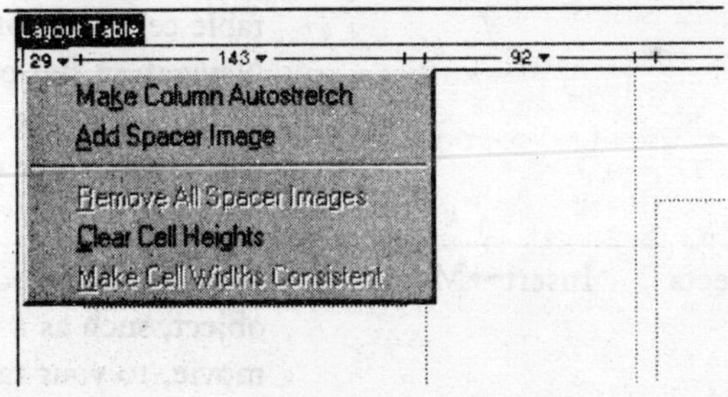

Figure L-13 The Layout Table contextual menu options.

Filling Layout Tables

You can add contents to your layout tables much as you can to a standard table. To add content, follow these steps:

1. Click inside a layout cell.
2. Your Properties inspector will give you a series of properties that will change depending upon the type of content that you add to your document.

The following table shows many of the options that you have for filling in your layout cells with content.

CONTENT	MENU OPTIONS	USE
Text	n/a	Just type in your text.
Formatted Text	Text menu options	Use all of these options to format your text, including font face, size, color, alignment, and style.
Images	Insert→Image	Adds any GIF, JPG, and PNG image to your table.
Forms	Insert→Form	Adds a form to your table.
Form Controls	Insert→ Form Objects	Adds individual Form objects to your table cells.
Interactive Images	Insert→ Interactive Images	Adds the selected interactive media to your table cell. Do not use Navigation Bar objects in Layout tables. They will create their own tables or layers.
Media Objects	Insert→Media	Adds the selected media object, such as a Flash movie, to your table cell.

Converting Tables to Layers

To convert a table, or series of tables, to a series of layers, select the Modify→Convert→Tables To Layers command. This will convert the existing tables in your document into series of layers. The Convert Tables To Layers dialog box, shown in Figure L-14, allows you to set the options controlling the conversion. These options control the appearance of Dreamweaver's layout tools after the conversion process is complete.

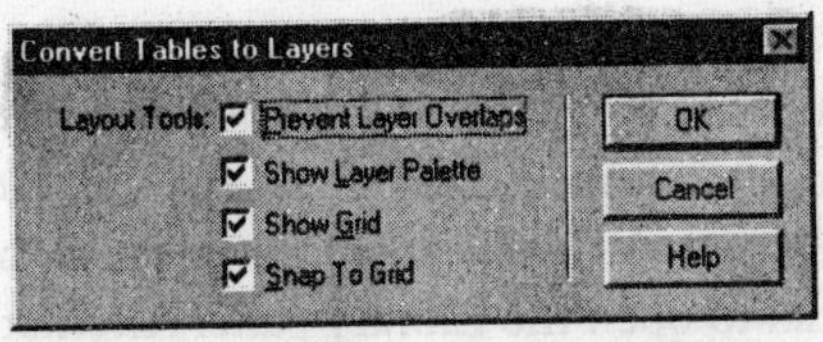

Figure L-14 The Convert Tables To Layers dialog box.

Figure L-15 shows our previous table converted to a series of layers. Only the areas of the document that contained tables cells with content were converted to layers with contents. All the rest of the table cells were ignored.

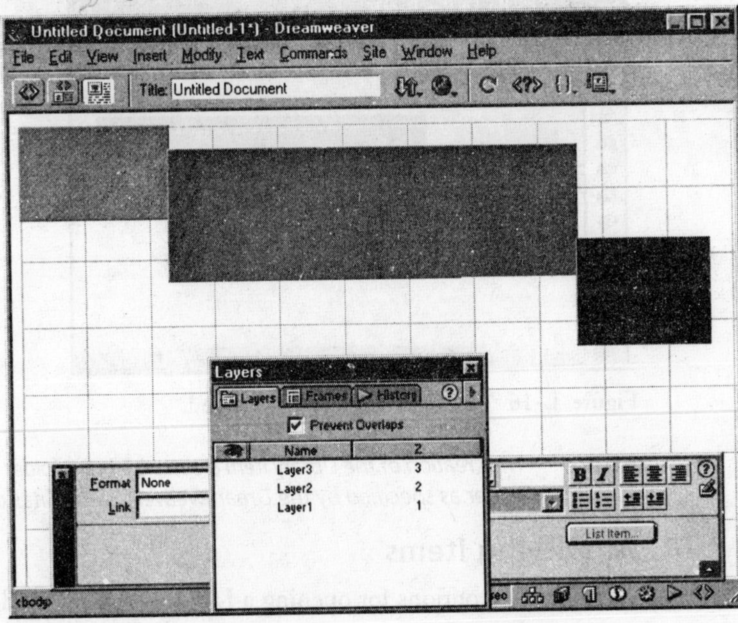

Figure L-15 Tables converted to a layers-based layout

NOTE *This command does not function in the Table Layout view.*

Library Items

Library items provide you with reusable sections of your document. For instance, a copyright statement should be applied to all of your documents in your site, but it might not always fit in the same spot on a document template. In this case, a Library item can be used, saving you the headache of updating each instance of that repeated text throughout your site.

Creating Items

You can create a Library item by selecting the portion of your document that you wish to be included in the item and then dragging it over the Library pane. Select Window→Library or select the Library tab on the Assets panel to open the Library pane. Alternatively, you can select Modify→Library→Add Object To Library. In Figure L-16 you can see the process of creating a Library item. Once you have dragged the item over to the Library pane, you must provide it with a name in the Name column. In the Full Path column, you can see the filename for this item.

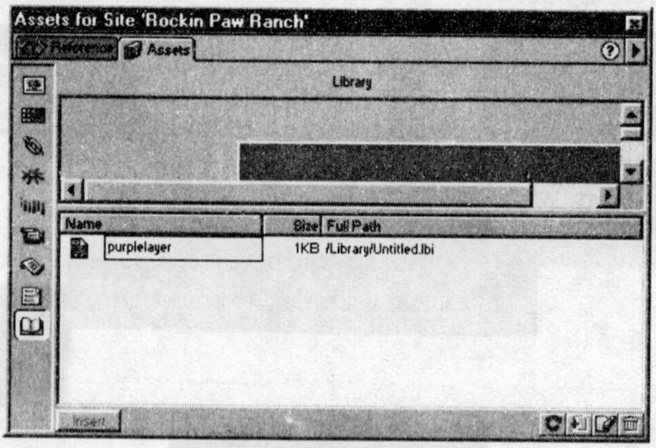

Figure L-16 A Library item being created.

NOTE *The creation of the Library item creates a Library folder in your site folder as specified by the Dreamweaver Define Sites dialog box.*

Modifying Items

You have two options for opening a Library item for modification:

- Double-click on the item in the Library pane.
- Select the Library item from the Library pane, and click the Edit button.

All Library items are stored as .lbi files. These files are HTML documents that store only the contents of that one Library item. You can modify the contents of these documents as you would any other HTML file. After modifying a Library item and saving it, all the documents in your site that use that item will also be updated. You can also update all the pages in your site by selecting Modify→Library→Updated Pages.

Adding Items to Documents

To apply a Library item to your document, drag the item from the pane to the document. You can't modify the Library item once it is added to the document. It must be modified prior to being added.

NOTE *If the Library item contains a layer, the location of the layer is static and you won't be able to change it.*

Removing Items from Documents

To remove a Library item from your document, you must open the Code view of your HTML document by using View→Code View. Once in Code view, you must select all the Library items, including the <!— Begin LibraryItem —> and the <!— End LibraryItem —> comment markers. This will completely remove the Library item from your document.

Deleting an Item

To remove a Library item from the Library pane, select the item and click the Delete Item icon (trashcan) on the pane. This will remove the Library item but not the content from documents to which it has been previously applied.

SEE ALSO *Assets Panel, Templates*

Library Pane

The Dreamweaver Library pane is part of the Assets panel, shown in Figure L-17, provides a list of all the Library items used within the current Web site, not just the current document. You can open the Library pane of the Assets panel by selecting Window→Library.

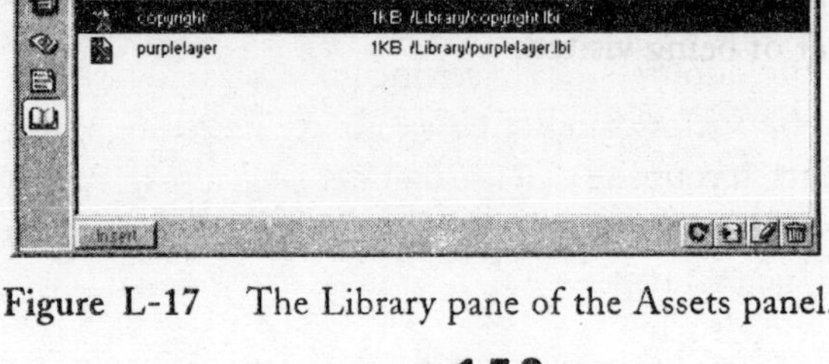

Figure L-17 The Library pane of the Assets panel.

Line Breaks

There are two types of line breaks in your document: a line break and a paragraph break.

Line Break

The line break code inserts an actual line break into your Web page. A line break doesn't insert additional white space around your text. It is a way to make text appear directly against each other, without adding extra space for between paragraphs.

To insert a line break into your document, place your cursor at its intended location and select either Insert→Special Characters→Line Break and press Shift+Enter (Return on the Macintosh) or click the Insert Line Break button in the Characters category of the Objects panel.

Paragraph Break

The paragraph break marks the end of your paragraph. A paragraph break doesn't insert additional white space around your text. Instead, two HTML elements are inserted around your text: <p> and </p> to mark the beginning and ending of a paragraph.

To insert a paragraph break into your document, place your cursor at its intended location and press Enter (Return on the Macintosh) or highlight the text and select the Text→Paragraph Format→Paragraph command.

SEE ALSO *Characters, Paragraphs*

Link Color

You can control the appearance of links in your documents by adjusting the Link and Text Color properties in your Page Properties dialog box, which is opened by selecting Modify→Page Properties. These three options, shown in Figure L-18, control the appearance of link text when it has been visited, when it has not been visited, and when it is in the act of being visited.

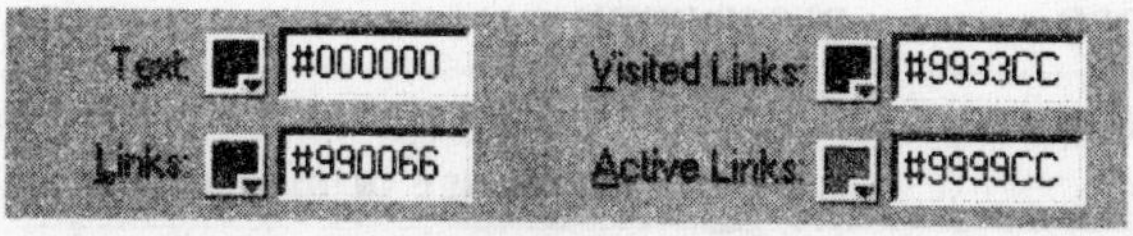

Figure L-18 Page options controlling the appearance of text links on your page.

However, you should control the colors of your link text using Cascading Style sheets rather than using the options available in the Page Properties dialog box.

SEE ALSO *Cascading Style Sheets, Color, Page Properties*

Link Element

The link element allows you to control the relationship between documents in your site. One of the most common uses for the link element is to add an external style sheet to your document.

To identify a link between the current document and its external style sheet, or another document, select the Insert→Head Tags→Link command to open the Link dialog box shown in Figure L-19.

Figure L-19 The Insert Link dialog box specifies a relationship between the two documents.

This dialog box allows you to specify the ID and URL of the document, the relationship of the document (stylesheet in this case), and a title for the related document.

```
<link href="rockinpaw.css" id="rpcss"
    rel="stylesheet" type="text/css"
    title="Rocking Paw Style Sheets">
```

The Rel and Rev attributes identify a document serving as one of the relationships listed in the following table:

KEYWORD	DESCRIPTION
Alternate	A substitute document, such as a document in a different language or media type.
Appendix	Appendix for a document collection.
Bookmark	Identifies a link to a key point in a document.
Chapter	A document chapter.
Contents	Table of contents.
Copyright	The copyright statement for the current document.
Glossary	Glossary of terms.
Help	Help documentation.
Index	Document index.
Next	Next document in a series.
Prev	Previous document in a series.
Section	Section within a chapter.
Start	The first document in a series.
Stylesheet	An external style sheet.
Subsection	A single portion of a document within a document section.

To modify an existing <link>, click on the Link icon on the Head Content bar. Selecting Insert→Head Tags→Link inserts a new, separate link element in your document. You can have as many link elements in your document as you wish.

Links

Links, also called hypertext, provide a document reader with the ability to quickly jump from one document to another at a click of the mouse. You can insert links into your HTML documents by adding the URL of a document to the Link field on the Properties inspector of each item you wish to serve as a jumping point to another document.

SEE ALSO *Absolute Links, Email Links, FTP Links, Named Anchors, Relative Links*

Macintosh see Apple Macintosh

Media Objects

Dreamweaver works with a variety of media types, many of which are created by Macromedia. Using Dreamweaver, you can automatically insert Flash buttons, Flash text, Flash movies, Generator files, ActiveX controls, applets, Server Side Includes, and even Shockwave programs.

SEE ALSO *ActiveX, Fireworks, Flash, Generator, Shockwave/Director*

Metadata

Metadata is information about information. It is information that provides supplemental support for your document, such as identifying the document author or the last time the document was edited. Dreamweaver can create four types of <meta> tags:-general meta tags, keywords, description, and refresh tags-without hand-coding. If you wish to create meta tags that can't be created using the Insert→Head Tags→Meta general meta tag creator, you can use Code view (View →Code View).

All <meta> elements follow this general format:

```
<head>

   <meta name="label" content="appropriate content">

   <meta http-equiv="instruction-name"
content="instructions">

</head>
```

As you can see, some meta tags use a name attribute, while others use the http-equiv attribute. These attributes aren't interchangeable. The http-equiv attribute identifies document languages and provides instructions for displaying documents using HTTP message headers. The name attribute provides information including keywords and document descriptions.

Each of the name and http-equiv attributes is also associated with a content attribute. The content attribute contains the content of the other meta tag. For instance, if the meta tag had a name="keywords" attribute, then the content attribute of that tag would contain keywords.

If the meta tag had a http-equiv="refresh" attribute, then the content attribute would contain the instructions for refreshing the document.

Keywords

Keywords for your document can be added using Insert→Head Tags→Keywords, which opens the Insert Keywords dialog box shown in Figure M-1. In the dialog box, type in your list of comma-separated keywords or phrases. Click OK when you are done.

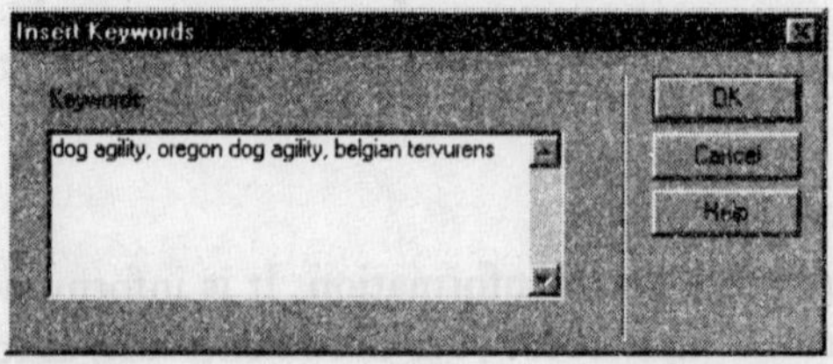

Figure M-1 The Insert Keywords dialog box.

To edit your keywords, select the Keyword icon from the Head Content bar (View→Head Content) and modify the settings in the Properties inspector. Selecting Insert→Head Tags→Keywords a second time will simply add an additional set of keywords to your document, which will confuse search engines.

Description

A description of your document can be added using Insert→Head Tags→Description, which opens the Insert Description dialog box shown in Figure M-2. In the dialog box, type in a short (25 words or so) description of your Web page. Click OK when you are done.

Figure M-2 The Insert Description dialog box.

To edit your description, select the Description icon from the Head Content bar (View→ Head Content) and modify the settings in the Properties inspector. Selecting Insert→Head Tags→Description a second time will simply add an additional description to your document, which will confuse search engines.

Refresh

You can automatically refresh your current document, or automatically load a new document using Insert→Head Tags→Refresh, which opens the Insert Refresh dialog box shown in Figure M-3. In the dialog box, specify the Delay, in seconds, that will occur before the document is refreshed. You then need to decide whether to select Refresh This Document or Go To URL. If you check Refresh This Document, the current document is reloaded at the specified time. If you check Go To URL, the other document is loaded after the specified delay.

Figure M-3 The Insert Refresh dialog box.

To edit your refresh meta tag, select the Refresh icon from the Head Content bar (View → Head Content) and modify the settings in the Properties inspector. Selecting Insert → Head Tags → Refresh a second time will simply add an additional refresh statement to your document which will create errors in the document browser.

Meta

Additional meta elements can be added using Insert→Head Tags→Meta, which opens the Insert Meta dialog box shown in Figure M-4. In the dialog box, select the Attribute type (either name or http-equiv), specify the attribute's Value (such as content-type), and specify the attribute's Content (such as "text/html; charset=iso-8859-1"). Each <meta> tag can also be edited in the Properties inspector (accessed by clicking the corresponding icon in the Head Content bar, opened by selecting View→Head Content).

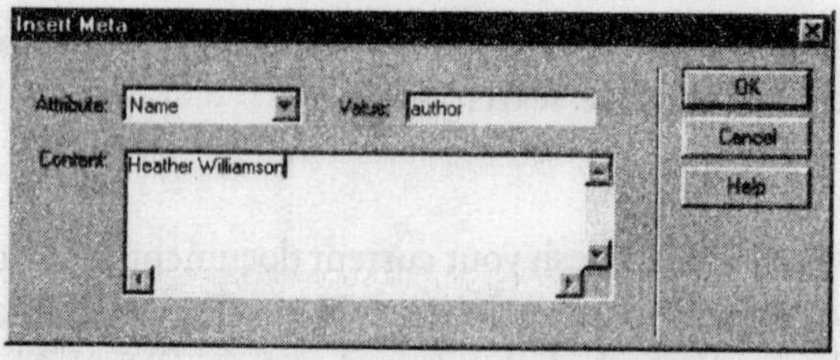

Figure M-4 The Insert Meta dialog box.

Viewing Meta Content

To view the meta content that you have added to your document select View→Head Content. This opens the Head Content display below your icon bar at the top of your Dreamweaver window, as shown in Figure M-5.

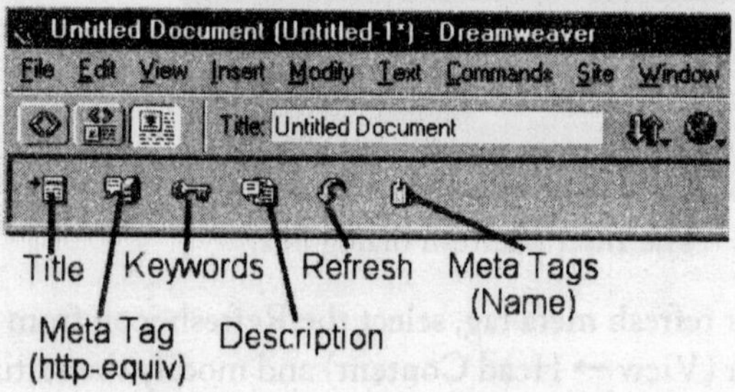

Figure M-5 The Head Content bar in your document.

Named Anchors

Named anchors are links that don't link to any other documents, but serve as a marker, like a bookmark, for the current document. You can insert a named anchor into your document by selecting Insert→Named Anchor. This opens the Insert Named Anchor dialog shown in Figure N-1.

Figure N-1 The Insert Named Anchor dialog box.

Type in the name of the anchor in the Name field, and then click OK. To reference a named anchor in your document, type in the name of the anchor, preceded by a pound sign, as shown in the text Link field in Figure N-2.

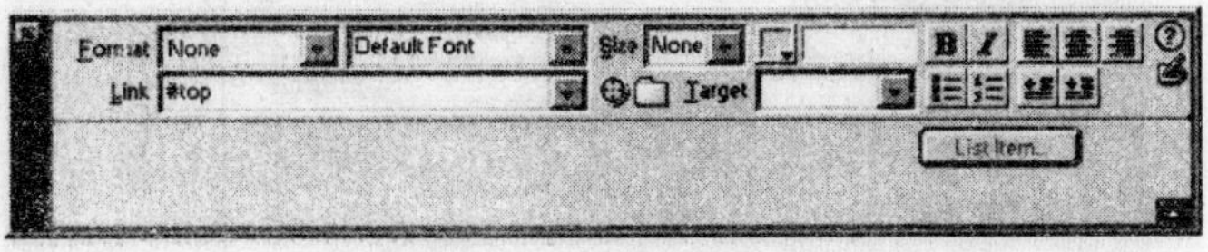

Figure N-2 The Link properties for referencing a named anchor from a text link.

SEE ALSO *Absolute Links, Email Links, FTP Links, Hypertext, Links, Relative Links*

Navigation Bars

Navigation bars provide a collection of interactive images whose sole purpose is to help visitors to your Web pages navigate your site. You can create a Navigation bar from your own images by selecting Insert→Interactive Images→Navigation Bar. Inserting a Navigation bar allows you to add multiple mouse-event states to a single image so that you can create a navigation system where visitors will always know where they are on your site.

In the Insert Navigation Bar dialog box, shown in Figure N-3, use the plus (+) and minus (-) buttons to add or remove elements from the Nav Bar Elements list. You can reorder the elements using the arrow buttons at the top of this screen.

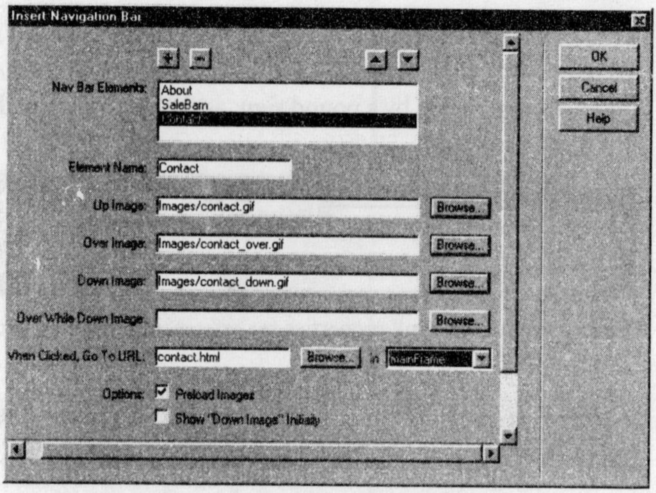

Figure N-3 The Insert Navigation Bar dialog box.

For each Navigation bar image, provide the following information:

- Element Name - Names the image button referenced by the image swapping script.
- Up Image (optional) - Contains the URL of the image displayed by default.
- Over Image (optional) - Contains the URL of the image displayed when mouse is over the image button.
- Down Image (optional) - Contains the URL of the image displayed when the image button is clicked.
- Over While Down Image (optional) - Contains the URL of the image displayed when the mouse button was pressed before the mouse was rolled over the image.
- When Clicked, Go To URL ... In - Contains the URL of the document opened when the image button is clicked.
- Options: Preload Images - Loads the images associated with the button when the page loads.
- Options: Show "Down Image" Initially - Uses the down image as the initial image for the button.

The following options apply to the Navigation bar as a whole:

- Insert - Specifies how the buttons in the Nav Bar Elements list are arranged: horizontally or vertically.
- Use Tables - Uses tables to position your buttons rather than layers, which are preferred for 4.0 and newer browser support.

Once you have completed your Navigation bar, it will appear with the same functionality as shown in Figure N-4, which shows the sample Web site.

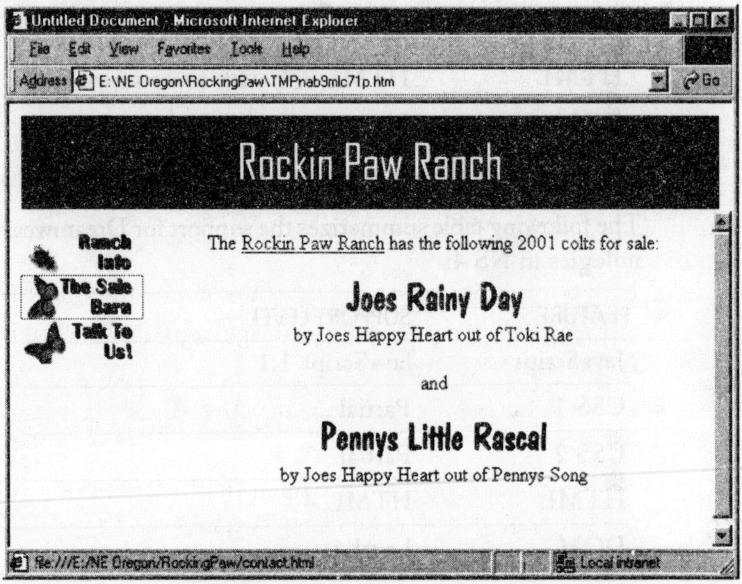

Figure N-4 The Rockin Paw Ranch Web site Navigation bar.

To modify a Navigation bar previously created, select either Modify→Navigation Bar, or Insert→Interactive Images→Navigation Bar and click OK when asked if you wish to modify the existing Navigation bar.

SEE ALSO *Behaviors, Rollover Images*

Netscape Navigator

Netscape Navigator used to be the most popular browser used on the Internet, but it has slipped in the last few years. Netscape browsers currently have approximately 30% of the browser market. There are currently three versions of Netscape Navigator still being used: NS 3, NS 4, and NS 6.

NS 3 Capabilities and Support

The following table summarizes the support for Dreamweaver's technologies in NS 3:

FEATURE	SUPPORT LEVEL
JavaScript	JavaScript 1
CSS 1	Partial
CSS 2	None
HTML	HTML 3.2, with some support for HTML 4
DOM	Partial Level 1

NS 4 Capabilities and Support

The following table summarizes the support for Dreamweaver's technologies in NS 4:

FEATURE	SUPPORT LEVEL
JavaScript	JavaScript 1.1
CSS 1	Partial
CSS 2	Partial
HTML	HTML 4
DOM	Level 1

NS 6 Capabilities and Support

The following table summarizes the support for Dreamweaver's technologies in NS 6:

FEATURE	SUPPORT LEVEL
JavaScript	JavaScript 1.5
CSS 1	Full
CSS 2	Partial
HTML	HTML 4 and XHTML
DOM	Full Level 1, Partial Level 2

SEE ALSO *Internet Explorer*

New Document

To open a new document in Dreamweaver, use one of the following methods:

- From the document window, select File→New.
- From the Site window, select File→New.

SEE ALSO *New from Template, Opening a Document, Opening Dreamweaver*

New from Template

To open a new document based on a Dreamweaver template, use one of the following methods:

- From the document window, select File→New From Template.
- From the Site window, select File→New From Template.

This opens the Select Template dialog box, shown in Figure N-5, which allows you to select the template to use. Select your template and click the Select button.

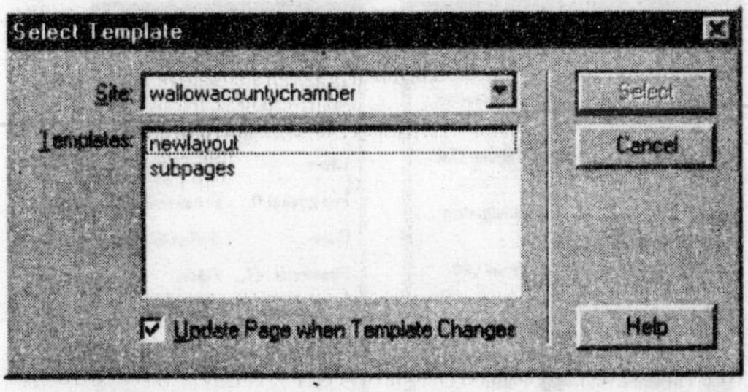

Figure N-5 The Select From Template dialog box.

Your template is automatically loaded so that you can create another document for your Web site.

SEE ALSO *New Document, Opening a Document, Opening Dreamweaver, Templates*

Non-breaking Spaces see Characters

Object

An object in an HTML document is typically any element or piece of text that has been added to the document content. Objects can be composed of images, Flash movies, buttons, frames, tables, or any other media type that can be displayed through a Web site. Objects that aren't part of the basic HTML package, such as images and text, are added using the <object> element.

SEE ALSO *Embed, Media Objects*

Objects Panel

The Objects panel contains icons representing the majority of the objects that can be added to your documents. The Objects panel, shown in all three modes in Figure O-1, can be opened by selecting Window→Objects. You can configure your Object Panel preferences by selecting Edit→Preferences. On the bottom of the General Preferences category is a listing for Object Panel. Select Icons and Text, Icons Only, or Text Only to suit the way you wish to work.

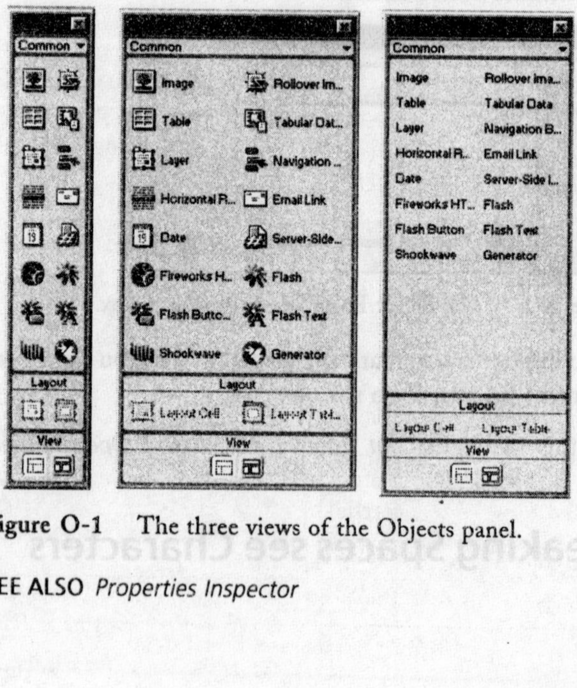

Figure O-1 The three views of the Objects panel.

SEE ALSO *Properties Inspector*

Open Browser Window see Behaviors

Opening a Document

To open a document in Dreamweaver, use one of the following methods:

- From the ocument window, select File→Open and select the file you wish to view.
- From the Site window, doubleclick on the name of the file that you wish to open from the Local Site side of the window.

SEE ALSO *New Document, New from Template, Opening Dreamweaver*

Opening Dreamweaver

To open Dreamweaver, choose the Dreamweaver icon from your Start menu (Windows) or select it from the Finder (Macintosh). Once open, you can open an individual file by selecting the File→Open command.

SEE ALSO *Closing Dreamweaver*

Opera

The Opera Web browser is slowly growing in popularity as it increases its installed base of users on operating systems such as Macintosh, BeOS, and Linux.

Opera 4.x

The following table summarizes the support for Dreamweaver's technologies in Opera 4:

FEATURE	SUPPORT LEVEL
JavaScript	JavaScript 1.2
CSS 1	All
CSS 2	Partial
HTML	HTML 4
DOM	Level 1

Opera 5.*x*

The following table summarizes the support for Dreamweaver's technologies in Opera 5:

FEATURE	SUPPORT LEVEL
JavaScript	JavaScript 1.3 and ECMAScript 2
CSS 1	All
CSS 2	All
HTML	HTML 4.1 and XHTML
DOM	Full Level 1, Partial Level 2

SEE ALSO *Internet Explorer, Netscape Navigator*

Page Properties

Dreamweaver provides a quick and easy interface to use when controlling the appearance of your individual document page. These properties are all accessible from the Modify→Page Properties command, as shown in Figure P-1.

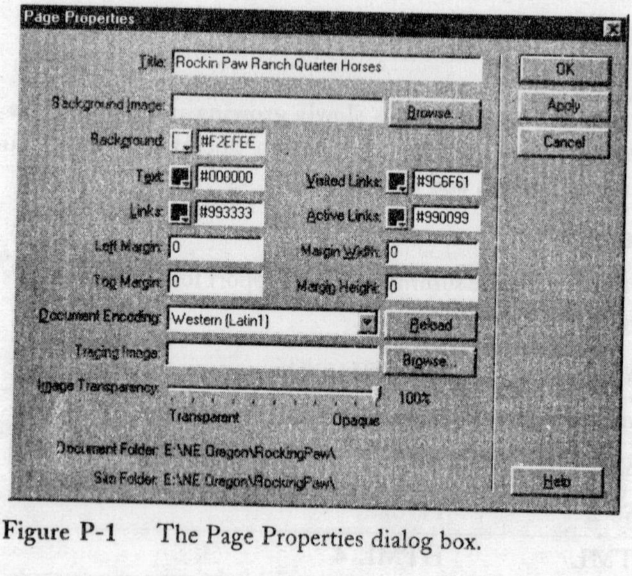

Figure P-1 The Page Properties dialog box.

Title

The field title must be set for each document. This is important because this is just one of the many items that search engines look at when manipulating your placements in their indexes. Your title should be less than 10 words and contain the key phrase that describes this particular page of your site. Each page of your site should have a separate title. This makes indexing the individual pages more efficient within the search engines.

Background Image and Color

The background image and color settings control the appearance of the "paper" on which you are creating your HTML document. You can set an image to be a background, or a solid color, both of which are shown in Figure P-2. The background behind the main text is set with the Bg Color settings, while the footprints behind the menu options are set with the Background Color option.

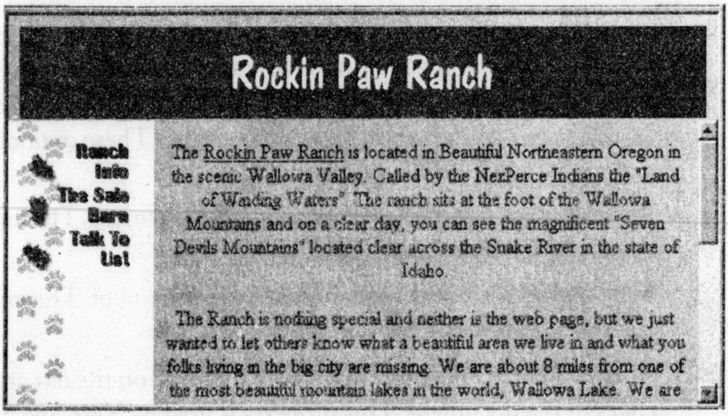

Figure P-2 Options for document backgrounds.

If you choose to set a background image, then use the Browse button to select an image file. When choosing a solid background color, use the color drop-down list to select the color from either the palette or the color chart. You can set both of these properties for browsers that don't show images or for those people who have the background images turned off in their browsers.

NOTE *Use Cascading Style Sheets to set these properties to be XHTML- and HTML 4-compliant and to take advantage of the features offered in the 4.0 and newer Web browsers.*

Text and Link Colors

Dreamweaver allows you to control the appearance of default document text and links. The colors of these items are available by setting the colors for the following fields: Text, Links, Visited Links, and Active Links. The Text color setting controls the appearance of all text on your document. The Links color setting controls the appearance of the links appearing on your document. The Visited Links color setting controls the appearance of your links after a visitor has viewed them, and the Active Links color setting controls the appearance of your links while in the process of selecting it. You can change the colors of your links or text at specific points in the document using Dreamweaver's font properties if you wish.

NOTE *Use Cascading Style Sheets to set these properties to be XHTML- and HTML 4-compliant and to take advantage of the features offered in the 4.0 and newer web browsers.*

Margins

Margins control the space around the outside of your document that is reserved against document content. Four options in the Page Properties dialog box control your document margins. These options, listed below, are all measured in pixels:

- Left Margin - Sets the left margin of the document. This property is used by Internet Explorer.
- Top Margin - Sets the top margin of the document. This property is used by Internet Explorer.
- Margin Width - Sets the width of the margin on the left and right edges of the document. This property is used by Netscape Navigator.
- Margin Height - Sets the height of the margin on the top and bottom edges of the document. This property is used by Netscape Navigator.

Tracing Image and Transparency

A tracing image is an image that can be placed in the background of your document, when viewed with Dreamweaver, so you can set items on specific areas of the image. For instance, if you have a complicated graphic for your background and you want to place layers in exact positions within the layout of that image, the Tracing Image option will let you see both the layer you are adjusting and the document background. This is also a handy tool to use when you are cutting apart an image to use inside of a layout table.

To specify a tracing image, either type in the address of the image or click the Browse button to select it. Then use the Transparency slider bar to control the opacity of the image.

Pane

An individual section of a panel. For instance, the Assets panel contains multiple panes, including the Library pane and the Template pane. Each of these panes shows information that is part of the complete panel of information.

SEE ALSO *Panel*

Panel

A panel is a selection of settings that has a series of controls representing one aspect of the Dreamweaver interface. Dreamweaver has a variety of panels, including those listed in the following table:

PANEL NAME	MENU OPTION
Assets	Windows→Assets
Behaviors	Windows→Behaviors
Code inspector	Windows→Code Inspector
CSS Styles	Windows→CSS Styles
Frames	Windows→Frames
History	Windows→History
HTML Styles	Windows→HTML Styles
Launcher	Windows→Launcher
Layers	Windows→Layers
Library	Windows→Library
Objects	Windows→Objects
Properties inspector	Windows→Properties

PANEL NAME	MENU OPTION
Reference	Windows→Reference
Templates	Windows→Templates
Timelines	Windows→Timelines

These panels are shown in their default installed position in Figure P-3.

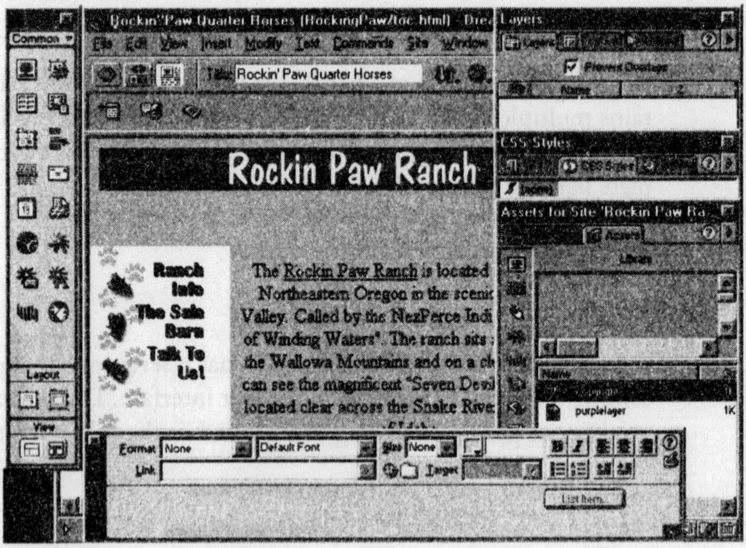

Figure P-3 The default Dreamweaver panels accessible from the document window.

SEE ALSO *Pane*

Paragraphs

The paragraph sections of your document are demarcated by two HTML elements around your text, <p> and </p>, to mark the beginning and ending of a paragraph.

To insert a paragraph break into your document, place your cursor at its intended location and press Enter (Return on the Macintosh) or highlight the text and select the Text→Paragraph Format→Paragraph command.

SEE ALSO *Characters*

Pasting Objects/Selections

To paste an object, such as a picture, into your document that has been cut or copied from another location in the document or another document, place your cursor at the point in your current document where you wish the item to appear. Click the Paste toolbar button or select Edit→Paste.

SEE ALSO *Copying Objects/Selections, Cutting Objects/Selections*

Play Sound see Behaviors

Play Timeline see Behaviors

PNG

Portable Network Graphics (PNG) is a graphics format that was created in the mid-1990s to avoid the licensing difficulties that developed out of the use of GIF images. PNGs can incorporate 16 million colors, like JPEG images, or transparent colors, like GIF images. Overall, PNGs could replace both JPEGs and GIFs, but their compression system isn't as good yet. For now, keep using JPEG images for photographs and GIF images for color graphics of under 256 colors. PNG is the default graphic format used by Macromedia Fireworks.

SEE ALSO *GIF, Images, JPEG*

Popup Message see Behaviors

POST

There are two methods for sending information to a web server using Forms: GET and POST. The POST method sends all of the information collected by the form to the server as part of a document.

SEE ALSO *Forms, GET*

Preferences

Dreamweaver incorporates a wide selection of preferences, accessible by selecting Edit→Preferences, which control the function and appearance of your Dreamweaver software. The Preferences dialog box is shown in Figure P-4.

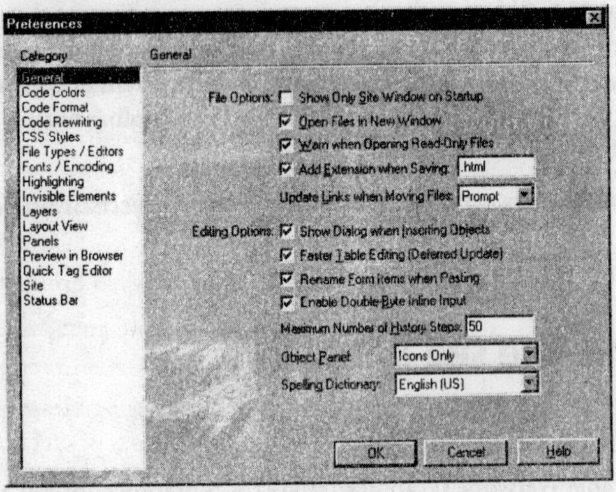

Figure P-4 The General Preferences dialog box.

The Preferences dialog box categories are described in the following list:

- General - Controls the default settings for file extensions, the appearance of the Objects panel, how new documents are opened, and how Dreamweaver works with changes that you make to documents.
- Code Colors - Controls the colors applied to specific terms and functions used within HTML, CSS, and JavaScript documents.
- Code Format - Controls the format of the elements and attributes used to create the HTML documents. These settings also control how the code is indented.
- Code Rewriting - Controls how programming information is dealt with on files that are not HTML, as well as how nested and unclosed HTML tags are treated.
- CSS Styles - Controls the use of shorthand CSS properties within your document. Shorthand properties are not supported by all Web browsers.
- File Types/Editors - Provides a list of external programs that can be used to modify the various types of media files used to create your Web pages.

- Fonts/Encoding - Controls the default text to use when creating documents. By default, these settings will match most installations of Internet Explorer and Netscape Navigator on both Windows and Macintosh platforms. If you change these settings, they will change the appearance of your Web document from within Dreamweaver, but not from within your Web browser.
- Highlighting - Sets the colors of editable and non-editable regions used with document templates and Library items.
- Invisible Elements - Allows you to decide which invisible elements will be visible to you in Dreamweaver while you are editing your documents. These are never visible in the Web browser.
- Layers - Controls the default appearance and code used to create a layer added to your document from the Insert→Layer command.
- Layout View - Controls the appearance of your tables when viewed in Layout view. This sets the colors for outlines of specific portions of your table that are selected, as well as creating and identifying spacer images used in the table.
- Panels - Allows you to select which panels to show in the Launcher, as well as which panels will appear on the top of your document when you are working within Dreamweaver.
- Preview In Browser - Allows you to configure a selection of Web browsers to use from within Dreamweaver for previewing and checking the layout of your document. You should have at least one version of Internet Explorer, Netscape Navigator, and Opera listed. Preferably, you will list both versions 4 and 5 of Internet Explorer and Opera and versions 4 and 6 of Netscape Navigator.
- Quick Tag Editor - Controls how the main document code window treats changes made in the Quick Tag Editor window.
- Site - Allows you to control the appearance and function of the site window.
- Status Bar - Controls the list of selectable window sizes for designing pages, as well as the estimated connection speed, so you can accurately judge how much time your pages are going to take to download.

After you have modified all your preferences, click OK. Depending on the options you adjusted, you will be able to see your changes immediately. To see others, you will need to restart Dreamweaver.

Preload Images see Behaviors

Properties Inspector

The Properties inspector's contents change as items within your HTML document are selected. Figure P-5 shows three different panels: text objects, layers, and images. There are many more configurations than these, of course. The upper half of the panel is the same for all text objects, no matter what their location. You can drop down or raise the lower half of the Properties panel by clicking the Expand/Contract button in the lower right corner of the panel.

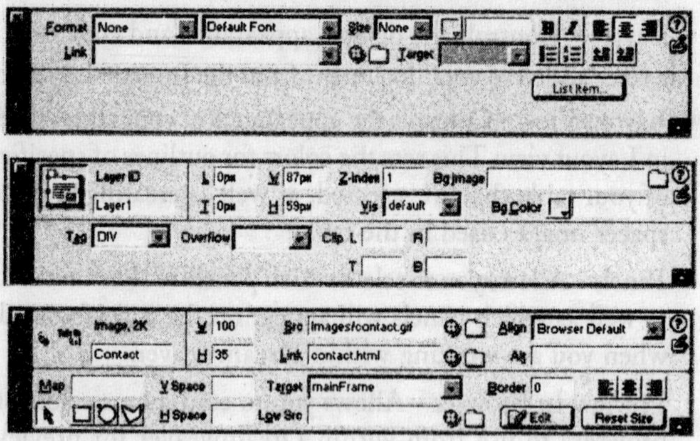

Figure P-5 The Properties inspector.

SEE ALSO *Panels*

Quick Tag Editor

The Quick Tag Editor gives you direct control over the HTML code used to format your Web page. There are a couple of ways to open the Quick Tag Editor:

- Select an element from the Tag Selector on your status bar and click your right mouse button. From the contextual menu, select Edit Tag.
- Select an item on your page, and click your right mouse button. From this contextual menu, select Edit Tag.

- Select an item on your page, and select Modify→Quick Tag Editor.

No matter how you open the Quick Tag Editor, it will look the same as that shown in Figure Q-1.

Figure Q-1 The Quick Tag Editor.

This window gives you the text content of the HTML tag you are editing, which allows you to make changes to the tag directly.

The Quick Tag Editor gives you the option of selecting additional attributes for the tag from a drop-down list. This list automatically appears after you have typed a space after a closing quotation mark from another attribute, or by letting your cursor pause in the empty element.

Once you are done making your changes in the Quick Tag Editor, click your mouse pointer onto any other area of the document. Any visible changes made to your document, such as changing font or image size, will be immediately visible. If you have made other changes, such as adding an event to a link, the results won't be seen until you have tested them in a browser.

SEE ALSO *Code Inspector, Code View*

Reference Panel

The Reference panel, which is new in Dreamweaver 4, provides detailed documentation on HTML, CSS, and JavaScript. All of this information originated from O'Reilly and Associates books and their Web site. Open the Reference panel using Window→Reference to see the Reference panel, as shown in Figure R-1. After choosing a Reference from the Book pop-up menu, use the Tag list to look up HTML tags and their attributes, CSS properties, or details on JavaScript objects, properties, and methods.

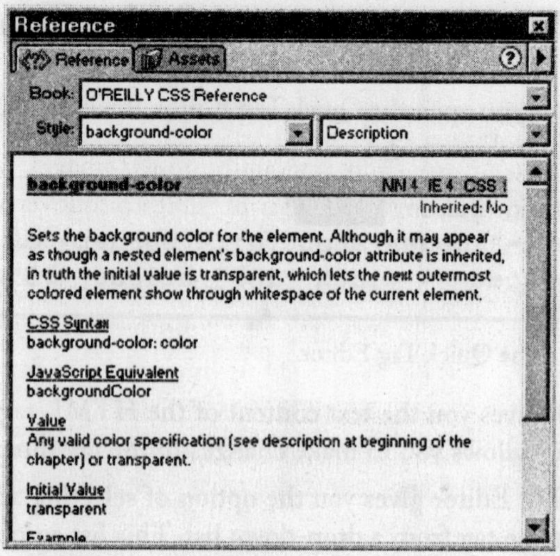

Figure R-1 The Reference panel.

SEE ALSO *Assets Panel, Help Files*

Relative Links

A relative link contains the address to another document or file, in relation to the current Web page. Relative links specify the location of the next file as a reference point, as shown in the following examples:

```
index.html

images/myfigure.gif

../styles/mystylesheet.css
```

Relative links, like absolute links, are entered into the Dreamweaver Properties inspector's Link field, as shown in Figure R-2.

Figure R-2 The Link field of the Property inspector.

SEE ALSO *Absolute Link, Hyperlink, Link*

Right-Click Menu see Contextual Menus

Rollover Images

Rollover images add a two-state interaction to the images on your pages in browsers that support JavaScript. With a rollover image, when the mouse rolls over an image object, another image is shown.

To add a rollover image to your document, select Insert→Interactive Images→Rollover Image to open the Insert Rollover Image dialog box, shown in Figure R-3.

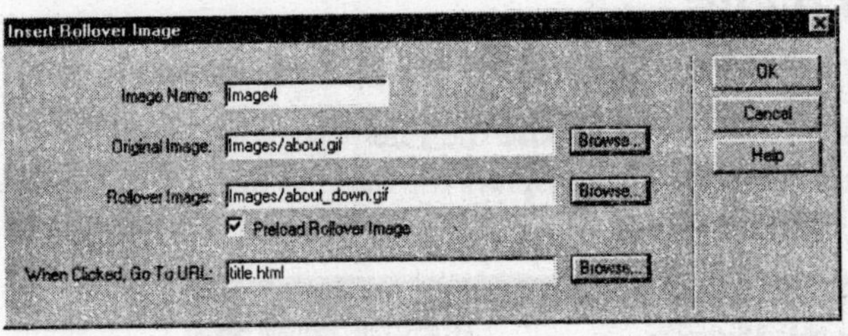

Figure R-3 The Insert Rollover Image dialog box.

The following options control which images are loaded and how the effect takes place:

- Image Name - Specifies the name of the image used by the JavaScript function. This field requires input.
- Original Image - Identifies the URL of the image displayed by default.
- Rollover Image - Identifies the URL of the image displayed when the mouse moves over the original image.
- Preload Rollover Image - Loads the rollover image(s) prior to its display. Check this box to ensure a smooth rollover transition.
- When Clicked, Go To URL - Identifies the URL of the document being linked by this button.

Images used in rollover effects should be the same size; otherwise, the Rollover Image will be scaled to fit in the Original Image's area.

NOTE *For browsers that don't support JavaScript, or when a visitor has disabled JavaScript in his or her Web browser, the visitor will not see the rollover effect (the button always displays the original image).*

SEE ALSO *Behaviors, Navigation Bars*

Roundtrip Graphics Editing

Roundtrip Graphics editing allows the Dreamweaver/Fireworks Studio to edit graphics created in Fireworks by Fireworks at Dreamweaver's request. When Dreamweaver asks that the graphic be edited, then Fireworks automatically opens the original PNG version of that graphic, if it is available, and makes the modifications to it before updating the image that Dreamweaver is actually using.

SEE ALSO *Dreamweaver Fireworks Studio*

Saving a File

To save a Web page, choose the File→Save command.

The first time you choose the File→Save command for a new document, Dreamweaver displays the Save As dialog box so you can name the file and specify where it should be saved, as shown in Figure S-1.

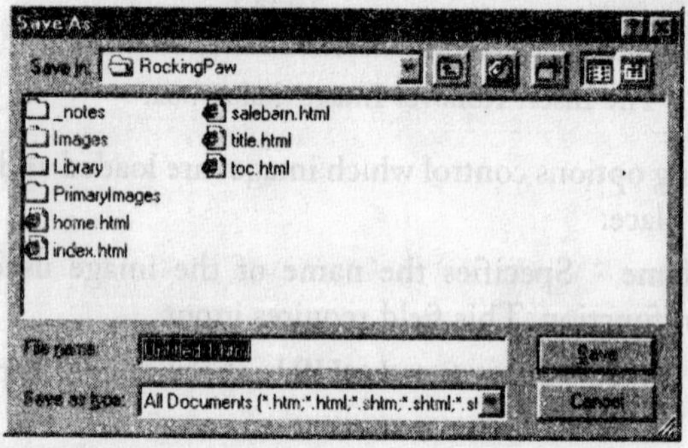

Figure S-1 The Save As dialog box.

To use the Save As dialog box, follow these steps:

1. Use the Save In box to pick the folder you want to save the document in.
2. Enter the name you want to use for the document into the File Name box.

NOTE *Dreamweaver creates HTML files readable by all other HTML or text editing programs.*

SEE ALSO *Closing Dreamweaver, New Document, New from Template, Opening Dreamweaver*

Scripting

Scripting is the process of adding JavaScript, JScript, ECMAScript, or VBScript code to your Web documents. These scripts can perform myriad tasks, including formatting, automatic testing of information contained within the document, and the update of that information as viewers interact with the information. Dreamweaver includes a variety of pre-made scripts, called behaviors, which can be added to your documents. These behaviors have already been tested for use with Internet Explorer, Netscape Navigator, and Opera.

SEE ALSO *Behaviors, ECMAScript, JavaScript, JScript*

Scripts see Scripting

Search and Replace

Dreamweaver allows you to manipulate your HTML documents by doing a series of Find and Replace searches on your document. Open the Find And Replace dialog box, shown in Figure S-2, by selecting Edit→Find And Replace or by pressing Ctrl+F (Windows) or Cmd+F (Macintosh).

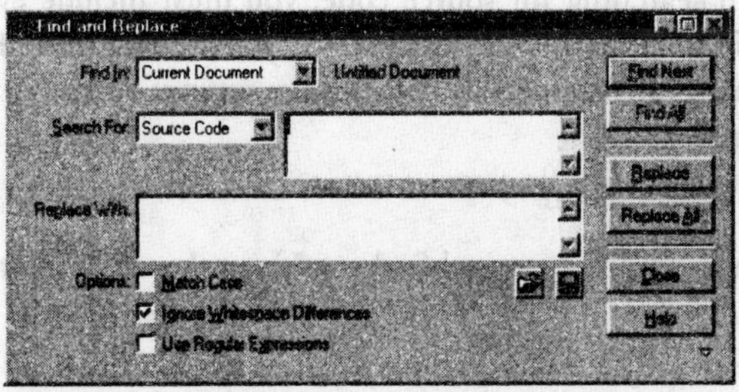

Figure S-2 The Find And Replace dialog box.

The Find And Replace dialog box has a variety of options, which are discussed in the following sections.

NOTE *Dreamweaver can't undo changes to closed documents made with the Find And Replace feature. Before making extensive changes to your documents, make a backup.*

Search Ranges

Dreamweaver provides a variety of searchable areas in the Find In drop-down list.

- Current Document - Searches the current open document only.
- Entire Local Site - Searches the entire site as defined in the Define Sites dialog box.
- Selected Files In Site - Searches only the files that you have specified.
- Folder - Searches only the specified folder, which may be all, or part of, another site.

Text or Source Code

Both of these options, available by adjusting the Search For field, provide only options for entering the text to search for and the text to be replaced. Figure S-2 shows the configuration of your screen when either Search For: Text or Search For: Source Code is selected.

To search your source code, follow these steps:

1. Select Search For: Source Code.
2. Type in the string of code to search for in the Search For field. When searching for source code, you must include everything within your search. For instance, if you are searching for a <p> element, you must specify the attribute settings of that <p> tag. For instance:

```
<p align="center">
```

You can't search for <p> and find anything other than an empty <p> tag. You must search for closing </p> elements separately.

3. Type the replace string in the Replace With field. This needs to be the full string, including any quotation marks and angle brackets.
4. Click the Find Next, Find All, Replace, or Replace All button that is most appropriate for your needs. Find Next finds only an instance of your Search For statement. Replace replaces only one instance of your Search For statement. Replace All replaces all the Search For statements found in your document.
5. Click Close when you are done.

To search the text of your document, independent of all HTML code, follow these steps:

1. Select Search For: Text.
2. Type in the string of code to search for in the Search For field. You must provide the exact string of text you are searching for. This search will ignore any HTML tags that might interrupt your search string, for instance, a Text search for "Dreamweaver A to Z" would find "Dreamweaver A to Z" as well as "<b>Dreamweaver</b> A to Z."
3. Type the replace string in the Replace With field. If you wish a section of this statement to be formatted in a specific way, you must add that HTML code to this statement.
4. Click the Find Next, Find All, Replace, or Replace All button that is most appropriate for your needs. Find Next finds only an instance of your Search For statement. Replace replaces only one instance of your Search For statement. Replace All replaces all the Search For statements found in your document. You can use your History to undo this action if necessary.
5. Click Close when you are done.

Text (Advanced)

If you have more advanced needs than the standard Source Code or Text search, try the Search For: Text (Advanced) option, whose settings are shown in Figure S-3. An advanced text search allows you to search for information inside a specific element tag or outside of the element markup altogether.

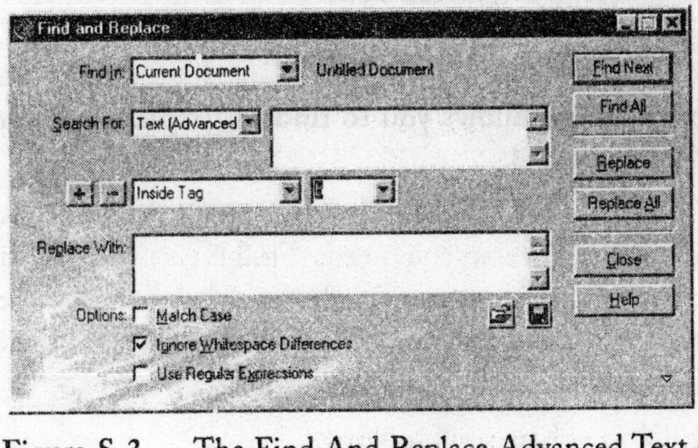

Figure S-3 The Find And Replace Advanced Text dialog box.

To search for a more complex string of text:

1. Type in the string of text to find in the Search For field.
2. To specify that this string occurs inside or outside of a specific element, select either Inside Tag or Outside Tag from the drop-down list.
3. Select the tag you wish to use as a reference point from the Tag drop-down list.
4. Use the Plus (+) and Minus (-) buttons to control the attribute settings of your specified tag, or add additional tags in the search string. When you add an additional attribute or tag search, you can control how the search will be performed based upon an attribute or attribute value's presence in the search tag (With Attribute / Without Attribute / Containing / Not Containing), and the specific options available with each of those settings. For example, these options can be used to find all the <font> elements with a color=""red" attribute, or all of the <p> elements not aligned left, but containing the word "George" in their contents.
5. Type the replace string in the Replace With field. If you wish a section of this statement to be formatted in a specific way, you must add that HTML code to this statement.
6. Click the Find Next, Find All, Replace, or Replace All button that is most appropriate for your needs. Find Next finds only an instance of your Search For statement. Replace replaces only one instance of your Search For statement. Replace All replaces all the Search For statements found in your document. You can use your History to undo this action if necessary.
7. Click Close when you are done.

Specific Tags

Dreamweaver also allows you to find and replace specific tags, as shown in Figure S-4.

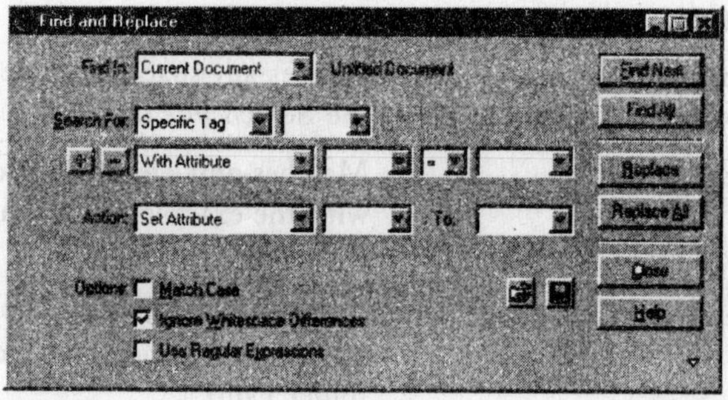

Figure S-4 The Find And Replace Tags dialog box.

You can search for a tag with a specific attribute, or a series of specific attributes, and then perform one of the following functions:

- Add After End Tag
- Add After Start Tag
- Add Before End Tag
- Add Before Start Tag
- Change Tag
- Remove Attribute
- Remove Tag And Content
- Replace Content
- Replace Tag And Content
- Set Attribute
- Strip Tag

Generic Search Controls

In addition to the specific search options discussed earlier, you can use the controls, listed in the following table, with all Find And Replace functions:

CONTROL	DESCRIPTION
Find Next	Finds the next instance of the Search For string.
Find	Finds the first instance of the Search For string.

CONTROL	DESCRIPTION
Ignore Whitespace Differences	Ignores any spacing differences in the Search For field.
Match Case	Matches only elements or content with the exact letter case used in the Search For field.
Open Query	Opens a saved Dreamweaver Find And Replace operation. (Yellow folder icon)
Replace All	Replaces all instances of the Search For string in the document range.
Replace	Replaces the first instance of the Search For string.
Save Query	Saves the current Find And Replace operation. (Floppy disk icon)
Use Regular Expressions	Allows you to use regular expressions (such as, ?, *, \w, and \b) in your search string.

Searching with Regular Expressions

Regular expressions assist you in performing searches for non-specified information, such as a <p> element with any content and any attributes. When the Use Regular Expression option is checked, the Regular Expressions, listed in the following table, are allowed in your Search For field:

EXPRESSION	DEFINITION
	'all finds call or tall but not all Any one character except the new line character.
$	$l finds call or tall but not look Finds the specified string at the end of a line.
*	l*k finds look or lake but not kale Finds the preceding characters zero or more times prior to the following character.

EXPRESSION	DEFINITION
?	la?k finds lake or talk but not lick Makes the preceding character optional or exist singularly. Other characters in the string must be present.
[^abc]	[^aei] finds stork or glyph but not cypher Matches any character other than those listed in the brackets.
[abc]	[aei] finds make or dale but not stork Matches any of the characters in the brackets.
\B	\Bq finds IQ but not queen Matches a letter not at the start or end of a word.
\b	\bq finds queen but not IQ Matches a letter at the start or end of a word.
\D	\D finds Han Solo but not C3PO Matches any non-numerical (digit) character.
\d	\d finds C3PO but not Han Solo Matches any numerical (digit) character.
\f	Represents a form feed.
\n	Represents a line feed.
\r	Represents a carriage return.
\s	\s finds the space in Han Solo Matches a single white-space character.
\S	\SSolo finds HanSolot but not Han Solo Matches a single non-white-space character in front of the specified string.
\t	Represents a Tab character.
\W	\Wq finds &q but not iq Matches any non-alpha-numeric character.
\w	q\w finds queen but not IQ& Matches any alpha-numeric character.

EXPRESSION	DEFINITION
^	^c finds call or cat but not tick Finds the specified string at the beginning of a word.
{i,n}	e{2,4} finds screech or creep but not creeeeepy Matches a minimum of i but no more n instances of the preceding letter.
{i}	e{2} finds screech or creep but not creepy Matches that number of the preceding character, no more, no less.
+	ow+l finds cowl or tool but not awl Finds the preceding character one or more times in the string.
x|y	el|al finds tell or tale but not wake Matches either statement.

Server Side Include

The computers that "serve up" documents stored for distribution are called servers. Server-side includes are statements that use documents stored on the server as inserts within the current document. For instance, you can use a server side include to add the controls for a server-side image map. You can use server side includes to insert automatically updated information, such as weather maps. You can insert a server side include into your HTML document by following these steps:

1. Place your cursor at the point in the document where the include should be placed.
2. Select Insert→Server-Side Include.
3. In the Select File dialog box, select the file that will be added, such as an image map document or other automatically updated file.
4. Click the Select button.

In Dreamweaver, the contents of the document will be displayed if it is a Dreamweaver readable file; otherwise, you will see the server-side icon representing the location where the include will be placed.

NOTE *If you add a server side include into your document, you must save it with the .shtml extension. This lets both the browser and the server know that you are using information off of the server and to look for the <!include > statements.*

SEE ALSO *Media Objects*

Set Nav Bar Image see Behaviors

Set Text of Frame see Behaviors

Set Text of Layer see Behaviors

Set Text of Status Bar see Behaviors

Set Text of Text Field see Behaviors

Shockwave/Director

Macromedia Director 8 Shockwave Studio is one of the tools used to develop multimedia Internet sites. Director combines graphics, sound, animation, text, and video to create a streaming, multi-user, interactive experience to be enjoyed through the Web or on CD-ROM or DVD-ROM. The Shockwave Player plug-in allows Web viewers to view the Director content.

To insert a Shockwave/Director object into your document, select the Insert→Media→ Shockwave command. In the Select File dialog box, choose a Shockwave file, such as a .shw or .dir movie file, and click Select. The properties for a Shockwave movie are similar to those available for a Flash movie, as shown in the Shockwave Properties panel shown in Figure S-5. For more information on these options, see the Flash entry.

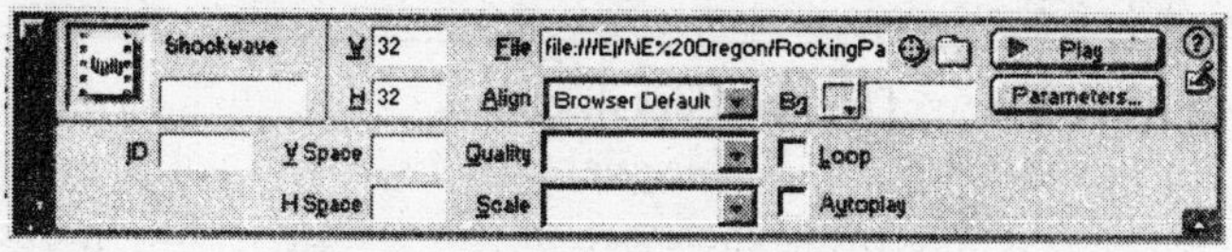

Figure S-5 The Shockwave Properties inspector.

SEE ALSO *Flash, Fireworks, Generator, Media Objects*

Shortcut Menus see Contextual Menus

Show-Hide Layers see Behaviors

Site Definitions see Defining Sites

Site Files

The Site window has two views: Site Files and Site Maps, as well as a combined view showing both. To view your site files in a fashion similar to Windows Explorer or Macintosh Finder, select Site→Site Files from your document window or Window→Site Files from your Site window on a Windows computer. You can also open this window by pressing F8.

The Site Files view, shown in Figure S-6, contains a listing of each document, image, folder, and auxiliary asset in the site. Each of the files listed can show information such as Modified, Size, Notes, Type, and Checked Out By. These options aren't available in the Site Map.

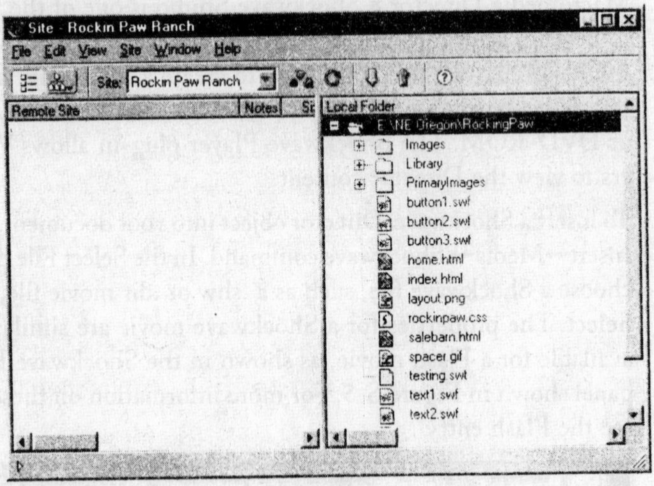

Figure S-6 The Site Files display.

NOTE *To move documents within your site, simply drag and drop them into your document structure. By moving the documents within Dreamweaver, your links will be kept intact, because Dreamweaver will automatically update the links in every document defined within the site structure. If you move documents associated with your Web site outside of Dreamweaver, you will have to reset the broken links manually.*

SEE ALSO *Defining Sites, Site Map, Site Window*

Site Map

The Site window has two views: Site Files and Site Map, and a combined view showing both. To view your site map, in a fashion similar to a flow chart, select Site→Site Map from your document window, or Window→Site Map from your Site Window on a Windows machine. You can also open this window by pressing Alt+F8 (Windows) or Opt+F8 (Macintosh).

The Site Map view, shown in Figure S-7, shows the hierarchical structure of your documents including links to other documents or e-mail addresses, images, and script programs that are used in the file. The Site Map view takes up a significant amount of screen space to view all of the documents in your site, so you may need to adjust the Zoom function located in the lower left corner of your Site window.

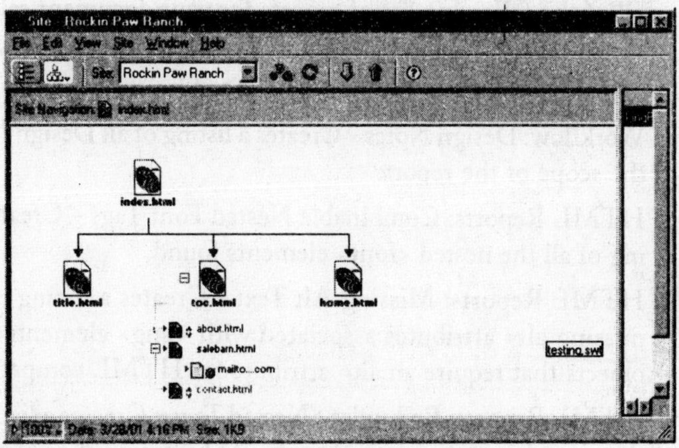

Figure S-7 The Site Map display.

SEE ALSO *Defining Sites, Site Files, Site Window*

Site Reports

Dreamweaver allows you to collect reports on the functioning and status of your site through the Site Reports dialog box, shown in Figure S-8. Open this dialog box by selecting Site→Reports from the document window.

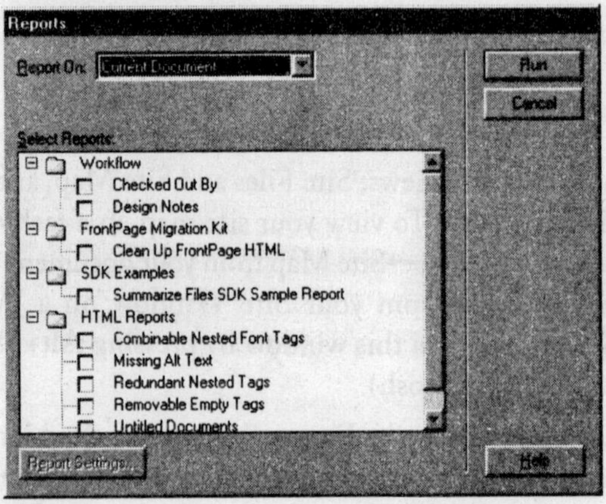

Figure S-8 The Site Reports dialog box.

Reports can be generated for the Current Document, the Entire Local Site, Selected Files In Site, or a specified Folder. You can generate any or all of the following list of reports for your document selection:

- Workflow: Checked Out By - Creates a listing of who has the selected document, documents, or site files checked out.
- Workflow: Design Notes - Creates a listing of all Design Notes for the scope of the report.
- HTML Reports: Combinable Nested Font Tags - Creates a listing of all the nested <font> elements found.
- HTML Reports: Missing Alt Text - Creates a listing of all the missing alt= attributes associated with <img> elements or other objects that require an alt= attribute for HTML compatibility.
- HTML Reports: Redundant Nested Tags - Creates a listing of all the nested repeating tags that should be removed or merged.
- HTML Reports: Removable Empty Tags - Creates a listing of all the empty elements to be removed.

- HTML Reports: Untitled Documents - Creates a listing of all documents that have either blank or Untitled Document in their <title> elements.

Generating a Report

To generate a report:

1. Select the scope of the report you wish to generate.
2. Select the report(s) that you wish to view.
3. Click OK.

A sample report is shown in Figure S-9. From this report you can learn what needs to be done for your site to make it glitch-free.

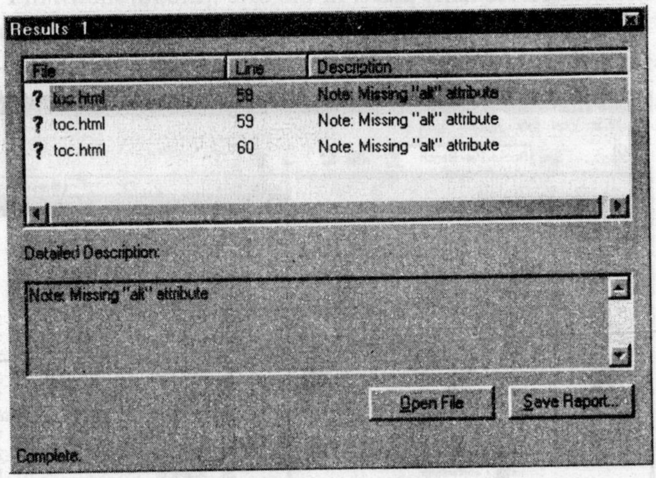

Figure S-9 A sample Missing Alt Attributes report.

Using Reports

To use a generated report, you need to read the report carefully and then follow these steps:

1. Select the file you need to edit, and click the Open File button in the Report Results dialog box shown in Figure S-9.
2. To make adjustments to the code directly, which is easiest if you know HTML, select View→Code and turn on Line Numbers by selecting View→Code View Options →Line Numbers.
3. Find the line in which the error occurred and alter your HTML text. Be sure to save your document when you are done by choosing File→Save.

To make the adjustments, use Design view and then you can edit your document like normal. To remove redundant tags, select the tag in the status bar, click the right mouse button, and select Remove Tag from the popup menu.

SEE ALSO *Checking Links*

Site Setup see Defining Sites

Site Window

The Site window is the primary location where communication with the Web server takes place. In the Site window, shown in Figure S-10, you can view the Site Files list, Site Maps, Checked Out By information, as well as the Design Notes available for each document.

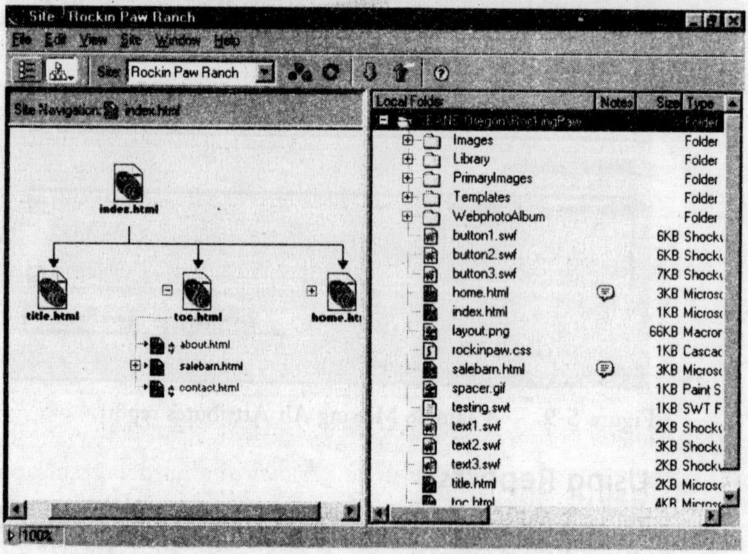

Figure S-10 The Dreamweaver Site window and major features.

SEE ALSO *Code And Design View, Code View, Design View, Document Window*

Special Characters see Characters

Status Bar

The status bar at the bottom of the document window, as shown in Figure S-11, contains the Tag selector, Window Size selector, and the Mini-Launcher. It also shows the current document's size and estimated download time. The status bar can be configured under Edit→Preferences→Status Bar.

Figure S-11 The status bar.

Tag Selector

The Tag Selector is visible only in Design view or when the Design pane is active in the Code And Design view. It displays the HTML tags that exist in the document hierarchy of the currently selected item. The tag representing the selected object is shown in boldface. You can change the selection by clicking the other tags appearing in the Tag Selector.

Window Size Selector

The Window Size Selector popup menu allows you to preview your pages at various screen sizes. The usable screen area is usually less than the monitor resolution due to toolbars and borders associated with typical browsers. HTML window sizes are fluid, therefore this setting has no bearing on the window size when the document is viewed in the user's browser. It is provided strictly as a potential test base. If necessary, use JavaScript to control the size of the window in which your HTML page is displayed.

Document Size and Estimated Download Time

The status bar shows the size of the HTML page plus any images or media files used in the document. By default, the estimated download time assumes a 28.8-Kbps connection, but the target connection speed can be configured under Edit→Preferences→Status Bar. If you choose to modify this setting, keep in mind that not everyone has a broadband connect, nor even a 56K dialup connection. Especially those of us in rural areas.

Mini-Launcher

The Mini-Launcher is a compact and convenient version of the Launcher.

SEE ALSO *Document Window, Launcher*

Stop Timeline see Behaviors

Swap Image see Behaviors

Swap Image Restore see Behaviors

Synchronize Site Files

Synchronizing Site Files is the easiest way to ensure that you are always working with the most current version of a document, especially if you have more than one team member working on a site. To synchronize your site files, select Site→Synchronize from the Site window in Windows or from the Site menu on a Macintosh. This opens the Synchronize Site dialog box shown in Figure S-12. When synchronizing your site, you have a variety of options.

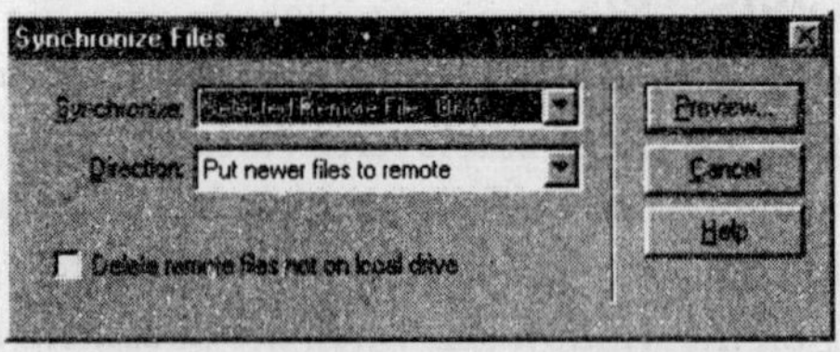

Figure S-12 The Synchronize Site dialog box.

The values available for the Synchronize option in this dialog box are listed below:

- Entire Site - Synchronizes both the remote and local sites to match.
- Select Files Only - Synchronizes only the selected files on both the remote and local server.

The values available for the Direction option are as follows:

- Put Newer Files To Remote - Puts the updated files onto the remote machine from the local machine.
- Get Newer Files From Remote - Updates the local machine to match the remote machine.
- Get And Put Newer Files - Updates both machines so that they are synchronized exactly.

Check the Delete Remote Files Not On Local Drive check box if you wish to remove the files on the Web server that are not on the local server. If you have a script or program that automatically generates pages, then do not select this option.

Once these selections have been made, click Preview to get a list of the pages that will be affected by the synchronization process. In the Synchronize dialog box, shown in Figure S-13, scroll through the file list to ensure that the files to be updated on either the local or remote servers are correct, and then click OK. When the site is fully synchronized, you will be returned to the Site window.

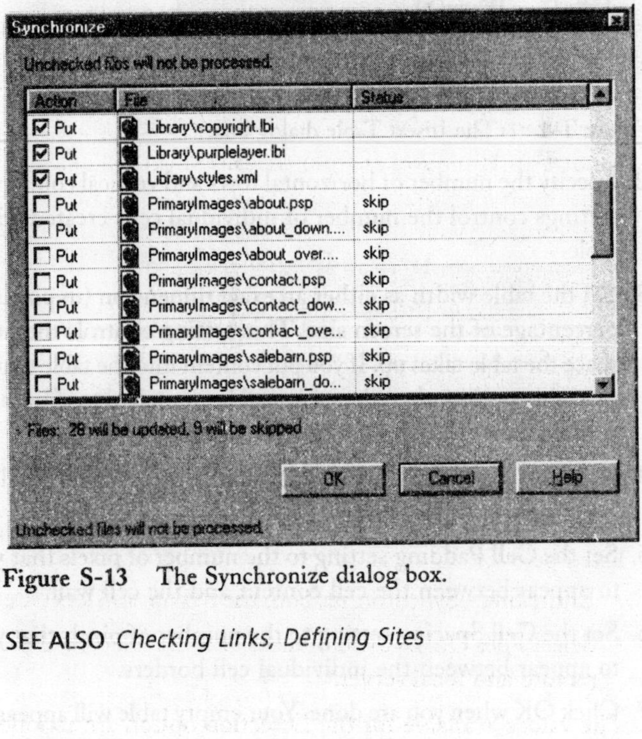

Figure S-13 The Synchronize dialog box.

SEE ALSO *Checking Links, Defining Sites*

Tables

Tables are used traditionally to hold information that is best formatted into rows and columns. HTML has expanded the use of tables to include the formatting of pages. When formatting your document, use Dreamweaver's Layout Tables feature. It provides more control over object placement than standard tables allow.

Creating a Table

To insert a table into a document, follow these steps:

1. Select Insert→Table or press Ctrl+Alt+T (Windows) or Cmd+Option+T (Macintosh). This opens the Insert Table dialog box shown in Figure T-1.

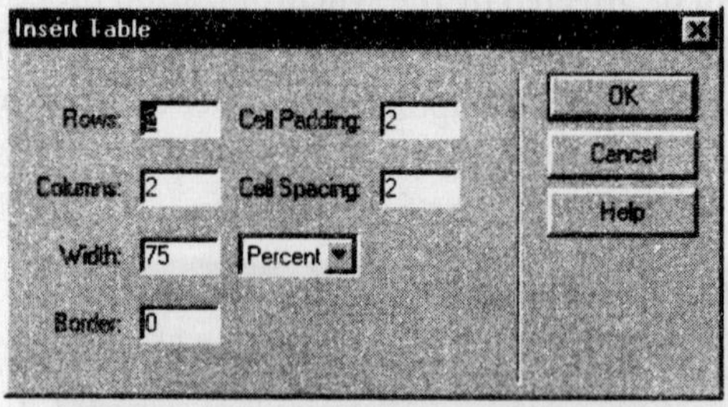

Figure T-1 The Insert Table dialog box.

2. Specify the number of horizontal tows and vertical columns. These settings control the number of individual cells created within the table.
3. Set the table width as either an exact dimension (in pixels) or as a percentage of the screen size. This setting controls the minimum space the table takes up. If you put content into the table that is wider than this setting, then the table will be stretched to show all of that content.
4. Set the table border dimensions as a measurement in pixels. When set to zero (0), the border is not visible.
5. Set the Cell Padding setting to the number of pixels that you wish to appear between the cell content and the cell wall.
6. Set the Cell Spacing setting to the number of pixels that you wish to appear between the individual cell borders.
7. Click OK when you are done. Your empty table will appear on your screen.

Table Properties

The selection of properties available for use with a table include those listed below and shown in Figure T-2. To select the table, either click on its border or select its element name from the Tag Selector on the status bar.

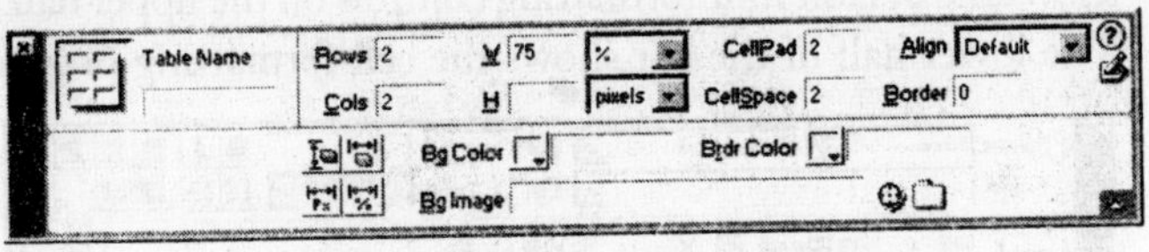

Figure T-2 The Table Properties inspector.

The Table Properties inspector has the following options:

- Table Name - Specifies the name of the table for scripting or style sheet purposes.
- Rows - Specifies the number of horizontal rows in the table.
- Columns - Specifies the number of vertical columns in the table.
- Width (W) - Specifies the width of the table as either a percentage of the document width or an exact pixel amount.
- Height (H) - Specifies the height of the table as an exact pixel amount.
- CellPad - Sets the number of pixels that appear between the cell content and the cell wall.
- CellSpace - Sets the number of pixels that appear between the individual cell borders.
- Align - Controls the alignment of the table on your document.
- Border - Specifies the width of the table borders.
- Brdr Color - Specifies the color of the border if the border value is greater than 0.
- Bg Color - Specifies the color of the table background.
- Bg Image - Specifies the image to use as the table background. This option doesn't display correctly in Netscape 4. The table background image is repeated in every cell.

Use these settings to control the appearance of your table in general. You can more closely control the appearance of individual cells by using the Cell Properties.

Cell Properties

The selection of properties available for use with an individual table cell includes those listed below and those shown in Figure T-3. To select the table, click within its borders or select its element name from the Tag Selector on the status bar. The Properties inspector for a table cell shows the default font formatting controls on the upper half of the bar. The lower half of the bar shows the cell formatting properties.

Figure T-3 The Cell Properties inspector.

The Cell Properties inspector has the following options:

- Horz - Specifies the default horizontal alignment of content placed in this cell.
- Vert - Specifies the default vertical alignment of content placed in this cell.
- Width (W) - Specifies the width of the cell as either a percentage of the table width or an exact pixel amount.
- Height (H) - Specifies the height of the cell as an exact pixel amount.
- No Wrap - Forces cell content not to wrap if the content is too large for the cell.
- Header - Sets the contents of the selected cell as a table heading.
- Brdr - Specifies the color of the border of the cell if the border value is greater than 0.
- Bg Color - Specifies the color of the cell background.
- Bg Image - Specifies the image to use as the cell background.

These settings control the appearance of your table cells, although their appearance can change remarkably by adding content to the tables, as shown in the filled table in Figure T-4.

Flight/Delivery Schedules

Date	Time	Destination
10/11/01	1203	Albany, Oregon
10/12/01	1540	Pendleton, Oregon
10/12/01	1730	La Grande, Oregon

Figure T-4 A simple data table containing a row of table headers and normal data.

Merging/Splitting Cells

Merging and splitting cells allows you to link multiple cells on a single axis, either horizontally (columns) or vertically (rows) into a single larger cell encompassing the area previously taken up by the two, or more, individual cells. Splitting cells allows you to separate a previously merged cell into its original parts, or any combination of those parts. Splitting a cell that has never been merged has the effect of creating a new row or column in your table.

To merge table cells highlight the cells to be merged and then select Merge Cells in one of the following four ways:

- Click the Merge Cells icon on the Properties inspector.
- Press Ctrl+Alt+M (Windows) or Cmd+Opt+M (Macintosh).
- Select Modify→Table→Merge Cells.
- Select Table→Merge Cells from the right-click contextual menu.

To split table cells, highlight the cell to split and then select Split Cells in one of the following four ways:

- Click the Split Cells icon on the Properties inspector.
- Press Ctrl+Alt+S (Windows) or Cmd+Opt+S (Macintosh).
- Select Modify→Table→Split Cell.
- Select Table→Split Cell from the right-click contextual menu.

This opens the Split Cells dialog box from which you need to select the number of rows or columns to create out of the split cell. Once you have clicked OK, you will be able to view your modified table.

SEE ALSO *Layers, Layout Tables*

Template Fields

Dreamweaver templates use a series of fields, as shown in the example in Figure T-5, that control the placement and formatting of information contained within your document. All areas outside of the Editable Regions, as Dreamweaver calls them, can't be edited. Each Editable Region on your Dreamweaver document will appear inside a blue box (default setting) with the field label above some holder

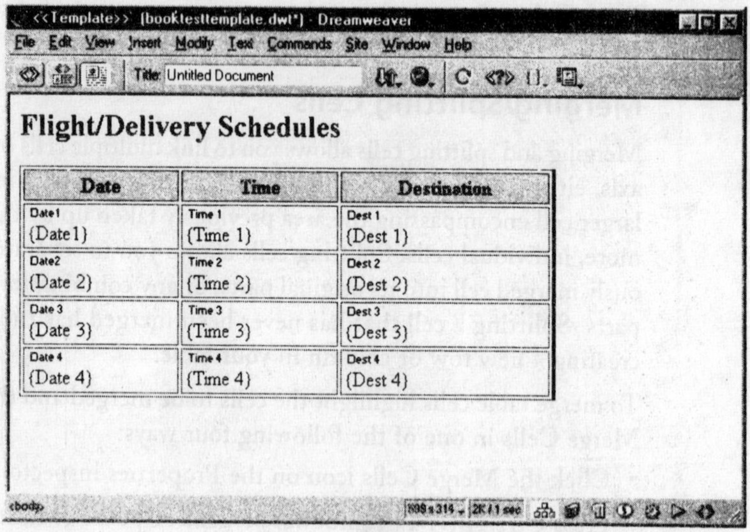

Figure T-5 A simple table with 12 editable fields/regions for customizing the table contents.

SEE ALSO *Library Items, Templates*

Templates

Dreamweaver's templates significantly increase the efficiency of Web developers when creating sites using the same format across a series of pages. Templates allow developers to quickly update the information on old pages and incorporate new pages as the site is being developed, or as the site grows over time.

When designing templates be sure to do the following:

- Place the information appearing on every page in the site on the template.

- Place editable regions in every area of the template that you may want to add content or modify.
- Test your template before creating an entire site.

Creating a Template

You have two options for creating a template: creating a document from scratch or modifying an existing document.

To create a template from a new document, follow these steps:

1. Select File→New to open a new blank document.
2. Add images, tables, text, etc. to complete the layout of the document. These pieces should be the ones that you wish to appear on every page. Anything that shouldn't be on every page using this template should be removed.
3. Select Save As Template to save the document as a Dreamweaver Template. This opens the Save As Template dialog box shown in Figure T-6.

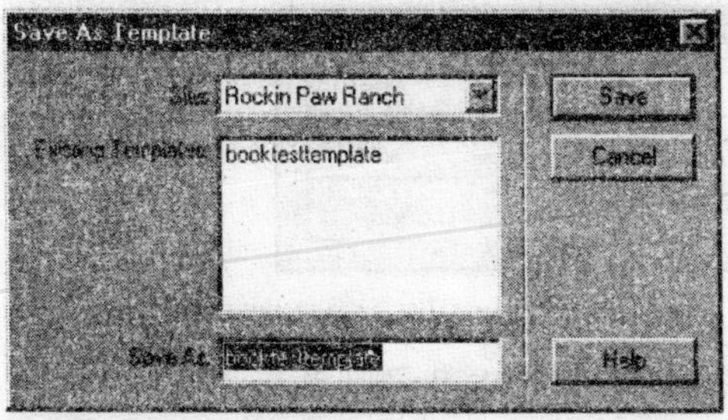

Figure T-6 The Save As Template dialog box.

4. In the Save As field, type in the name of the template.
5. Click the Save button.

To create a template from an existing file, follow these steps:

1. Select File→Open and select an existing document from the Select File dialog box.
2. Modify the content of your page, removing everything that shouldn't be on the template. Do not include or leave any content that you do not want to appear on all pages made with this template

3. Select Save As Template to save the document. This opens the Save As Template dialog box shown in Figure T-6. Select the site you wish to associate the template with, type the name of the template in the Save As field, and then click OK.

After saving your document as a template, you will be able to add template fields, also called Editable Regions, to your template.

Adding Editable Regions

Editable Regions added to your document make it editable when it is used as the foundation for other documents in your site. To add an Editable Region, place your cursor where a template field is required and select Modify→Templates→New Editable Region, or press Ctrl+Alt+V (Windows) or Cmd+Opt+V (Macintosh). In the New Editable Region dialog box shown in Figure T-7, type the name for the template field, and click OK. Repeat this process for each new template field. The template field appears on your document in a light blue outline.

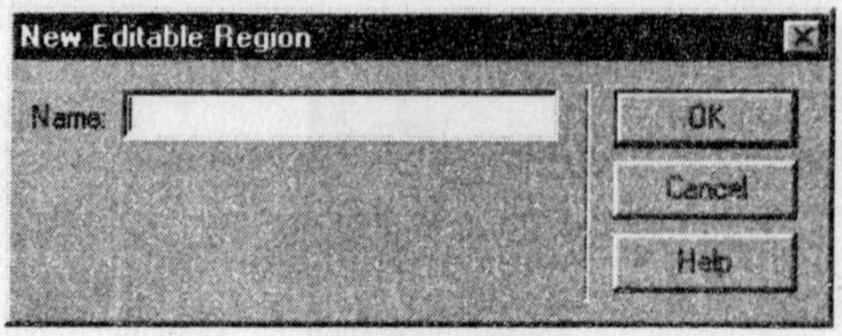

Figure T-7 The New Editable Region dialog box.

When creating a template using layout tables, use the entire table cell as the Editable Region. To do this, select the <td> element from the Tag Selector on the status bar and select Modify→Templates→New Editable Region.

You can control the appearance of text in your Editable Region by formatting the region on the template. Simply highlight each Editable Region and use the formatting options on the Properties inspector to configure the appearance of your text. The style applied to your template fields serves as the default for your document objects, but can be further modified during page development.

NOTE *You must place a block level object within each of your Editable Regions or else you will not be able to add a new paragraph within that region.*

Removing Editable Regions

To remove an Editable Region from your document template, select Modify→Templates→Remove Editable Region. This opens the Remove Editable Region dialog box shown in Figure T-8.

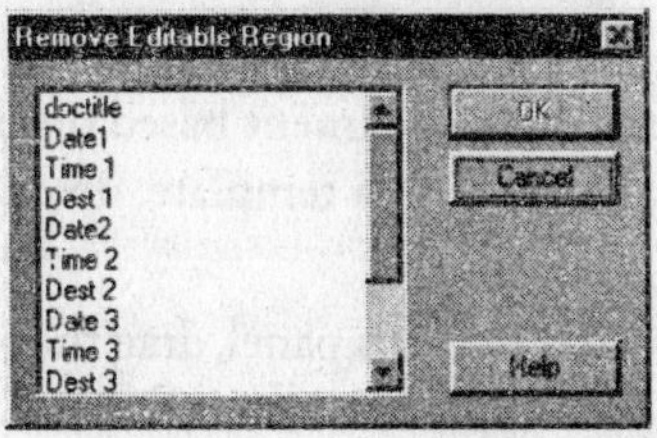

Figure T-8 The Remove Editable Region dialog box.

To remove an Editable Region, select it and click OK. You can select multiple regions by selecting them with your mouse while holding down the Ctrl key.

Using the Assets Panel

Dreamweaver templates are readily accessible from the Assets panel, Templates category. From this location, as shown in Figure T-9, you can alter the name of your template, open it for editing, or even apply it to a document.

Figure T-9 A simple template shown in the Assets panel.

- To change the name of your template, click twice on the template name and then change the name of the template.
- To open a template for editing, select the template name and then click the Edit button.
- To apply a template to the document, select it and click the Apply button, or drag it over the existing document.

Using Templates in a Document

Before you can use your template in your document, you must first apply it to a document or create a new document based on the template. To get a document ready to use with a template, do one of the following:

- From the Templates category of the Assets panel, drag the template onto the document or click the Apply button.
- Select File→New From Template to open a new document based on the template.
- Select Modify→Templates→New Apply Template in the current document.

Once you have a document open that is based upon a template, you can modify the contents of the editable fields using the following steps:

1. Select the editable region and highlight the placeholder text.
2. Type your content, or insert your images, over the placeholder text.
3. Use the formatting options on the Text menu and the Properties inspector to modify the appearance of your text.
4. Save the document with a new name. Do not save it as a template.

SEE ALSO *Library Items*

Timelines

Dreamweaver's timelines provide a third dimension to your Web, allowing you to move and alter objects, including images and layers, based upon the passage of time rather than the interactions with visitors. These effects use complex Java scripts to measure a series of discrete intervals, called frames, to provide a document with a sense of timing. By default, each second has 15 frames. An individual frame that has specific contents, such as an associated behavior, is a keyframe, or a frame that provides a key point within the timeline.

Creating

Both layers and images can be added to timelines and some of their properties can be manipulated as the timeline progresses. You can add an object to a timeline in a variety of fashions:

- Select the object to add and select Modify→Timeline→Add Object To Timeline.
- Click your right mouse button and select Add Object To Timeline from the contextual menu.
- Drag and drop an object from the document to the Timelines panel.
- Press Ctrl+Alt+Shift+T (Windows) or Cmd+Opt+Shift+T (Macintosh).

NOTE *To add objects to a timeline in a document based upon a template, you will need to add those objects to the timeline in the template itself.*

When the object is added to the timeline, you will see it appear as one of the objects in the Timelines panel, as shown in Figure T-10.

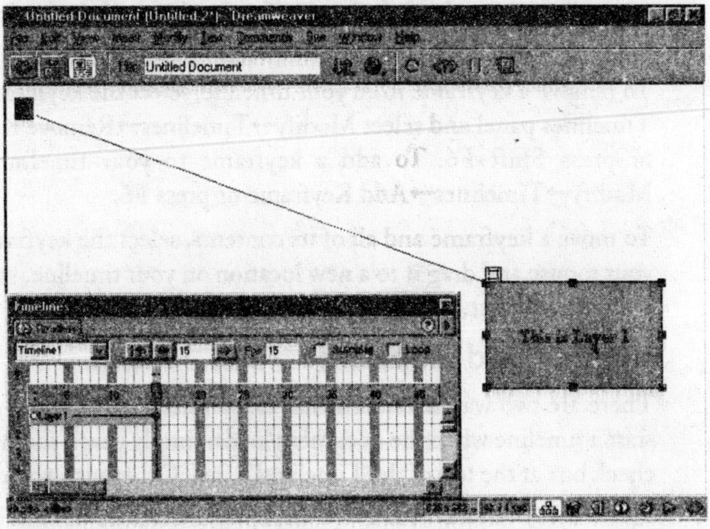

Figure T-10 The Timelines panel showing a layer being dragged across the screen.

NOTE *When selecting a frames-per-second (fps) setting for your timeline, keep in mind that the lower the fps setting, the more jerky the movement of your timeline animation. Feature films run at 24 fps, while Dreamweaver's default 15 fps setting should be appropriate for most Web browsers. Because the browsers have a lot of information to redraw every time a frame occurs, setting your fps setting higher may make your timeline run rougher, not smoother.*

Using KeyFrames to Modify Timelines

Properties of your objects are modified at keyframes in the timeline. In order to adjust the properties of your objects for each of these keyframes, you must select the keyframe and then adjust the property value on the Properties inspector. For example, if you adjust the src attribute in the first keyframe, it will be returned to the original value in the next keyframe. You can avoid this occurrence by planning your keyframes carefully and making all of the changes to the image properties at the same time that you originally make the keyframe. Any attempt to change a property value outside of a keyframe will make your adjustments the default value for the object when the document loads.

To remove a keyframe from your timeline, select the keyframe in the Timelines panel and select Modify→Timelines→Remove Keyframe or press Shift+F6. To add a keyframe to your timeline, select Modify→Timelines→Add Keyframe or press F6.

To move a keyframe and all of its contents, select the keyframe with your mouse and drag it to a new location on your timeline, within its associated object.

Starting and Stopping

There are two ways to start a timeline and two ways to end one. To start a timeline when the document loads, simply check the AutoPlay check box at the top of the Timelines panel. Otherwise, you can start your timeline by applying the Play Timeline behavior to an event, such as the click of a button on your page.

You can stop the timeline by simply letting it run itself out or by associating the Stop Timeline behavior to an event on your Web page.

SEE ALSO *Behaviors, Layers*

Timelines Panel

The Dreamweaver Timelines panel is the nerve center of Dreamweaver timed events. To view the Timelines panel, shown in Figure T-11, select Window→Timelines.

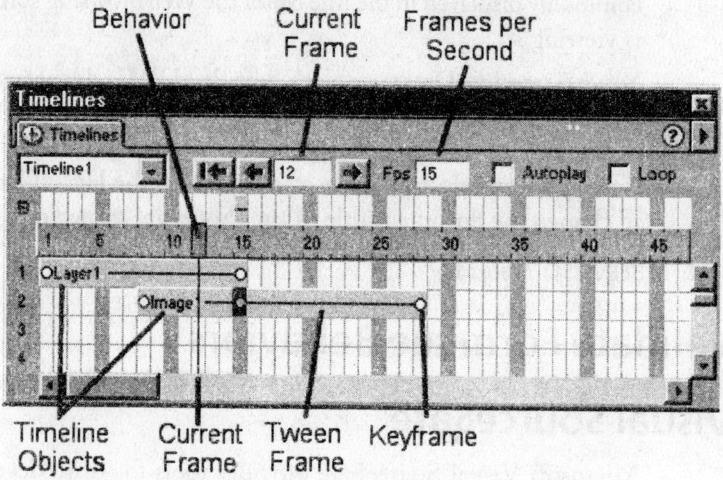

Figure T-11 The Timelines panel.

The options in this panel have the following functions:

- Behavior Marker - Shows where a behavior will be run during the course of the timeline.
- Current Frame - Identifies the currently selected frame.
- Frames Per Second - Shows the current number of frames that will run each second.
- Timeline Objects - Shows the items that have been applied to the timeline, as well as when they come under the control of the timeline and when they leave.
- Current Frame - Identifies the current frame that is selected.
- Tween Frame - Identifies a frame with no activity specifically taking place.
- Keyframe - Identifies a frame that has a specific action taking place, such as a behavior running, or an adjustment to make on the document objects.

SEE ALSO *Behaviors, Behaviors Panel*

Title Bar

The title of a document provides an overall view of the document. In HTML, the title is written using the <title> element, which is used by search engines when indexing pages. The <title> element is also commonly displayed in the title bar of the Web browsing software that is viewing it.

You can modify Dreamweaver's default HTML document title by selecting Modify→Page Properties. This opens the Page Properties dialog box, allowing you to type a title into the document. Alternatively, you can select the Title icon, shown in the Head Content bar, to change the document title in the Properties inspector.

SEE ALSO *Status Bar*

Validate Form see Behaviors

Visual SourceSafe

Microsoft Visual SourceSafe provides tools for team development environments to track and protect your document structures. Visual SourceSafe includes tools for version control, including tracking changes to all aspects of each document. Different administrator access levels allow you to assign users and project-specific file authorizations, allowing for secure administration of the information contained in your system. Visual SourceSafe even includes controls for reconciling changes made to document code at similar times from multiple users and prevents the information from being overwritten.

SEE ALSO *Defining Sites, FTP, WebDAV*

Web Links see Links

WebDAV

The Web-based Distributed Authoring and Versioning (WebDAV) system is a set of extensions to the HTTP protocol allowing users to collaboratively edit and manage files on Web servers no matter their location.

WebDAV provides a network-based protocol for creating collaborative applications, which includes the following features:

- Concurrency Control - WebDAV provides a system for managing both exclusive and shared locks on files to prevent the problem of overwriting, where multiple development team members write to the same document without first merging changes.
- File Manipulation - WebDAV supports standard file manipulations, including copy and move operations, without creating inconsistencies in your code.
- Properties: WebDAV - Uses XML properties to provide metadata information on your documents, such as a list of team members working on a single site or document. WebDAV can be used to set, delete, and retrieve these properties.

SEE ALSO *Defining Sites, FTP, Visual SourceSafe*

Web Photo Album

The Web Photo Album command creates a document showing a thumbnail-sized selection of images stored on your computer. The Create Web Photo Album option requires all of your images to be in a single folder. This command is ideal for sharing images from your latest vacation, business convention, or dog show. To create a Web Photo Album, select Commands→Create Web Photo Album to open the Create Web Photo Album dialog box shown in Figure W-1.

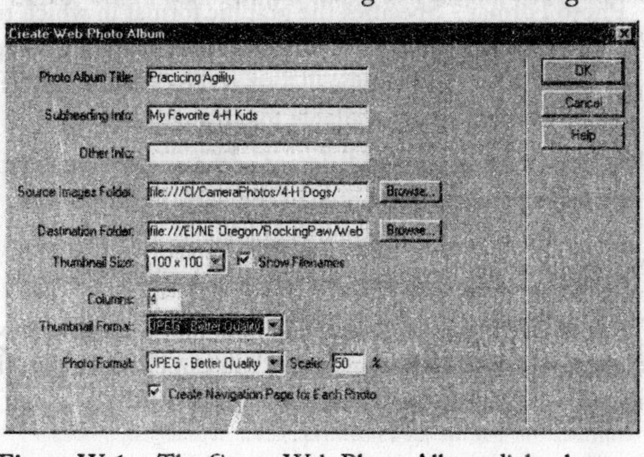

Figure W-1 The Create Web Photo Album dialog box.

NOTE *You must have Fireworks 3 or later installed on your computer for this option to be available from your Dreamweaver menus.*

Provide the following requested information:

- Photo Album Title - Identifies your Web Photo Album. This value also serves as the document title.
- Subheading Info (optional) - Places a subheading beneath the page title.
- Other Info (optional) - Stores additional information about your Photo Album.
- Source Images Folder - Identifies the location of the images for the photo album, which must all reside in a single directory.
- Destination Folder - Identifies the destination directory for storing the completed photo album documents and modified images.
- Thumbnail Size - Specifies the size of each thumbnail image, in pixels, such as 36 x 36, 72 x 72, 100 x 100, 144 x 144, or200 x 200.
- Show Filenames - Shows the filenames on the opening thumbnail page of the Photo Album.
- Columns - Specifies the number of columns of photos to be created.
- Thumbnail Format - Specifies the graphic format of the thumbnails to be created, such as Web Snap 128, Web Snap 256, JPEG-Better Quality, JPEG-Smaller file
- Photo Format - Specifies the graphic format in which to save the original photographs used for the Photo Album. The options are the same as for the Thumbnail format. The PNG format (Fireworks' native format) is not available for this purpose.
- Scale - Controls the size (percent of the original photo) that is used to display individual photos in the Web Photo Album.
- Create Navigation Page For Each Photo - Creates an individual navigation page for each photograph in the album.

Figure W-2 displays a completed Web Photo Album showing four columns of 100 x 100 thumbnails. You can click on each thumbnail and open up a larger version of the image file.

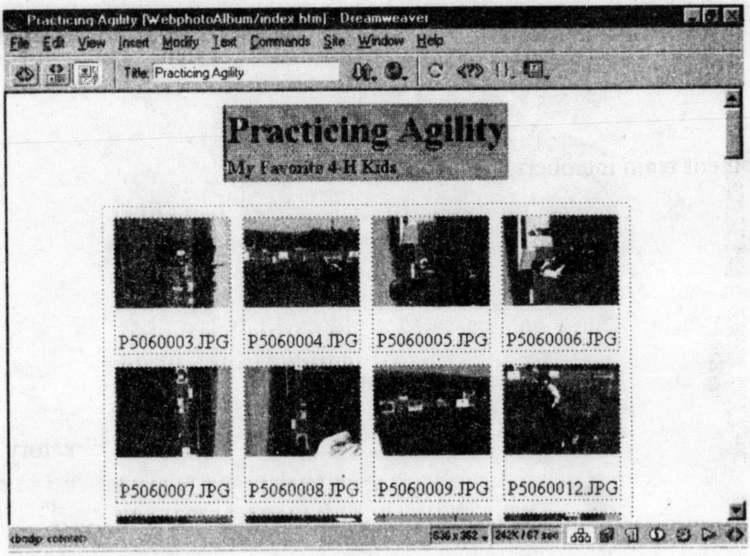

Figure W-2 A Web Photo Album.

SEE ALSO *Behaviors, Dreamweaver Exchange*